Logic Puzzles

Logic Puzzles

200 Challenging Puzzles

ARCTURUS

ARCTURUS
This edition published in 2012 by Arcturus Publishing Limited
26/27 Bickels Yard, 151–153 Bermondsey Street,
London SE1 3HA

ISBN: 978-1-84858-623-9
AD002258EN

Printed in China

Contents

WHERE DO THEY LIVE?

Each of the four women in this puzzle lives in a different house
(as seen on the plan below). Every woman has a different job and a
different number of children to the other women. Use the clues to
find out the facts relating to the occupant of each house.

1

1   Lorna has two more children than the waitress, who lives directly east of Sophie.
2   Sophie has one more child than the accountant, who lives directly north of Angela.
3   Joanne lives directly north of the teacher.
4   The teacher has two more children than the journalist.

Lorne not waitress
Sophie not accountant
Joanne not teacher

	Name				Job				Children				
	Angela	Joanne	Lorna	Sophie	Accountant	Journalist	Teacher	Waitress	2	3	4	5	
No 1													
No 2													
No 3													
No 4													
2 children													
3 children													
4 children													
5 children													
Accountant													
Journalist													
Teacher													
Waitress													

House

N
W — E
S

| 1 | | 2 |
| 3 | | 4 |

House No	Name	Job	Children

PENFRIENDS

2 Mark has five penfriends living abroad, former schoolfriends, to whom he regularly writes. Discover the city in which each is now living, together with his occupation.

1 Adrian lives in Paris; he isn't the analyst.
2 Arnold isn't the author (who lives in Rome), nor is he the analyst.
3 Alistair is a successful artist.
4 Ambrose lives in Madrid.
5 Arnold isn't the architect and doesn't live in Lisbon.

	City					Occupation				
	Lisbon	Madrid	Munich	Paris	Rome	Accountant	Analyst	Architect	Artist	Author
Adrian				O			X			
Alistair	O		O						O	
Ambrose		O						O		
Arnold	X			O	O	O	X	X	X	
Arthur		O					O			
Accountant										
Analyst										
Architect										
Artist										
Author										

Penfriend	City	Occupation
Adrian	Paris	
Allistar		Art
Ambrose	Madrid	
Arnold	Rome	Accunt
Arter		

BED COVERS

Five women are sewing designs onto old bed covers, to give them a new look. Every woman has chosen a different shape for the pieces she is stitching. What is the colour of each woman's bed cover, and what shape are the pieces she is using?

3

1　Mary's bed cover isn't pink and she isn't using square pieces, nor are the square pieces being used by Chris.

2　Neither Barbara nor Chris is using diamond-shaped pieces.

3　The pentagons are being stitched onto the cream-coloured cover, but not by Chris.

4　No-one is stitching triangular pieces onto the lemon-coloured bed cover.

5　Barbara's bed cover is turquoise. Chris's bed cover isn't pink.

6　Ellen isn't the woman currently sewing square shaped pieces on to the lilac bed cover.

	Colour					Pieces				
	Cream	Lemon	Lilac	Pink	Turquoise	Circles	Diamonds	Pentagons	Squares	Triangles
Barbara										
Chris										
Ellen										
Mary										
Stephanie										
Circles										
Diamonds										
Pentagons										
Squares										
Triangles										

Name	Colour	Pieces

DRINKS AFTER WORK

4 After a busy week at the office, four friends met up for a drink last Friday evening. Can you link each to his surname, job, and the drink each prefers?

1 Peter's surname is Fletcher.

2 Ralph is the salesman. He isn't Mr Davis who drank gin and tonic.

3 Tim drank rum and cola, and the accountant drank whisky and ginger ale.

4 Michael isn't Mr Goring, the manager. Nor is Michael the accountant.

	Surname				Job				Drink			
	Davis	Fletcher	Goring	Johnston	Accountant	Clerk	Manager	Salesman	Brandy/soda	Gin/tonic	Rum/cola	Whisky/ginger
Michael												
Peter												
Ralph												
Tim												
Brandy/soda									
Gin/tonic									
Rum/cola									
Whisky/ginger									
Accountant					
Clerk					
Manager					
Salesman					

Name	Surname	Job	Drink

10

SHOWERED WITH GIFTS

Four women recently received flowers and chocolates sent by their boyfriends. What type of chocolates and flowers did each get, and what is the name of the man who sent them?

5

1. Pamela isn't the woman to whom Ian sent a box of milk chocolates and a bunch of tulips.
2. Shirley received a box of assorted chocolates and a bouquet of roses, but not from Gordon.
3. David's girlfriend is Barbara, to whom he didn't send any lilies.
4. The man who sent white chocolates didn't also send a bunch of asters.

	Chocolates				Flowers				Sender			
	Assorted	Dark	Milk	White	Asters	Lilies	Roses	Tulips	David	Gordon	Ian	Michael
Barbara												
Jenny												
Pamela												
Shirley												
David												
Gordon												
Ian												
Michael												
Asters												
Lilies												
Roses												
Tulips												

Woman	Chocolates	Flowers	Sender

TOY CARS

6

Each of the little boys in this puzzle owns a different number of toy cars. Discover the full name of each boy, together with the quantity of cars he possesses, by carefully negotiating a way through these clues:

1 Dean has one fewer car than the number owned by the boy surnamed Cross.

2 Pierre has the lowest number of cars, while the boy surnamed Williams has the highest number.

3 The child surnamed Robson has one fewer car than the number owned by the child surnamed Hart.

4 Tony owns one more car than Alan.

	Cross	Hart	Porter	Robson	Williams	15	16	18	19	20
Alan										
Dean										
Frank										
Pierre										
Tony										
15 cars					
16 cars					
18 cars					
19 cars					
20 cars					

Boy	Surname	No of cars

DOGS' PLAYTIME

David has five dogs, all of different breeds, and each of which has a different favourite plaything. Can you discover the facts from the clues below?

7

1. The collie's favourite toy is an old rag doll that used to belong to David's sister when she was a child.
2. The rubber bone is not the favourite plaything of Spot, who is an Alsatian.
3. Patch is a poodle.
4. The whippet (whose name isn't Sammy) plays with the rubber ring.
5. Bobby's favourite plaything is a much-chewed rubber ball.

	Breed					Toy				
	Alsatian	Collie	Dachshund	Poodle	Whippet	Rag doll	Rubber ball	Rubber bone	Rubber ring	Teddy bear
Bobby										
Patch										
Sammy										
Spot										
Zeus										
Rag doll										
Rubber ball										
Rubber bone										
Rubber ring										
Teddy bear										

Dog	Breed	Toy

CHARITY COLLECTION

8 Four friends, each wearing a different costume, spent the day in town, collecting money for charity. At what location did each stand, as what was he dressed, and how much did he raise?

1 Clive raised seven dollars less than the man dressed as a gorilla, who stood outside the bus station.

2 The man dressed as a pirate raised less money than the one who visited the library.

3 Henry who collected money on the steps of the town hall didn't dress as a pirate or as a punk rocker.

4 Samuel collected money from shoppers as they left the supermarket.

	Location				Dress				Amount			
	Bus station	Library	Supermarket	Town hall	Dracula	Gorilla	Pirate	Punk rocker	$35	$40	$42	$47
Clive												
Henry												
Peter												
Samuel												
$35												
$40												
$42												
$47												
Dracula												
Gorilla												
Pirate												
Punk rocker												

Friend	Location	Dress	Amount

SUNDAY LUNCH

The British tradition of Sunday lunch is the best meal of the week according to the Smith family. Each of the members of the family has a favourite meat and a favourite pudding, so discover what was served on four consecutive Sundays last month, together with the person in whose opinion the combination of the two constitutes the best meal possible!

9

1   Bread and butter pudding was served two weeks earlier than roast pork, which wasn't served at the same day as the apple pie.

2   Rice pudding was served on the same day as roast chicken, which was two weeks earlier than Mr and Mrs Smith's son's favourite meal.

3   Roast beef is the favourite of Mr and Mrs Smith's daughter. It didn't form part of the meal served the week before Mrs Smith's favourite meat.

4   Apple pie was served on the 23rd of the month.

	Beef	Chicken	Lamb	Pork	Apple pie	Bread and butter	Rice	Spotted dick	Mr Smith	Mrs Smith	Son	Daughter
2nd												
9th												
16th												
23rd												
Mr Smith												
Mrs Smith												
Son												
Daughter												
Apple pie												
Bread and butter												
Rice												
Spotted dick												

Date	Meat	Pudding	Favourite of

MUSIC LESSONS

10 Each of the five Player children has a music lesson starting at a different time on Saturday mornings, so it's always a bit of a rush for their parents to get them to the lessons (in different locations, naturally!) on time. What instrument does each child play, and at what time is his or her lesson?

1 The clarinet lesson takes place either one hour earlier or one hour later than Tina's music lesson.

2 The flute lesson is earlier than William's lesson, which is one hour earlier than Lucy's music lesson.

3 Brian's lesson starts at half past ten.

4 The saxophone lesson doesn't start at ten o'clock.

5 Frank is learning to play the piano.

	Clarinet	Flute	Piano	Saxophone	Violin	9.30am	10.00am	10.30am	11.00am	11.30am
Brian										
Frank										
Lucy										
Tina										
William										
9.30am					
10.00am					
10.30am					
11.00am					
11.30am					

Child	Instrument	Time

Soft Cocktails

Five friends have each made a new cocktail. Can you discover what liquid each used, and what fruit each added to flavour it?

11

1 One of the friends (not Diane) made a peculiar cocktail of cold tea and pineapple juice.

2 No-one mixed strawberries with milk; nor did Louise add strawberries to her drink, which she made using cola.

3 Stanley added crushed gooseberries to flavour his concoction.

4 The man who mixed soda and blackcurrant juice together isn't Terence.

	Liquid					Fruit				
	Cola	Cold tea	Lemonade	Milk	Soda water	Banana	Blackcurrants	Gooseberries	Pineapple	Strawberries
Diane										
Harry										
Louise										
Stanley										
Terence										
Banana										
Blackcurrants										
Gooseberries										
Pineapple										
Strawberries										

Friend	Liquid	Fruit

RELATIVE POSITIONS

12 Four cousins all own small businesses located in the same building, although on different floors. On which floor does each work, what is the nature of his or her business, and how many staff does he or she employ?

1 The cousin with the highest number of staff works on a floor directly between two others: that on which Martin runs his business, and that of the publishing company.

2 The legal business employs one fewer person than Susan's company, which is situated on a lower floor than that with the highest number of staff.

3 The millinery business employs one fewer person than Francesca's company.

4 The company with the fewest employees is situated either one floor above or one floor below the accountancy firm, which isn't on the second floor.

	Floor				Business				Staff			
	First	Second	Third	Fourth	Accountancy	Legal	Millinery	Publishing	11	12	14	15
Francesca												
Martin												
Richard												
Susan												
11 staff								
12 staff								
14 staff								
15 staff								
Accountancy				
Legal				
Millinery				
Publishing				

Cousin	Floor	Business	Staff

BEACH BUDDIES

Four women met up for a day on the beach. Each brought along a different item and all used towels of different colours. Can you link together the facts, as well as the total amount of time each friend spent swimming in the sea that day?

13

1 The woman who brought along a bucket and spade (for the purpose of a sandcastle-building contest with her friends) spent less time in the sea than the one with a pink towel, but longer in the sea than Dora.

2 Cora spent thirty minutes less time in the sea than the woman with the orange towel.

3 The woman who brought the sun umbrella spent fifteen minutes less time in the sea than the one who brought along her surfboard.

4 The woman with the brown towel spent fifteen minutes less time in the sea than Flora.

		Item				Towel			Swam for			
	Beachball	Bucket/spade	Surfboard	Umbrella	Brown	Orange	Pink	Scarlet	1 hour	1¼ hours	1½ hours	2 hours
Cora												
Dora												
Flora												
Nora												
1 hour												
1¼ hours												
1½ hours												
2 hours												
Brown												
Orange												
Pink												
Scarlet												

Name	Item	Towel	Swam for

19

CARDS SCENT

14 Jenny received five scented cards on her birthday. What was the picture and perfume (not necessarily associated with the picture on the card) relating to the card each person gave?

1 Jenny received a pine-scented card (not the one with a picture of butterflies) from her grandfather.

2 Jenny's brother sent a card featuring a country scene, which wasn't patchouli perfumed.

3 The lavender-scented card from her grandmother didn't have a picture of butterflies or kittens.

4 The card showing a river scene (which was scented with honeysuckle) wasn't given to Jenny by her mother.

	Picture					Perfume				
	Butterflies	Country scene	Kittens	Mountains	River scene	Honeysuckle	Lavender	Patchouli	Pine	Roses
Brother										
Father										
Grandfather										
Grandmother										
Mother										
Honeysuckle										
Lavender										
Patchouli										
Pine										
Roses										

From	Picture	Perfume

JEWELLERY

Margot received five items of jewellery last Christmas, each made of a different metal. Can you decide the metal from which each item is made, as well as the stones set into each piece?

15

1. The peridots are set into stainless steel, which isn't the metal from which the earrings are made.

2. The garnet necklace isn't made of silver.

3. Margot's favourite piece of jewellery is her titanium ring.

4. The agates are set in gold, which isn't the metal from which the bracelet was fashioned.

5. The stones set in the bracelet are neither peridots nor amethysts.

	Metal					Stones				
	Gold	Platinum	Silver	Stainless steel	Titanium	Agates	Amethysts	Garnets	Jade	Peridots
Bracelet										
Brooch										
Earrings										
Necklace										
Ring										
Agates										
Amethysts										
Garnets										
Jade										
Peridots										

Item	Metal	Stones

HONEYMOON ACTIVITIES

16 Four couples who were married last week are currently on honeymoon in different countries. Their honeymoons all involve a different activity, but you, however, need to exercise only your mind in order to discover who is married to whom, the country in which they are holidaying, and the type of activity in which they are engaged.

1 Opal and her husband are enjoying their canoeing holiday, which isn't in Portugal or Italy.

2 James and his wife Melissa booked their holiday six months ago. They aren't honeymooning in Italy or Scotland.

3 Adam and his wife chose the walking holiday.

4 The couple who are spending their honeymoon diving are neither Penny and her husband Neil, nor the couple who are honeymooning in Portugal.

	Wife				Country				Activity			
	Melissa	Nadine	Opal	Penny	France	Italy	Portugal	Scotland	Canoeing	Diving	Horse-riding	Walking
Adam												
James												
Neil													
Philip													
Canoeing												
Diving												
Horse-riding												
Walking												
France												
Italy												
Portugal												
Scotland												

Husband	Wife	Country	Activity

CLASS REUNION

Rick tried to organize a class reunion with his former schoolmates, some of whom he hadn't seen for a good many years, but due to work, holiday and family commitments, only four people eventually made it. Can you discover the name of the wife of each of Rick's former friends, the number of children they have, and what each man now does for a living?

1   The plumber (who isn't married to Patricia) has either one more or one fewer child than Kevin.

2   Patricia has at least two fewer children than the electrician's wife.

3   The doctor (who isn't Gordon) has at least two more children than Vera's husband.

4   Jeff has one fewer child than the chef.

5   Willow's husband used to sit next to Rupert when they were at school together.

	Patricia	Tamsin	Vera	Willow	2	3	4	5	Chef	Doctor	Electrician	Plumber
Wife					**Children**				**Job**			
Gordon												
Jeff												
Kevin												
Rupert												
Chef												
Doctor												
Electrician												
Plumber												
2 children												
3 children												
4 children												
5 children												

Name	Wife	Children	Job

23

FRUIT TREES

18 Five neighbours recently planted new fruit trees in their gardens. What type of tree did every person plant, and on which day last week?

1 Miss Bishop planted her apple tree earlier in the week than Ms Fisher planted a tree, but later in the week than the greengage tree was planted.

2 Mr Coutts is very much looking forward to a crop of pears from the tree he planted.

3 Mr Evans didn't plant a tree on Monday, but he did plant a tree the day before Mrs Dean's damson plum tree went into the ground.

4 The cherry tree was planted on Saturday.

	Tree					Day				
	Apple	Cherry	Damson	Greengage	Pear	Monday	Tuesday	Wednesday	Friday	Saturday
Miss Bishop										
Mr Coutts										
Mrs Dean										
Mr Evans										
Ms Fisher										
Monday										
Tuesday										
Wednesday										
Friday										
Saturday										

Name	Tree	Day

DON'T BE SCARED!

Five women were talking together yesterday, discussing the methods each uses to try to combat what scares them the most. Can you link each woman to her particular fear and the method she uses to try to overcome it?

19

1 The woman who is scared of spiders is undergoing hypnotherapy to try to cure her of her problem.

2 Verna (who is frightened of the dark) is the sister of the woman who attends a support group.

3 Sharon isn't the woman who uses the power of prayer to overcome her fear of heights.

4 Toni insists that herbal tea is a great help in dealing with her particular fear.

5 Yolande's greatest fear is of snakes.

	Fear					Method				
	Dark	Flying	Heights	Snakes	Spiders	Herbal tea	Hypnotherapy	Prayer	Support group	Yoga
Rachel										
Sharon										
Toni										
Verna										
Yolande										
Herbal tea										
Hypnotherapy										
Prayer										
Support group										
Yoga										

Woman	Fear	Method

SPLIT PERSONALITIES

20 Silly Simon has taken photographs of four of his aunts and uncles, cutting each into four pieces (head, body, legs and feet) and then reassembling them in such a way that each 'new' picture contains pieces of four 'old' ones. How have the pictures been reassembled?

1 Aunt Claire's head is in the same picture as the body of a man.
2 Uncle John's legs are now attached to Aunt Anne's body.
3 Aunt Anne's head isn't in the same picture as Uncle John's feet.

		Body				Legs				Feet			
		Aunt Anne	Aunt Claire	Uncle Bill	Uncle John	Aunt Anne	Aunt Claire	Uncle Bill	Uncle John	Aunt Anne	Aunt Claire	Uncle Bill	Uncle John
Head	Aunt Anne												
	Aunt Claire												
	Uncle Bill												
	Uncle John												
Feet	Aunt Anne												
	Aunt Claire												
	Uncle Bill												
	Uncle John												
Legs	Aunt Anne												
	Aunt Claire												
	Uncle Bill												
	Uncle John												

Head	Body	Legs	Feet

26

PLAYING CARDS

The women in this puzzle are playing a game of cards and each has three in her hand: one club, one diamond and one spade. Can you discover which three cards are in each woman's hand? (NB – A=ace, J=jack, Q=queen and K=king; and in the game ace=1, jack=11, queen=12, king=13 and the values of the other cards are as per their numbers.)

21

1 Teresa's club has a value two higher than that of Margaret's spade.

2 Margaret's diamond has a value one higher than that of her club.

3 Jacqueline's club has a higher value than that of her diamond, but a lower value than that of her spade.

4 The woman with the two of diamonds is also holding the seven of spades in her hand, but not the eight or nine of clubs.

5 Elizabeth isn't holding the queen of clubs. Teresa isn't holding the jack of spades.

	Club				Diamond				Spade			
	8	9	J	Q	A	2	Q	K	6	7	J	K
Elizabeth												
Jacqueline												
Margaret												
Teresa												
Spade 6												
Spade 7												
Spade J												
Spade K												
Diamond A												
Diamond 2												
Diamond Q												
Diamond K												

Player	Club	Diamond	Spade

A GLUT OF PEAS

22 Pamela and her family adore pea soup, which Pamela makes in vast quantities during the growing season, freezing it for use during the year. Over the past five weeks, she combined the peas with other ingredients, just for a change. Can you discover the variety of peas she used each week, together with the other ingredient she combined with the peas each week to make the batches of soup?

1. Mint was added to the peas (not the variety named Ambassador) used in the soup Pamela made in week 5.

2. Carrots were added to the batch of soup made later than the soup that combined potatoes and Hurst Greenshaft peas.

3. The variety of pea named Onward was used in a batch of soup made earlier than that to which crushed garlic was added.

4. Parsley was added to the soup made in week 4 and the Kelvedon Wonder variety of pea was used for the soup Pamela made in week 3.

	Variety					Other				
	Ambassador	Hurst Greenshaft	Kelvedon Wonder	Little Marvel	Onward	Carrots	Garlic	Mint	Parsley	Potatoes
Week 1										
Week 2										
Week 3										
Week 4										
Week 5										
Carrots										
Garlic										
Mint										
Parsley										
Potatoes										

Week	Variety	Other

TV CHOICE

Each of these five people prefers a different type of television programme. Which is each person's favourite, and at what time this evening will he or she be viewing it?

23

1   Suzanne's favourite type of programme will be broadcast one hour later than Linda's choice.

2   The cartoons will be shown 30 minutes later than the documentary. Neither Linda nor Robert enjoys cartoons.

3   The wildlife programme is scheduled for a time two hours later than the type of programme (not cartoons) enjoyed by David.

4   Terence prefers game shows to all other types of programme.

	Cartoons	Documentary	Game show	Soap opera	Wildlife	7.00pm	7.30pm	8.00pm	9.00pm	9.30pm
David										
Linda										
Robert										
Suzanne										
Terence										
7.00pm										
7.30pm										
8.00pm										
9.00pm										
9.30pm										

Viewer	Programme	Time

HOMEMADE GIFTS

24 Four women each made a present for her husband on his birthday last year. What did each woman make, to whom was it given, and in which month is his birthday?

1 The jumper was knitted for the man (not Peter) whose birthday falls in November.

2 The woman whose pottery skills enabled her to make the mug isn't married to the man who celebrates his birthday in July.

3 Harriet's husband's birthday is in February. John's birthday is in September.

4 Dorothy put her carpentry skills to use by making a bookcase for her husband.

5 Judy (who didn't knit the jumper) is married to Steven.

	Made				Given to				Birthday			
	Bookcase	Jumper	Paperweight	Mug	John	Malcolm	Peter	Steven	February	July	September	November
Beryl												
Dorothy												
Harriet												
Judy												
February												
July												
September												
November												
John												
Malcolm												
Peter												
Steven												

Woman	Made	Given to	Birthday

30

PLENTY OF PENS

Four children compared the number of black, green and red pens they possess. Every child has three different quantities of the colours of pens, so use the clues to determine how many of each kind every child has.

1   Sharon has three green pens, which is lower than the number of green pens that Lucy owns.

2   Neil hasn't five pens in any single colour. The child with five red pens also has two green pens.

3   The child with four black pens has the same number of green pens as the number of red pens owned by Jamie.

	Black				Green				Red			
	2	3	4	5	2	3	4	5	2	3	4	5
Jamie												
Lucy												
Neil												
Sharon												
Red 2												
Red 3												
Red 4												
Red 5												
Green 2												
Green 3												
Green 4												
Green 5												

Child	Black	Green	Red

Monster Mix

26 Mona Lott has just finished writing her latest horror story, *Monster Mix*, in which five characters change into various forms at certain phases of the moon. Who transforms into each creature, and at what stage in the moon's cycle?

1 Whenever there is no moon at all, one of the five characters (not Neil) turns into a werewolf.

2 Philip is affected when the moon is three-quarters full, unlike the character who becomes a vampire.

3 The character who transforms into a malevolent goblin when the moon is in its first quarter isn't Abigail. Nor is Abigail affected when the moon is full or when there is no moon.

4 Samuel becomes a yeti (abominable snowman) at a certain stage of the moon's cycle.

	Creature					Moon				
	Goblin	Troll	Vampire	Werewolf	Yeti	Quarter	Half	Three-quarters	Full	No moon
Abigail										
Caroline										
Neil										
Philip										
Samuel										
Quarter										
Half										
Three-quarters										
Full										
No moon										

Name	Creature	Moon

CHICKENS

Five smallholders who live near the village of Cluckingford specialize in raising chickens and selling eggs. What breed of fowl does each keep, and how many eggs did they sell last week?

1   The smallholder who keeps Australorp chickens sold ten dozen more eggs than Mitch, who keeps Sussex chickens.

2   Clarice (who sold fewest eggs last week) isn't the smallholder who keeps Dorking chickens.

3   The Leghorn chickens are kept by the person who sold ten dozen more eggs than Bill.

4   George sold ten dozen fewer eggs than Juliette.

	Breed					Eggs sold				
	Australorp	Dorking	Leghorn	Sussex	Welsummer	50 dozen	60 dozen	70 dozen	80 dozen	90 dozen
Bill										
Clarice										
George										
Juliette										
Mitch										
50 dozen					
60 dozen					
70 dozen					
80 dozen					
90 dozen					

Smallholder	Breed	Eggs sold

ORDERS IN ORDER

28 Phil's Fast Food outlet currently has four customers waiting to order. Each knows precisely what he or she wants by way of food and drink, but can you work out what they will have, together with each customer's position in the queue?

1   The customer who wants chicken nuggets is second in the queue, which is further ahead than Catherine's position.
2   The person who wants cola to drink is third in the queue, which is further back than the position of the customer who will order a hamburger.
3   Dean (who intends to order fried fish) is standing directly behind the person who will order lemonade.
4   The person who wants a milkshake is further ahead in the queue than Moira.

	Food				**Drink**				**Position**			
	Cheeseburger	Chicken nuggets	Fried fish	Hamburger	Coffee	Cola	Lemonade	Milkshake	First	Second	Third	Fourth
Catherine												
Dean												
Fred												
Moira												
First												
Second												
Third												
Fourth												
Coffee												
Cola												
Lemonade												
Milkshake												

Customer	**Food**	**Drink**	**Position**

TALENTED ARTISTS

Tanya has no artistic talents at all, but her two siblings and parents have just won major prizes for theirs, in a recent national competition! Can you work out the name of each member of Tanya's family (take care, these are all names which can be given to both men and women), the field in which each excels and the prize each gained?

29

1   Pat is delighted with the prize of money, which will be spent on some new equipment related to the field in which he or she excels.

2   The man who entered the painting competition is called Jo.

3   Tanya's mother isn't the person who entered the photography competition and won the holiday.

4   Tanya's brother will be making a television appearance in connection with his particular field of expertise.

5   Tanya's father is Lee, who won a car, but whose field of interest isn't sculpture.

	Name				Field				Prize			
	Chris	Jo	Lee	Pat	Painting	Photography	Pottery	Sculpture	Car	Holiday	Money	TV appearance
Brother												
Father												
Mother												
Sister												
Car												
Holiday												
Money												
TV appearance												
Painting												
Photography												
Pottery												
Sculpture												

Relation	Name	Field	Prize

PRESENT PROBLEM

30 Having wrapped up her Christmas presents earlier in the year, Gayle has just discovered that five have lost their tags, and she is having difficulty in remembering what is in each of the differently-coloured paper parcels, and to whom it should be given. Can you help?

1 The parcel wrapped in shiny green paper contains a book.
2 The parcel in gold paper (which doesn't contain a scarf) is for Gayle's sister.
3 The watch is a present for her grandfather. It isn't wrapped in purple paper.
4 The parcel wrapped in silver paper contains the present for Gayle's mother.
5 Her uncle will receive a pair of gloves for Christmas.

	Gift					For				
	Book	Gloves	Pen	Scarf	Watch	Aunt	Grandfather	Mother	Sister	Uncle
Green										
Gold										
Purple										
Silver										
Red										
Aunt					
Grandfather					
Mother					
Sister					
Uncle					

Paper	Gift	For

CAMPING FUN

Five boys are all about to enjoy a week's stay at the Young Adventurers' Campsite. They all drew lots to decide who should undertake each different task prior to settling down for the night. What additional task will each boy perform, and what is the colour of his sleeping bag?

1   The boy who will cook supper has a brown sleeping bag, unlike Zach.

2   The boy with the red sleeping bag won't be fetching water.

3   Jim (whose sleeping bag isn't orange) will either be fetching water or lighting a fire.

4   Stuart's job is to erect the tent in which the boys will be sleeping. Either Stuart or the boy who will fetch wood has a black sleeping bag.

5   Thomas (who won't be fetching water) has a green sleeping bag.

	Cook supper	Erect the tent	Fetch water	Fetch wood	Light a fire	Black	Brown	Green	Orange	Red
Task						**Sleeping bag**				
Jim										
Robbie										
Stuart										
Thomas										
Zach										
Black										
Brown										
Green										
Orange										
Red										

Boy	Task	Sleeping bag

A PREVIOUS LIFE

32

The four women in this puzzle strongly believe in reincarnation; in fact, each says that she knows who she was in the past. Can you discover the name by which each woman believes she was previously known, her role in life, and the year in which she believes she died?

1   The woman who believes she was Maud died 39 years after Naomi's character and 78 years later than the servant girl.

2   Karen believes her character died 39 years after the seamstress and 78 years later than Joan.

3   The woman who believes she was a queen in a previous life says that she died 39 years later than Alice and 78 years later than Lesley's character.

4   Marcia is convinced that she was a milkmaid in a previous existence. She doesn't believe that she died in 1742, however.

	Named				Role				Died			
	Alice	Catherine	Joan	Maud	Milkmaid	Queen	Seamstress	Servant girl	1742	1781	1820	1859
Karen												
Lesley												
Marcia												
Naomi												
1742												
1781												
1820												
1859												
Milkmaid												
Queen												
Seamstress												
Servant girl												

Woman	Named	Role	Died

LOUSY LUNCHES!

Penny and three other women decided to get their lunch from the new potato shop in town, which specializes in providing fillings and sauces chosen by the customer. However, all of the women decided that their lunches were inedible, as the sauce each had chosen was not, after all, to her taste. What is each woman's full name, and what did each woman choose by way of filling and sauce?

1 The potato filled with ham was topped with cheese sauce.

2 The one filled with baked beans wasn't chosen by Ms Phillips.

3 Ms Purser's potato (not topped with tomato sauce) was filled with salad, unlike that chosen by Penny, whose potato was topped with chilli sauce.

4 Pippa chose the potato filled with tuna.

5 Polly's surname is Pelling.

	Surname				Filling				Sauce			
	Parsons	Pelling	Phillips	Purser	Baked beans	Ham	Salad	Tuna	Chilli	Cheese	Mayonnaise	Tomato
Pauline												
Penny												
Pippa												
Polly												
Chilli												
Cheese												
Mayonnaise												
Tomato												
Baked beans												
Ham												
Salad												
Tuna												

Name	Surname	Filling	Sauce

BIRTHDAY CARDS

34 Mary has just received a birthday card from each of her five children. She has the cards on a shelf, as shown in the picture below, and has given the following clues, so that you can determine the name and age of the child who gave every card:

1 William is two years older than the child who gave card A in the picture below.

2 The card from Ellen is larger than the one Mary received from her youngest child, which is directly next to and left of the card given by the child who is one year younger than Simon.

3 Greta is three years younger than Chris.

4 The child aged seven gave Mary the card which is next to and left of the card given to her by the child aged eight.

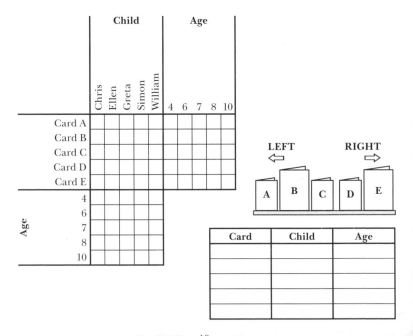

WEDDINGS GALORE

Mrs Jones's five granddaughters were married last year; luckily each in a different month. What is the name of each one's husband, and in which month were they married?

35

1 One of Mrs Jones's granddaughters (not Angela) married Angus in April of last year. Avril's husband is Alan.

2 Andrea was married earlier in the year than Anthony, but later in the year than Arnold.

3 Abigail's wedding was three months before that of Alison.

	\multicolumn{5}{c}{Husband}	\multicolumn{5}{c}{Month}

	Adrian	Alan	Angus	Anthony	Arnold	April	May	June	July	August
Abigail									☆	
Alison			✗							
Andrea						✗				✗
Angela			○							
Avril		✗								
April			✗							
May										
June										
July										
August										

Name	Husband	Month

SMELLS GOOD

36 Lorraine has four sisters, each of whom prefers to scent her bedroom with a different perfumed spray. Can you discover each sister's age, the spray she prefers to use, and the colour (not necessarily linked to the spray she uses!) of her room?

1 The girl who prefers the scent of lilies is younger than Leanne, but older than the sister whose bedroom is pink.

2 Laura is two years younger than the girl (not Lola) whose bedroom is green.

3 The sister who prefers lavender spray is one year younger than the girl who uses lemon-scented spray.

4 The oldest girl's name has the same number of letters as the name of her sister, and one of these two girls has a white bedroom.

	Age				Spray				Bedroom			
	12	14	15	16	Lavender	Lemon	Lilac	Lily	Blue	Green	Pink	White
Laura												
Leanne												
Lola												
Lucy												
Blue												
Green												
Pink												
White												
Lavender												
Lemon												
Lilac												
Lily												

Sister	Age	Spray	Bedroom

FAMILY FEUDS

Four families living in Dry Gulch during the 19th century had been involved in feuds with families from the neighbouring town of Silver City for a very long time, until the women of the families decided it was time to patch things up. What was the surname of each brave woman's family, for what reason had they originally started fighting, and for approximately how many years had the feud continued?

37

1. Mrs Dayton put an end to her family's feud seven years later than that over mining rights was brought to a close, but seven years earlier than Eliza's feud.

2. The feud over cattle rustling involved Bella's family and was brought to a satisfactory conclusion seven years earlier than the Hancock family's dispute, which wasn't resolved by Eliza.

3. The Lowell family feud was over the theft of some horses and was ended seven years later than that in which Helen intervened.

	Surname				Reason				Years			
	Dayton	Giles	Hancock	Lowell	Cattle rustling	Gambling debt	Horse theft	Mining rights	38	45	52	59
Bella												
Eliza												
Helen												
Verity												
38 years												
45 years												
52 years												
59 years												
Cattle rustling												
Gambling debt												
Horse theft												
Mining rights												

Woman	Surname	Reason	Years

BROTHERS AND SISTERS

38 Can you pair up each brother with his sister in this puzzle, and discover their surname?

1 No boy has a sister whose name begins with the same letter as the initial letter of his own name.

2 Of the five boys: one is the brother of Mary; one is Mark; one is the boy surnamed Chester; one is Steven; and the other is the boy surnamed Dale.

3 Of the five boys: one is Richard; one is the boy surnamed Atkins; one is Terence; one is the boy surnamed Brown; and the other is the brother of Wendy.

4 Of the five boys: one is the brother of Sandra; one is the boy surnamed Atkins; one is Terence; one is the boy surnamed Chester; and the other is nine years old today!

		Sister					Surname			
	Mary	Ruth	Sandra	Tanya	Wendy	Atkins	Brown	Chester	Dale	Evans
Mark										
Richard										
Steven										
Terence										
William										
Atkins										
Brown										
Chester										
Dale										
Evans										

Brother	Sister	Surname

CLOUD WATCHING

Five children of different ages lay on their backs in a meadow, idly watching the clouds drifting by. Each child picked out a cloud which had the shape or form of something. Use the clues to find out the children's ages, and what his or her chosen cloud looked like.

1   Gina is younger than Lynne, who is one year younger than the child who thought that one of the clouds resembled a dog.

2   Timmy is three years older than the child who thought one of the clouds looked like a castle.

3   Edward is one year older than the child who saw a cloud shaped like a wheelbarrow.

4   Vincent is one year younger than the child who spotted a cloud resembling a ship in full sail.

| | Age | | | | | Cloud | | | | |
	7	8	10	11	12	Castle	Dog	Pyramid	Ship	Wheelbarrow
Edward										
Gina										
Lynne										
Timmy										
Vincent										
Castle					
Dog					
Pyramid					
Ship					
Wheelbarrow					

Child	Age	Cloud

BEAR COLOUR

40 Babs owns four teddy bears, each of which wears a coat, hat and trousers in three different colours. Can you work out the colours of the clothes they are wearing, given these clues?

1 Sukie's trousers are blue, but nothing worn by Bernie is blue.

2 Sukie's coat isn't green.

3 Pebble's hat and Candy's trousers are red.

		Coat				Hat				Trousers			
		Blue	Green	Red	Yellow	Blue	Green	Red	Yellow	Blue	Green	Red	Yellow
	Bernie												
	Candy												
	Pebble												
	Sukie												
Trousers	Blue								
	Green								
	Red								
	Yellow								
Hat	Blue								
	Green								
	Red								
	Yellow								

Bear	Coat	Hat	Trousers

Hardware Sales

A new hardware store in the High Street opened its doors to customers for the first time yesterday morning. Follow the clues to discover the full name of each of the shop's first four customers, together with their purchases and the order in which each was served.

41

1 Mrs Parker was served immediately before the customer who purchased a can of paint, but later than Tony.

2 Mr Dale bought a new stepladder.

3 Marc was served later than the customer surnamed Bartlet, but earlier than the person who bought a saw.

4 Pamela wasn't the third customer to be served.

	Surname				Purchased				Order			
	Bartlet	Dale	Morton	Parker	Nails	Paint	Saw	Stepladder	First	Second	Third	Fourth
Marc												
Pamela												
Tony												
Wilma												
First												
Second												
Third												
Fourth												
Nails												
Paint												
Saw												
Stepladder												

Name	Surname	Purchased	Order

TOY SHOP TREAT

42 Aunt Sally took her five nieces and nephews to the local toy shop yesterday, to buy each a present. How old is each child, and what kind of toy did he or she choose?

1 Lucy, who chose a bat and ball, is two years older than the child who wanted the doll.

2 Peter is four years younger than the child for whom Aunt Sally purchased the building bricks.

3 Modelling clay was chosen by the youngest of Aunt Sally's nieces and nephews, who isn't Tammy.

4 Rebecca is one year older than the child who chose the teddy bear.

	Age					Toy				
	4	5	6	8	9	Bat and ball	Building bricks	Doll	Modelling clay	Teddy bear
Lucy										
Martin										
Peter										
Rebecca										
Tammy										
Bat and ball										
Building bricks										
Doll										
Modelling clay										
Teddy bear										

Child	Age	Toy

FOOD ORDERS

In a small cafe in town, Mary has just taken five orders for coffee and cake. Can you discover who is seated at each numbered table, as well as work out what type of cake each wants?

1 The customer at table No 4 has ordered coconut cake.

2 Mrs Brown is at a table with a number three higher than that at which Mr Chapman is seated.

3 Mrs Lane's table has a number two higher than that of the person who has ordered a slice of sponge cake.

4 Mr Phillips is at a table with a number one lower than that at which Mrs Rothman is seated. Neither has ordered coconut cake.

5 The person who ordered chocolate cake is at a table with a number one lower than that at which the person who ordered cherry cake is seated.

	Name					Cake				
	Mrs Brown	Mr Chapman	Mrs Lane	Mr Phillips	Mrs Rothman	Cherry	Chocolate	Coconut	Fruit	Sponge
Table No 1										
Table No 2										
Table No 3										
Table No 4										
Table No 5										
Cherry					
Chocolate					
Coconut					
Fruit					
Sponge					

Table No	Name	Cake

PLAYING CARDS

44 The men in this puzzle are playing a game of cards and each has three in his hand: one heart, one club and one spade. Can you discover which three cards are in each man's hand? (NB – A=ace, J=jack, Q=queen and K=king; and in the game ace=1, jack=11, queen=12, king=13 and the values of the other cards are as per their numbers.)

1   Alan's heart has a value four higher than that of Clive's heart. Clive's heart has a value three lower than that of his club, which has a higher value than that of Alan's club.

2   Clive's spade has a value two higher than that of Darren's spade.

3   The man with both the three of hearts and the five of clubs isn't Darren.

4   Alan's spade has a value four higher than that of the spade held by Robin.

		Heart				Club				Spade			
		3	4	7	J	5	6	10	Q	A	3	5	9
	Alan												
	Clive												
	Darren												
	Robin												
Spade	A								
Spade	3								
Spade	5								
Spade	9								
Club	5				
Club	6				
Club	10				
Club	Q				

Player	Heart	Club	Spade

TRIP TO THE ZOO

Four friends each persuaded their mothers to take them on a day out to the zoo. Each child was captivated by a different animal there. What is the name of each child's mother, what animal did he or she like best, and what item did each purchase at the gift shop at the end of the visit?

45

1   The child who bought the colouring book didn't much care for the lizards and isn't the son or daughter of Felicity.

2   Felicity's child didn't like the lizards or the chimpanzees as much as another type of animal.

3   Cheryl's daughter is Hilary, whose favourite animals aren't lizards.

4   The child (not Florence) who adores tigers bought a tiger-striped mug at the gift shop.

5   Florence (whose mother isn't Anita), didn't buy a pencil case at the end of her visit to the zoo.

6   Anita's child isn't Benny, who fell in love with the chimpanzees.

	Mother				Animals				Bought			
	Anita	Cheryl	Felicity	Martina	Chimpanzees	Lizards	Polar bears	Tigers	Colouring book	Mug	Pencil case	Postcards
Benny												
Florence												
Hilary												
Jimmy												
Colouring book												
Mug												
Pencil case												
Postcards												
Chimpanzees												
Lizards												
Polar bears												
Tigers												

Child	Mother	Animals	Bought

51

IN COMPETITION

46 Five people recently entered a pottery competition. What did each make, and in which position did he or she finish?

1 The finishing position of the person (not Doris or Douglas) who made the vase was three higher than that achieved by the person who made the mug.

2 Diane made the figurine. Her finishing position was one higher than that of the person who made the plate.

3 Damian (who made the bowl) finished one place higher than that awarded to Doris.

	Bowl	Figurine	Mug	Plate	Vase	First	Second	Fifth	Seventh	Eighth
Damian										
Deirdre										
Diane										
Doris										
Douglas										
First										
Second										
Fifth										
Seventh										
Eighth										

Entrant	Item	Position

HOLIDAYS

The people in this puzzle all went on holiday last month, each for a different number of days, and each in a different country. Can you discover the facts from the clues?

1 The person who went to New Zealand was away for four days longer than Mitch.

2 Patricia (who went to France) was away for longer than Florence.

3 Andrew's holiday was shorter than that taken by the person (not Mitch) who visited Jordan.

4 The holiday in Mexico was longer than Patricia's holiday.

	Days away					Location				
	7	10	14	18	21	France	Italy	Jordan	Mexico	New Zealand
Andrew										
Eric										
Florence										
Mitch										
Patricia										
France										
Italy										
Jordan										
Mexico										
New Zealand										

Name	Days away	Location

New Homes

48 Four people last week adopted cats from their local rescue centre, from which they also purchased an item. What has each person decided to name the new pet, which item was bought at the rescue centre, and on what day of the week did each person take his or her cat home?

1 The person who adopted Cookie bought her a nice new blanket. Cookie was collected the day after Lynne's cat, but earlier in the week than the cat whose owner bought the leather collar.

2 Nigel adopted Katie, taking her home later in the week than Anne collected her pet, but earlier in the week than the day on which the oldest cat (for whom the food bowl was bought) was taken home.

3 The toy mouse wasn't purchased by Sooty's new owner.

	Cat's name				Bought				Day			
	Cookie	Dizzy	Katie	Sooty	Blanket	Collar	Food bowl	Toy mouse	Tuesday	Wednesday	Thursday	Friday
Anne												
Charles												
Lynne												
Nigel												
Tuesday												
Wednesday												
Thursday												
Friday												
Blanket												
Collar												
Food bowl												
Toy mouse												

Owner	Cat's name	Bought	Day

54

SPLIT PERSONALITIES

Sandie has taken photographs of four of her friends, cutting each into four pieces (head, body, legs and feet) and then reassembling them in such a way that each 'new' picture contains pieces of four 'old' ones. How have the pictures been reassembled?

49

1   Ben's legs are now attached to Sue's feet.
2   Lucy's legs are now attached to Sue's body.
3   Richard's legs and Lucy's body are in two different pictures.
4   Richard's head and Sue's feet are in two different pictures.
5   Ben's feet and Sue's legs are in two different pictures.

		Body				Legs				Feet			
		Ben	Lucy	Richard	Sue	Ben	Lucy	Richard	Sue	Ben	Lucy	Richard	Sue
Head	Ben												
	Lucy												
	Richard												
	Sue												
Feet	Ben												
	Lucy												
	Richard												
	Sue												
Legs	Ben												
	Lucy												
	Richard												
	Sue												

Head	Body	Legs	Feet

55

SUITCASE SHUFFLE

50

Having arrived at the airport, five people discovered on leaving the train that they had placed their suitcases next to one another. This wouldn't have been a problem, except that all of the suitcases were identical, and their labels had all become detached. A picture of the cases is below. Can you discover which belongs to each person, as well as work out everyone's country of destination?

1   Sean's suitcase is next to and between Mark's and that of the person travelling to Switzerland.

2   Linda's suitcase is further right than Paul's, but further left than that of the person travelling to South Africa.

3   Ruth's suitcase is further left than that of the person (not Sean) travelling to India.

4   The suitcase belonging to the person travelling to Denmark is next to and to the left of that of the person travelling to China; neither suitcase belongs to Ruth.

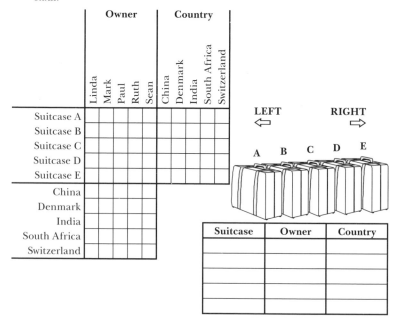

	Linda	Mark	Paul	Ruth	Sean	China	Denmark	India	South Africa	Switzerland
Suitcase A										
Suitcase B										
Suitcase C										
Suitcase D										
Suitcase E										
China										
Denmark										
India										
South Africa										
Switzerland										

Suitcase	Owner	Country

TROLL BRIDGES

Long ago, in a land that time has forgotten, there were five trolls, each of whom dwelt beneath a bridge, allowing people to cross once they had paid a certain number of silver coins. Over which river was the bridge where each troll lived, and what number of silver coins did each extract from travellers trying to get from one side to the other?

51

1   Travellers crossing the River Flowwin were required to pay more than the price charged by Hagrim, but less than the price expected by Frimbi.

2   The toll extracted from those crossing the Crashen River was three silver coins.

3   Blaggitt charged one more coin than it cost to cross the Dropyn River.

4   It cost travellers less to cross the Runnin River than to cross the River Spurton (which wasn't spanned by the bridge beneath which Frimbi dwelt).

5   Zwerg charged one fewer silver coin than Dwivolt charged for the privilege of using his bridge.

	Crashen	Dropyn	Flowwin	Runnin	Spurton	2	3	4	5	6
Blaggitt										
Dwivolt										
Frimbi										
Hagrim										
Zwerg										
2 coins										
3 coins										
4 coins										
5 coins										
6 coins										

Troll	River	Coins

LIBRARY BOOKS

52 The first four people to visit Little Lake Lending Library yesterday morning borrowed different numbers of books. Each person's reading choice is limited to one particular genre, so see if you can discover the full name of each borrower, the type of reading matter each prefers, and how many books each took away to read.

1 Science fiction (sci-fi) is the reading matter preferred by the person who borrowed either one more or one fewer book than the person surnamed Pugh and either one more or one fewer book than Keith (who surname isn't Pugh or Stoner).

2 The borrower surnamed Lawson took away more books than Ivan, but fewer than the person whose favourite genre is romance.

3 Humorous books are preferred by Helen, who borrowed more books than those chosen by the person who prefers crime novels.

4 Neither the borrower surnamed Stoner nor the one surnamed Morgan ever reads crime novels.

	Lawson	Morgan	Pugh	Stoner	Crime	Humour	Romance	Sci-fi	2	3	4	5
Helen												
Ivan												
Janice												
Keith												
2 books												
3 books												
4 books												
5 books												
Crime												
Humour												
Romance												
Sci-fi												

Borrower	Surname	Genre	No of books

A FAMILY MATTER

Each of the four families in this puzzle consists of a husband, wife, son and daughter, whose names begin with four different letters of the alphabet. Can you discover who is related to whom?

53

1 Adam (whose mother is Freda) is not related to Carol.
2 Amy (whose brother is Christopher) isn't Jack's daughter.

		Wife				Son				Daughter			
		Anna	Colette	Freda	Julia	Adam	Christopher	Ferdy	James	Amy	Carol	Faye	Jodie
Husband	Alan												
	Colin												
	Fred												
	Jack												
Daughter	Amy												
	Carol												
	Faye												
	Jodie												
Son	Adam												
	Christopher												
	Ferdy												
	James												

Husband	Wife	Son	Daughter

FIVE WISHES

54 Granny Cauldron practises witchcraft. On different days last week, she received a visit from each of the five girls in the village, who sought a potion to bring her what she desired. Naturally Granny obliged... for a price. On which day did each girl call, and what is her desire?

1 Beth isn't the girl who desires employment (preferably part-time and at a high salary), who visited Granny Cauldron on Friday to collect her potion.

2 Cordelia (who wishes to be cured of her current, and largely imaginary, health problems) called to see Granny Cauldron later in the week than the girl who professed a desire to travel the globe.

3 Dulcie's visit was earlier in the week than that of the girl who desires wealth.

4 Flora visited Granny Cauldron on Wednesday.

5 The girl who came on Thursday was looking for a potion that would guarantee love.

	Day					Desire				
	Monday	Tuesday	Wednesday	Thursday	Friday	Employment	Health	Love	Travel	Wealth
Beth										
Cordelia										
Dulcie										
Edna										
Flora										
Employment										
Health										
Love										
Travel										
Wealth										

Visitor	Day	Desire

PRESENTS PLEASE!

Five children each wrote a letter to Santa Claus, requesting certain presents. What is the surname of each child, and how many presents did he or she ask for?

55

1. No child has a name that begins with the same letter as that of his or her surname.

2. Danny (whose surname isn't Lister) asked for one fewer present than the number on the list compiled by the child surnamed Thorpe.

3. The child surnamed Jarvis requested twice as many presents as the number on Raymond's list. Larry's surname isn't Jarvis.

4. Jane asked for two more presents than the number on Tina's list.

	Day	Jarvis	Lister	Raven	Thorpe	3	4	6	7	8
Danny										
Jane										
Larry										
Raymond										
Tina										
3										
4										
6										
7										
8										

Child	Surname	Presents

61

SLEEP-OVER PARTY

56 Mary invited three of her friends to stay last night: a mini sleep-over party! Each girl wore a pair of pyjamas of a different colour, has a toothbrush of a different colour, and chose a different bedtime drink. Sort out the facts from the clues below.

1 No girl has a toothbrush of the same colour as that of her pyjamas.

2 The girl who drank cocoa has a toothbrush of the same colour as that of the pyjamas worn by Mary, who drank neither hot nor cold milk last night.

3 Molly's pyjamas are of the same colour as that of Mary's toothbrush.

4 The girl whose choice of bedtime drink was cold milk has a turquoise toothbrush.

5 Milly's toothbrush is blue and Mandy's pyjamas are pink.

	Pyjamas				Toothbrush				Drink			
	Blue	Pink	Red	Turquoise	Blue	Pink	Red	Turquoise	Cocoa	Cold milk	Hot milk	Water
Mandy												
Mary												
Milly												
Molly												
Cocoa												
Cold milk												
Hot milk												
Water												
Blue												
Pink												
Red												
Turquoise												

Girl	Pyjamas	Toothbrush	Drink

ALL CHANGE

Fed up with no-one being able to remember, pronounce, or even spell their names, four aliens decided to change them to something more appropriate for Earth. At the same time, each changed the colour of his or her hair to match that of the populace. All this paid off, as they are now making friends and being invited to dinner parties. Discover each alien's new name, home planet, and original hair colour…

1   The alien from the distant planet of Rezel has changed her name to Polly.

2   Bxcn changed her name to Louise. She isn't from Breel or Degrex. Nor is Nzdf from Breel.

3   The alien from Breel (who used to have violet hair) didn't change his or her name to Bill. Nor was Bill's original hair colour green.

4   The alien who used to have shiny gold hair was originally called Lgrt, but didn't come from the planet Degrex.

	New name				Planet				Hair colour			
	Bill	Louise	Polly	Norman	Breel	Degrex	Rezel	Wargis	Gold	Green	Purple	Violet
Bxcn												
Grvl												
Lgrt												
Nzdf												
Gold												
Green												
Purple												
Violet												
Breel												
Degrex												
Rezel												
Wargis												

Planet

Alien	New name	Planet	Hair

Naughty Teddies

58 Young Terry regularly blames his five teddy bears for getting him into trouble with his mum! Yesterday was no exception, and he had to give each a mild telling-off after he was, in turn, told off by his mother. What is the colour of each bear, and what kind of 'trouble' was he involved with?

1 According to Terry, Brian had informed him that it was no longer thought necessary for children to brush their teeth!

2 Neither Billy nor Brian is blue. Neither Bamber nor Billy is brown.

3 Apparently, the buff-coloured teddy bear told Terry that he didn't have to make his bed yesterday morning, after his mother had expressly told Terry to do just that.

4 Despite his mother calling and calling, Terry was late for dinner yesterday because he was busy attending to the needs of the brown teddy bear.

5 The black bear is Bobby, who wasn't involved in the incident concerning wearing shoes in the house, which resulted in Terry getting mud on the floor.

	Colour					Trouble				
	Beige	Black	Blue	Brown	Buff	Late for dinner	Mud on floor	Spilt milk	Unbrushed teeth	Unmade bed
Bamber										
Bernie										
Billy										
Bobby										
Brian										
Late for dinner										
Mud on floor										
Spilt milk										
Unbrushed teeth										
Unmade bed										

Bear	Colour	Trouble

APPRENTICES

Five skilled employees of Clore and Ball, renowned cabinetmakers, have just been assigned an apprentice apiece, who will be working with them for the next few months, before moving to a different area of the company. Can you discover how long each employee has worked for Clore and Ball, together with the name of his apprentice?

59

1   Noel will be working with an employee who has been with the company for two fewer years than the man with whom Liam will be working.

2   Robert's mentor has been employed at Clore and Ball for ten fewer years than Albert.

3   Eddie has been at Clore and Ball for two years longer than the man with whom Max will be working.

4   Joe has been at Clore and Ball for two years longer than George.

	No of years					Apprentice				
	15	17	19	23	25	Liam	Max	Noel	Pete	Robert
Albert										
Charlie										
Eddie										
George										
Joe										
Liam										
Max										
Noel										
Pete										
Robert										

Employee	No of years	Apprentice

PUZZLE FANS

60 Four fans of logic puzzles managed to complete quite a few last week. Can you discover their full names, the number of puzzles each finished and the longest amount of time every person took to solve a puzzle he or she found particularly challenging?

1 The solver surnamed Peterson took 20 minutes longer to solve a challenging puzzle than the time taken by the solver surnamed Trotter.

2 Darren Sharp solved four more puzzles last week than the solver surnamed Vance, who took longer to solve a challenging puzzle than the time taken by Darren.

3 Ellen solved two more puzzles last week than Pamela, who solved more puzzles than the person who took 35 minutes to solve a particularly challenging puzzle.

	Surname				Solved				Time			
	Peterson	Sharp	Trotter	Vance	38	40	42	44	25 minutes	35 minutes	45 minutes	55 minutes
Darren												
Ellen												
Michael												
Pamela												
25 minutes												
35 minutes												
45 minutes												
55 minutes												
38												
40												
42												
44												

Puzzler	Surname	Solved	Time

HOMEWARD BOUND

Mr and Mrs Worth were at the airport this morning, seeing off their four daughters and respective sons-in-law, who all left for home after attending Mr and Mrs Worth's golden wedding anniversary party last Saturday. Can you link each daughter to her husband, the country in which they live and the time at which their flight departed?

61

1 Nicola and her husband Colin took a later flight than that going to Venezuela, but an earlier flight than the one taken by Jean.

2 The daughter married to Micky departed on the next flight after that to Germany.

3 Mr and Mrs Worth's daughter Sue left on a later flight than that taken by Shane and his wife, who live in Belgium.

	Husband				Country				Flight time			
	Colin	Micky	Ray	Shane	Belgium	Germany	New Zealand	Venezuela	0930 hours	1015 hours	1100 hours	1145 hours
Angela												
Jean												
Nicola												
Sue												
0930 hours												
1015 hours												
1100 hours												
1145 hours												
Belgium												
Germany												
New Zealand												
Venezuela												

Daughter	Husband	Country	Flight time

WEDDING HELPERS

62 Caroline's five sisters were all more than happy to help her to organize her wedding reception last summer. Each is of a different age and helped with a different aspect of planning the wedding: and now you can put your skills to the test, by organizing the facts.

1 Shelley is 25 years old. The sister aged 28 made all of the table decorations.

2 Kate, who kindly volunteered to stamp all of the wedding invitation envelopes and to post them, is older than the sister (not Moira) who helped Caroline to find and book a location for the reception.

3 Vera, who is older than Kate, helped Caroline to organize all of the catering for the event.

	Age					Helped with				
	22	24	25	28	29	Catering	Decorations	Invitations	Location	Music
Deborah										
Kate										
Moira										
Shelley										
Vera										
Catering										
Decorations										
Invitations										
Location										
Music										

Sister	Age	Helped with

PANDORA'S BOXES

Pandora has five boxes on her shelves (a plan of which can be seen below). What is the colour of each box and what does Pandora keep inside it?

1   The gold box which contains stamps is further right than the box in which Pandora keeps pens.

2   The box of coins is further left than the red box, which is on a lower shelf than the box in which Pandora keeps coins.

3   The box containing candies is directly below the green box.

4   The purple box is directly next to the silver box, which isn't directly next to the red box.

	Colour					Contents				
	Gold	Green	Purple	Red	Silver	Buttons	Candies	Coins	Pens	Stamps
Box A										
Box B										
Box C										
Box D										
Box E										
Buttons										
Candies										
Coins										
Pens										
Stamps										

LEFT ⇦   **RIGHT** ⇨

A		B

C	D	E

Box	Colour	Contents

FRESHENING UP

64 Four people who live in neighbouring apartments decided to spruce up their lounges last December, in order that they would look fresh and bright for Christmas and the New Year. Each painted the walls a different colour and bought one new item for the room. Can you decide who lives in each numbered apartment, the colour he or she chose for the walls and the new item each purchased?

1 The occupant of apartment 1 is Geraldine, who didn't choose white paint for her walls.

2 Henry isn't the occupant of apartment 3, where the lounge walls are cream.

3 The person who lives in apartment 2 purchased a new carpet for his or her lounge.

4 Grant (who painted his lounge walls a fetching shade of grey) lives in an apartment with a number either two higher or two lower than that for which someone purchased a new television.

5 Heather didn't buy new curtains for her lounge.

	Occupant				Colour				Item			
	Geraldine	Grant	Heather	Henry	Beige	Cream	Grey	White	Carpet	Curtains	Light fitting	Television
Apartment 1												
Apartment 2												
Apartment 3												
Apartment 4												
Carpet									
Curtains									
Light fitting									
Television									
Beige									
Cream									
Grey									
White									

Apartment	Occupant	Colour	Item

70

PARTY TIME

Four children celebrated their birthdays last week and had parties on different days. What is each child's full name, how many guests were invited, and on which day was his or her party?

1   Pippa's party was later in the week than that of the child surnamed Fisher.

2   Larry's party was either two days before or two days after that of the child who invited most guests.

3   The child surnamed Best invited twice as many children as the number attending Warren's party on Friday.

4   The child surnamed Parry had his or her party later in the week than Candice's party, which was later in the week than that to which ten guests were invited.

5   There were more guests at Larry's party than the number invited by Pippa.

	Surname				Guests				Day			
	Best	Fisher	Flynn	Parry	5	6	10	12	Monday	Tuesday	Wednesday	Friday
Candice												
Larry												
Pippa												
Warren												
Monday												
Tuesday												
Wednesday												
Friday												
5 guests												
6 guests												
10 guests												
12 guests												

Child	Surname	Guests	Day

71

Essay Overkill

66
Miss Penn set her pupils the task of writing essays about what they did during the summer. However, once they started, five of them didn't want to stop, with the result that they wrote too much and handed in their essays two weeks late. How many pages did each write, and on which day last week did he or she eventually hand in the work to Miss Penn?

1 Maurice handed in his essay three days later than Naomi, who wrote three fewer pages than Patrick.

2 Patrick handed in his work two days later than Pauline, who wrote two fewer pages than Joseph.

3 Patrick wrote fewer pages (and handed in his essay earlier in the week than) the tallest child.

| | Pages | | | | | Day | | | | |
	15	16	17	18	19	Monday	Tuesday	Wednesday	Thursday	Friday
Joseph										
Maurice										
Naomi										
Patrick										
Pauline										
Monday					
Tuesday					
Wednesday					
Thursday					
Friday					

Pupil	Pages	Day

POTS OF HERBS

Basil has five pots of herbs (as you can see from the picture below) growing on his patio. Each herb was planted on a different day last week. Can you discover the facts by following the clues?

1   The chives are in the pot next to and right of the pot next to and right of that planted three days after the dill.

2   Basil planted parsley in pot E four days before the herb in pot B was planted.

3   Pot A isn't the one containing thyme, which Basil planted on Monday.

	Herb					Day				
	Chives	Dill	Garden mint	Parsley	Thyme	Monday	Tuesday	Wednesday	Friday	Saturday
Pot A										
Pot B										
Pot C										
Pot D										
Pot E										
Monday										
Tuesday										
Wednesday										
Friday										
Saturday										

LEFT ⇐   **RIGHT** ⇒

A   B   C   D   E

Pot	Herb	Day

73

TREE HOUSES

68 The map below shows four houses, each with gardens containing just one type of tree. Who lives at each address, and how many trees of a particular type grow there?

1   There are five fewer trees in Rachel's garden than the number of willows in the garden of the house directly east of Ruth's.

2   Ralph has two fewer trees than the number of elms in the garden of the house directly north of Rodney's.

3   There are two more oak trees than the number of trees in the garden of the house owned by the tallest of the four neighbours.

		Occupant				Quantity				Type			
		Rachel	Ralph	Rodney	Ruth	3	5	8	10	Ash	Elm	Oak	Willow
	No 5												
	No 6												
	No 7												
	No 8												
Type	Ash												
	Elm												
	Oak												
	Willow												
Quantity	3												
	5												
	8												
	10												

N
W—E
S

| 5 | | 6 |
| 7 | | 8 |

House No	Occupant	Quantity	Type

QUICK SERVICE

The Systems Department at Quickforce Ltd has recently instigated a new method of logging and responding to calls for assistance with computer problems. Four people called the helpdesk this morning with different problems. At what time did each call, with what was he or she experiencing difficulties, and what was the response time in each case?

69

1   The caller who had the shortest response time rang half an hour later than the person who had trouble with a monitor, who didn't have the longest response time. Martha didn't report a problem with her monitor.

2   Neil rang to report a non-functioning keyboard. The response time to his call was one minute less than to the call made by Karen, who rang 15 minutes later than the person whose mouse had stopped working.

3   The person whose mouse had stopped working had a quicker response time than that of the person who called at 11.00am.

	Called at				Problem				Time (minutes)			
	10.00am	10.30am	10.45am	11.00am	Keyboard	Memory stick	Monitor	Mouse	4	5	6	7
Antony												
Karen												
Martha												
Neil												
4 minutes												
5 minutes												
6 minutes												
7 minutes												
Keyboard												
Memory stick												
Monitor												
Mouse												

Caller	Called at	Problem	Time

75

WAYS TO WORK

70

Shortly after moving to a new neighbourhood, Shirley discovered that there were five different routes she could take to work. She tried them all, to see which was quickest, on different days last week. Can you discover which route was taken each day, and the amount of time it took?

1 Shirley took route A two days later than the one that took two minutes longer to travel than route D.

2 The route that took 13 minutes to travel was taken the day after route B, but the day before route C.

3 Route D was taken later in the week than the one which took the shortest time to travel, but earlier in the week than route E.

4 Thursday's journey didn't take one minute less time than Tuesday's journey to work.

	Day					Time (minutes)				
	Monday	Tuesday	Wednesday	Thursday	Friday	11	12	13	14	15
Route A										
Route B										
Route C										
Route D										
Route E										
11 minutes					
12 minutes					
13 minutes					
14 minutes					
15 minutes					

Route	Day	Time

Mr and Mrs

This puzzle concerns four sisters, all of whom took the surnames of their husbands when they married. No man has a name which begins with the same letter as that of his surname. Who is married to each man, and what is his surname?

71

1 Neither Glenda nor Rosemary is Mrs Walker.

2 Neither William nor Lee is married to Glenda, whose husband's name starts with the same letter as that of Fiona's surname.

3 Nancy Stanford is married to the man whose name begins with the same letter as that of Glenda's surname.

4 Neither Hal nor Lee is married to Lydia, whose husband's name starts with the same letter as that of Sean's surname.

		Husband				Surname				
	Chris	Hal	Lee	Sean	William	Connor	Holmes	Lacey	Stanford	Walker
Fiona										
Glenda										
Lydia										
Nancy										
Rosemary										
Connor										
Holmes										
Lacey										
Stanford										
Walker										

Sister	Husband	Surname

ROOM SERVICE

72 Last night, four guests staying at the Tower Hotel rang down to reception to request certain items. What did each person want, in which numbered room is he or she staying, and at what time was each guest's call?

1 The woman in room 267 called later than the person who wanted more towels.

2 Mrs Gates asked for an extra blanket, as she feels the cold at night. Her call wasn't at half past eight.

3 Mr Jackson rang half an hour earlier than Mr Sands, who requested a pot of coffee.

4 The woman in room 309 wasn't the guest who called an hour earlier than the man in room 134.

	Wanted				Room No				Time			
	Blanket	Coffee	Pillow	Towels	134	267	282	309	8.30pm	9.30pm	10.00pm	10.30pm
Mrs Gates												
Mr Jackson												
Miss Milton												
Mr Sands												
8.30pm												
9.30pm												
10.00pm												
10.30pm												
Room No 134												
Room No 267												
Room No 282												
Room No 309												

Guest	Wanted	Room No	Time

LITTLE STITCHES

Four little girls sewed their first garments, aprons, at school. They took them home today to show their parents, who were delighted to view their daughters' talents. What colour is each girl's apron, what flower did she embroider onto its pocket, and how long did it take her to make?

73

1   The girl who made an apron in the shortest time stitched a daisy onto its pocket.

2   Tracey made the blue apron, which didn't have a daisy on its pocket.

3   Cara stitched a buttercup onto the pocket of her apron, which didn't take six weeks to make.

4   The green apron took one week longer to make than the pink apron.

5   Jenny (who took four weeks to make her apron) didn't stitch a primrose onto its pocket. Jenny didn't make the pink apron.

	Blue	Green	Orange	Pink	Buttercup	Daisy	Poppy	Primrose	3 weeks	4 weeks	5 weeks	6 weeks
Alice												
Cara												
Jenny												
Tracey												
3 weeks												
4 weeks												
5 weeks												
6 weeks												
Buttercup												
Daisy												
Poppy												
Primrose												

Girl	Colour	Flower	Time

FORMIDABLE TASKS

74 The five women in this puzzle today each tackled two different tasks they don't enjoy, which they've been putting off for a very long time. What did every woman do this morning and this afternoon?

1 Donna cleaned her house this afternoon. The woman who cleaned her house this morning went shopping this afternoon, unlike Georgina.

2 Cora spent this morning in the garden, but didn't do any baking this afternoon. The job tackled by Cora this afternoon was different to the one Naomi did this morning.

3 The woman who did the ironing in the morning didn't do any baking this afternoon.

4 Naomi hasn't been shopping today.

	Morning					Afternoon				
	Baking	Cleaning	Gardening	Ironing	Shopping	Baking	Cleaning	Gardening	Ironing	Shopping
Cora										
Donna										
Georgina										
Naomi										
Patricia										
Afternoon Baking										
Cleaning										
Gardening										
Ironing										
Shopping										

Woman	Morning	Afternoon

EGG COLLECTING

The Faverolle children are currently staying on holiday at their
grandparents' chicken farm. Every morning they go out to collect the
eggs. Work through the clues to discover the colour of each child's
basket as well as the number of eggs collected this morning.

75

1   Edward (whose basket isn't black) collected the fewest eggs.

2   Paul collected four fewer eggs than the child with the red basket.

3   The child with the green basket collected 17 eggs.

4   The child with the blue basket collected four fewer eggs than Sally, whose
    basket is brown.

5   Helen isn't the child who collected the highest number of eggs this morning.

	Black	Blue	Brown	Green	Red	11	15	17	19	21
Edward										
Helen										
John										
Paul										
Sally										
11 eggs										
15 eggs										
17 eggs										
19 eggs										
21 eggs										

Child	Basket	No of eggs

QUADRUPLETS

76 Four brothers were all born at the same time, but share nothing in common with one another in terms of appearance. Can you work out each man's hair colour, height and weight?

1 The man with blond hair weighs ten pounds more than Ralph.

2 Ralph is taller than the heaviest man.

3 The shortest man weighs ten pounds less than the man with red hair (who isn't Rupert).

4 Rory is taller than his brother Rupert, who is taller than Richard.

5 Rupert is shorter than the man with brown hair (who isn't Rory).

	Hair				Height				Weight			
	Black	Blond	Brown	Red	5 feet 8 inches	5 feet 9 inches	5 feet 10 inches	5 feet 11 inches	160 pounds	165 pounds	170 pounds	180 pounds
Ralph												
Richard												
Rory												
Rupert												
160 pounds												
165 pounds												
170 pounds												
180 pounds												
5 feet 8 inches												
5 feet 9 inches												
5 feet 10 inches												
5 feet 11 inches												

Brother	Hair	Height	Weight

PIRATES' TALES

One night back in March 1822, four captains of pirate ships found themselves seated around the same table in an ale house. After they had introduced themselves, they boasted of their ships and the number of other vessels they had looted and sunk so far that year. What was the name of each captain's ship, how many crew had he, and how many ships had they raided?

1   Bad Bill's ship had a higher number of crew members than sailed aboard the *Barbaric*, but fewer than worked for the man who had raided seven ships so far that year. Bad Bill had raided more than six ships.

2   Dirty Dan's men had raided two more vessels than the crew of the *Golden Doe*, who numbered one fewer than the crew aboard the ship that had raided six vessels.

3   The crew of the *Swordfish* numbered two fewer than the number who sailed with Terrible Tom.

	Ship				Crew				No of ships			
	Barbaric	*Golden Doe*	*Katrina*	*Swordfish*	28	29	30	31	6	7	8	9
Bad Bill												
Dirty Dan												
Horrible Harry												
Terrible Tom												
Ships 6												
7												
8												
9												
Crew 28												
29												
30												
31												

Captain	Ship	Crew	No of ships

New Neighbours

78 Five couples have recently moved into houses in Corner Street. Using the clues and the map below will help you to determine their names.

1   Rory and his wife Molly live further east than Moira and her husband who don't live directly south of Muriel and her husband.

2   Rupert and his wife live directly north of Megan and her husband Raymond.

3   Robert's wife isn't Mandy, who lives with her husband in a house with a number two lower than that which Richard and his wife moved into last month.

	Husband					Wife				
	Raymond	Richard	Robert	Rory	Rupert	Mandy	Megan	Moira	Molly	Muriel
No 1										
No 2										
No 3										
No 6										
No 8										
Mandy										
Megan										
Moira										
Molly										
Muriel										

House No	Husband	Wife

BUSY MORNINGS

Louise had five appointments on different mornings last week. At what time and on which day were her appointments?

1   The appointment Louise made to see the optician was at a time three quarters of an hour later in the morning than that of her Thursday appointment.

2   Louise kept an appointment with her hairdresser last Monday morning.

3   The 11.15am appointment with the doctor was the day before Louise saw the chiropodist.

4   The 9.15am appointment was the day before the 10.30am appointment.

	Time					Day				
	9.15am	9.45am	10.30am	11.15am	11.45am	Monday	Tuesday	Wednesday	Thursday	Friday
Chiropodist										
Dentist										
Doctor										
Hairdresser										
Optician										
Monday					
Tuesday					
Wednesday					
Thursday					
Friday					

Appointment	Time	Day

SPLIT PERSONALITIES

80 Maurice has taken photographs of four of his teachers, cutting each into four pieces (head, body, legs and feet) and then reassembling them in such a way that each 'new' picture contains pieces of four 'old' ones. How have the pictures been reassembled?

1 Miss Owen's head is in the same picture as Mr White's legs.

2 Mrs Rose's legs are now attached to Miss Owen's feet.

3 Mr White's feet are in the same picture as Miss Owen's body.

4 Mr Potter's feet and Miss Owen's legs are in two different pictures.

5 The person whose feet are in the same picture as Miss Owen's legs isn't the one whose legs are now attached to Mr White's body.

		Body				Legs				Feet			
		Miss Owen	Mr Potter	Mrs Rose	Mr White	Miss Owen	Mr Potter	Mrs Rose	Mr White	Miss Owen	Mr Potter	Mrs Rose	Mr White
Head	Miss Owen												
	Mr Potter												
	Mrs Rose												
	Mr White												
Feet	Miss Owen												
	Mr Potter												
	Mrs Rose												
	Mr White												
Legs	Miss Owen												
	Mr Potter												
	Mrs Rose												
	Mr White												

Head	Body	Legs	Feet

Playing Cards

The people in this puzzle are playing a game of cards and each has
three in his or her hand: one heart, one club and one diamond.
Can you discover which three cards are in each person's hand?
(NB – A=ace, J=jack, Q=queen and K=king; and in the game ace=1,
jack=11, queen=12, king=13 and the values of the other cards are as
per their numbers.)

81

1   James's heart has the same value as the club held by the player who has the three of diamonds.

2   James's diamond has a value higher than that of Ruby's heart, which has a value two higher than that of her club.

3   The player with the ace of hearts has a club with a value two lower than that of Maria's club.

4   The person with the queen of hearts has a diamond with a lower value than that held by Kevin.

	Heart				Club				Diamond			
	A	4	8	Q	4	6	8	10	3	6	J	K
James												
Kevin												
Maria												
Ruby												
Diamond 3												
6												
J												
K												
Club 4												
6												
8												
10												

Player	Heart	Club	Diamond

No Smoking

82 Five women recently gave up smoking. Each now chews on something whenever she has a craving for a cigarette. Find out how many cigarettes per day each woman used to smoke, as well as what she uses to combat the desire to light up again.

1 The woman who chews toffees smoked fewer cigarettes per day than Nadine.

2 Vera (who used to smoke 16 cigarettes per day) is the sister of Claire, who uses peppermints as a way of combatting her craving.

3 The woman who chews gum once smoked four more cigarettes per day than Sonja, who doesn't eat apples.

4 The woman who munches apples once smoked fewer cigarettes than Brenda, who smoked fewer cigarettes than the woman who crunches her way through several packets of peanuts per day.

	Cigarettes					Chews				
	10	12	14	16	18	Apples	Gum	Peanuts	Peppermints	Toffees
Brenda										
Claire										
Nadine										
Sonja										
Vera										
Apples										
Gum										
Peanuts										
Peppermints										
Toffees										

Name	Cigarettes	Chews

NICELY WRAPPED UP

The picture below shows five presents, all nicely wrapped and waiting to be given to people. Can you determine the contents of each, as well as the colour of its bow?

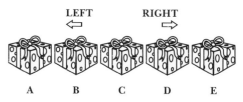

LEFT ⇐ **RIGHT** ⇒

A B C D E

1 The present of cosmetics is directly next to and left of the one with a yellow bow, which is further left than the parcel containing an ornament.

2 The parcel containing books has a blue bow and is further right than (and not next to) the present with a scarlet bow, which doesn't contain cosmetics.

3 The present of perfume is further left than the one with a pink bow, which is further left than at least one other present.

4 The present that is furthest right doesn't have a blue bow.

	Contents					Bow colour				
	Books	Coffee set	Cosmetics	Ornament	Perfume	Blue	Pink	Purple	Scarlet	Yellow
Present A										
Present B										
Present C										
Present D										
Present E										
Blue										
Pink										
Purple										
Scarlet										
Yellow										

Present	Contents	Bow colour

GRANDPARENTS

84 Four couples were talking about their families yesterday afternoon. Each couple has a different number of grandchildren, the latest additions to their numbers all being born last year. Who is married to whom, how many grandchildren have they, and in which month last year was their latest grandchild born?

1 Fred has either one or two more grandchildren than George, whose latest grandchild was born in July.

2 The man with the most grandchildren is grandfather to a baby born either two months before or two months later than the latest addition to Fred's family. Fred's wife isn't Rosie.

3 Bob's youngest grandchild was born later than that of the couple who have eight grandchildren, but earlier than the latest addition to Susan's family.

4 Ann has twice as many grandchildren as George and his wife.

	Grandma				G'children				Born			
	Ann	Jane	Rosie	Susan	4	5	8	10	March	April	May	July
Bob												
Fred												
George												
Tony												
March												
April												
May												
July												
4												
5												
8												
10												

G'children

Grandpa	Grandma	G'children	Born

PARACHUTE DROP

On a moonless night during the war that raged between two countries, four soldiers headed off in different directions after being parachuted into enemy territory, their mission being to find the nearest town and see if there was any military installation nearby. Every man was successful, and you can count your mission successful if you discover the direction in which each went, together with the other details.

85

1 Bob (who didn't travel north) located the town of Gunnerford.

2 The man who went south found the tanks, despite their heavy camouflage.

3 The soldier who walked east to Battlebury was neither Johnnie nor Tommy.

4 The missile launcher was hidden just outside of Trenchbridge. It wasn't located by the man who travelled north from the dropping zone.

5 The ammunition ('ammo') dump wasn't found by the soldier who went east.

6 West wasn't the direction in which Tommy walked after landing.

	Direction				Town				Found			
	North	South	East	West	Battlebury	Gunnerford	Sapper's Wood	Trenchbridge	Ammo dump	Field guns	Missile launcher	Tanks
Albert												
Bob												
Johnnie												
Tommy												
Ammo dump												
Field guns												
Missile launcher												
Tanks												
Battlebury												
Gunnerford												
Sapper's Wood												
Trenchbridge												

Soldier	Direction	Town	Found

TEENAGE DREAM

86 Madeline and her four friends were delighted when their favourite band, *Teenage Dream*, came to town. Each bought a ticket to the first night's concert and spent most of the evening drooling at the sight of her favourite group member (and, fortunately, each girl has a different favourite). Can you discover which boy is the idol of each girl, together with his position in the group?

1 Lyndsey's heartthrob is Gary, who isn't the lead guitarist.

2 Poppy prefers the keyboard player, and doesn't think Errol is at all attractive.

3 Leroy is Holly's idol. He doesn't play the guitar.

4 Catherine's idol isn't Ashley, who is the vocalist with the band.

	Favourite					Position				
	Ashley	Ben	Errol	Gary	Leroy	Bass guitarist	Drummer	Keyboard player	Lead guitarist	Vocalist
Catherine										
Holly										
Lyndsey										
Madeline										
Poppy										
Bass guitarist										
Drummer										
Keyboard player										
Lead guitarist										
Vocalist										

Girl	Favourite	Position

VALUABLE FINDS

Whilst sorting through the contents of their attics, which contain the accumulated junk of previous generations, five people came across items which are now collectors' pieces, and worth considerably more than they were when discarded. What did each person find, and how much is it worth?

1   The slightly faded and moth-eaten tapestry is worth more than the rickety old chair.

2   The item found by Boris is worth $1,000 more than the silver candelabra, but $1,000 less than the item found by Caitlin, which isn't the marble figurine.

3   The portrait discovered by Arthur is worth less than the marble figurine, which isn't the item valued at $6,000.

4   Martin discovered an item worth less than the amount the silver candelabra is expected to fetch when it is put up for auction next month.

	Item					Value				
	Candelabra	Chair	Figurine	Portrait	Tapestry	$3,000	$4,000	$5,000	$6,000	$7,000
Arthur										
Boris										
Caitlin											
Gloria											
Martin											
$3,000											
$4,000											
$5,000											
$6,000											
$7,000											

Finder	Item	Value

A FAMILY MATTER

88 Each of the four families in this puzzle consists of a husband, wife, son and daughter whose names begin with four different letters of the alphabet. Can you decide who is related to whom?

1 John's son has a name which begins with the same letter as that of Marian's daughter.

2 Nancy's mother has a name which begins with the same letter as that of Melissa's father.

		Wife				Son				Daughter			
		Glenda	Jennifer	Marian	Norma	Gerry	Joe	Mitch	Neil	Gemma	Joelle	Melissa	Nancy
Husband	Geoff												
	John												
	Malcolm												
	Nigel												
Daughter	Gemma												
	Joelle												
	Melissa												
	Nancy												
Son	Gerry												
	Joe												
	Mitch												
	Neil												

Husband	Wife	Son	Daughter

94

MOVIE TIME

Four couples each went to one of four different cinemas in town last night, to see a movie. Can you link each couple together with the title of the film they saw and its genre?

1 Nicholas took his girlfriend to see the romance. His girlfriend isn't Josie, who saw *Aunt Agatha*.

2 *The Question* is a murder mystery. It was seen by neither Vernon nor Sarah.

3 Verity and her boyfriend went to see *Gordon's Goal*. Verity's boyfriend is neither Nicholas nor Brian.

4 Brian and his girlfriend saw the western. He enjoyed it immensely; she didn't!

	Girlfriend				Title				Genre			
	Josie	Marcia	Sarah	Verity	Aunt Agatha	Gordon's Goal	Heaven Scent	The Question	Murder mystery	Romance	Science fiction	Western
Brian												
Nicholas												
Rupert												
Vernon												
Murder mystery												
Romance												
Science fiction												
Western												
Aunt Agatha												
Gordon's Goal												
Heaven Scent												
The Question												

Boyfriend	Girlfriend	Title	Genre

FISH PONDS

90 Five friends all have fish ponds in their gardens, in which they have various quantities of koi carp and tench. How many fish of each type has each person?

1 Lynne has two fewer tench than Tricia, who has two more koi carp than Barry.

2 Norman has three fewer tench than koi carp. He also has fewer tench than Lynne.

3 No pond contains precisely the same number of koi carp as tench.

4 One of the ponds contains three koi carp and two tench.

5 No pond contains two koi carp and four tench.

	Koi carp					Tench				
	2	3	4	5	6	2	3	4	5	6
Barry										
John										
Lynne										
Norman										
Tricia										
Tench 2					
Tench 3					
Tench 4					
Tench 5					
Tench 6					

Friend	Koi carp	Tench

WINNING STREAKS

The five Streak brothers all bet on horses in different races last Saturday afternoon, and all of them won a small amount. What was the name of the horse on which each placed a bet, and how much did each brother win?

1   The man who won $140 didn't place a bet on Minaret.

2   Seth didn't win the highest amount, but was very happy nonetheless!

3   Stan won twenty dollars more than Steve, who had placed a bet on West Hope.

4   One of the Streak brothers won $100 as the result of a bet on Good Will.

5   The man who put his money on Sunrise won forty dollars more than Saul, who won twenty dollars more than Simon.

	Bay Laurel	Good Will	Minaret	Sunrise	West Hope	$100	$120	$140	$160	$180
Saul										
Seth										
Simon										
Stan										
Steve										
$100					
$120					
$140					
$160					
$180					

Brother	Horse	Won

FATHERS IN WAITING

92

The four women in this puzzle are all expecting babies. Shortly after telling their husbands the good news, the men all went shopping, each returning home with something for the baby, although it may be some time before the baby can play with it! What is the name of each woman's husband, when is their baby due, and what did each man buy?

1 Marie's baby is due in July. Hoping for a girl, her husband bought a doll's house.

2 Ben's baby is due before that of the man who purchased a train set.

3 Tim's wife is Tina.

4 Ross bought a very large teddy bear.

5 Jack's wife is due to give birth either the month before or the month after Kirsty.

	Ben	Jack	Ross	Tim	March	April	June	July	Bicycle	Doll's house	Teddy bear	Train set
Jenny												
Kirsty												
Marie												
Tina												
Bicycle												
Doll's house												
Teddy bear												
Train set												
March												
April												
June												
July												

Woman	Husband	Baby due	Bought

RELATIVES ABROAD

Last year, Trevor visited four relatives who live abroad. Can you discover each woman's relationship to Trevor, the month he visited, and the country in which she lives?

93

1　Trevor visited Gloria earlier in the year than he went to see his sister, who lives in Portugal.

2　December's trip was to Poland, which isn't where his grandmother lives.

3　Belinda received a visit from Trevor earlier than December of last year. She doesn't live in Italy or Portugal.

4　Trevor visited his aunt in Italy later than January of last year.

5　Isabel isn't Trevor's cousin.

	Relation				Month				Country			
	Aunt	Cousin	Grandmother	Sister	January	April	August	December	Italy	Mexico	Poland	Portugal
Belinda												
Gloria												
Isabel												
Katrina												
Italy												
Mexico												
Poland												
Portugal												
January												
April												
August												
December												

Name	Relative	Month	Country

It's a Hold-up

94 Five commuters who take different routes to work were stuck in traffic jams this morning, for various lengths of time. What held up each traveller, and for how long?

1 Ms Dawlish was held up for longer than the commuter (not Miss O'Hare or Mr McNab) who was held up due to an accident.

2 A slow-moving caravan caused a delay of ten minutes less than the breakdown of a large lorry at a roundabout.

3 Mr Evans was held up by a herd of cattle on the road. His delay wasn't as long as that of the commuter (not Mr McNab) who was held up by the lorry breakdown.

4 Miss O'Hare was held up for a quarter of an hour less time than Mr Church.

	Reason					Time				
	Accident	Breakdown	Caravan	Cattle	Roadworks	10 minutes	15 minutes	20 minutes	25 minutes	30 minutes
Mr Church										
Ms Dawlish										
Mr Evans										
Mr McNab										
Miss O'Hare										
10 minutes										
15 minutes										
20 minutes										
25 minutes										
30 minutes										

Commuter	Reason	Time

PARKING LOT

Five cars are in the parking lot you see depicted below. All of the cars are of different colours. Who owns each, and what is its colour?

95

1. Mr Porter's car is further west than the green car, and both are further south than the car driven by Mrs Scott.

2. The driver of the red car is a man. He has parked his vehicle either directly north or directly south of the one belonging to Miss Young, and both he and Miss Young have parked further west than Mr Warner.

3. Miss Young's car has a number three higher than that of the black car.

4. The blue car is parked further east than the white car. Both are driven by members of the opposite sex.

	Owner					Colour				
	Mr Berry	Mr Porter	Mrs Scott	Mr Warner	Miss Young	Black	Blue	Green	Red	White
Car 1										
Car 2										
Car 3										
Car 4										
Car 5										
Black										
Blue										
Green										
Red										
White										

Car	Owner	Colour

3D PUZZLE

96 Each of the four listed boxes has different dimensions (height, width and depth) to the other three boxes. Can you work out the size of each box? (NB – Any box may have the same height as width or depth, or the same width as depth: for example, any box may be 29 cm high, 25 cm wide and 25cm deep.)

1   Box B has a height two centimetres more than its depth, and isn't as wide as the box that is 26 cm in height.

2   Box C is one centimetre deeper than its width, and isn't as tall as the box that is 24 cm wide.

3   Box D has a depth one centimetre more than its height, and isn't as wide as the box that is 25 cm deep.

		Height (cm)				Width (cm)				Depth (cm)			
		26	28	29	30	24	25	26	27	25	26	27	29
	Box A												
	Box B												
	Box C												
	Box D												
Depth	25 cm												
	26 cm												
	27 cm												
	29 cm												
Width	24 cm												
	25 cm												
	26 cm												
	27 cm												

Box	Height	Width	Depth

TESTING TIMES

It was exam time at St Custard's Elementary School last week, and the brightest pupils from the four classes comprising Year Six were striving hard to be 'top of the form'. Study the clues to work out each pupil's class together with his or her year position and most successful subject.

1 The child in Class 1 attained a higher position than the pupil whose most successful subject is science.

2 Fiona (who is a pupil in Class 4) achieved a higher position than the child who does best in mathematics.

3 The Class 2 pupil came first, getting the highest marks, unlike Nick (whose top subject is English).

4 Jane excels in geography and hopes to be a teacher when she grows up.

	Class				Position				Subject			
	1	2	3	4	First	Second	Fourth	Fifth	English	Geography	Mathematics	Science
Fiona												
Jane												
Neil												
Nick												
English												
Geography												
Mathematics												
Science												
First												
Second												
Fourth												
Fifth												

Pupil	Class	Position	Subject

DRIFTWOOD ART

98 Jonathan carves ornaments from driftwood he finds on the beach near his workshop: Jennifer makes collage pictures from sand, seashells and dried seaweed, which she also finds on the beach. Together they own a small shop on the seafront, selling their art. How many collages and ornaments did they sell from Monday to Friday of last week?

1 On the day that Jonathan and Jennifer sold six ornaments, they didn't also sell seven collages.

2 They sold the same number of ornaments on Friday as the number of collages sold on Wednesday, which was two more than the number of ornaments they sold on Wednesday.

3 Jonathan and Jennifer sold five ornaments the day after they sold eight collages.

4 Jonathan and Jennifer sold four collages the day before they sold seven ornaments. They sold seven ornaments two days after they sold ten ornaments.

	Collages					Ornaments				
	4	5	7	8	9	5	6	7	9	10
Monday										
Tuesday										
Wednesday										
Thursday										
Friday										
Ornaments 5										
6										
7										
9										
10										

Day	Collages	Ornaments

THE HOMEWORK TABLE

Five boys are each seated around a table (as shown in the picture below), all doing their homework. Can you name the occupant of every chair, and the subject on which he is working? (NB - the words 'seated around the table in a clockwise direction' do not imply starting at any particular chair.)

99

1   Seated around the table in a clockwise direction are: the boy studying drama; Dave; Roger (who isn't in seat B or seat D); the boy doing English homework; and John.

2   Seated around the table in a clockwise direction are: the boy doing history homework; Eddie; the boy studying mathematics; Thomas; and another boy (who isn't in seat B or seat E).

	Dave	Eddie	John	Roger	Thomas	Drama	English	Geography	History	Mathematics
Chair A										
Chair B										
Chair C										
Chair D										
Chair E										
Drama										
English										
Geography										
History										
Mathematics										

Clockwise

Chair	Occupant	Subject

CANS OF PAINT

100

On the shelves below are a dozen cans of paint. Each shelf has cans containing four different colours of paint, and every colour is in cans identified by three different letters. Can you decide the contents of each can on the top, middle and bottom shelves?

1   On the bottom shelf, the yellow paint is further left than the red paint; however, on the middle shelf, the yellow paint is further right than the red paint.

2   On the top shelf, the cans containing red and blue paint have one can of paint between them; however, on the middle shelf, the blue paint is directly next to (and right of) the red paint.

3   On the top shelf, the green paint isn't in can D, but it is further right than the blue paint; however, on the middle shelf, the blue paint is further right than the green paint.

		Top				Middle				Bottom			
		Blue	Green	Red	Yellow	Blue	Green	Red	Yellow	Blue	Green	Red	Yellow
	Can A												
	Can B												
	Can C												
	Can D												
Bottom	Blue												
	Green												
	Red												
	Yellow												
Middle	Blue												
	Green												
	Red												
	Yellow												

LEFT ⇐   **RIGHT** ⇒

A   B   C   D

A   B   C   D

A   B   C   D

Can	Top	Middle	Bottom

THE ROKKET SISTERS

The five members of the band The Rokket Sisters all have day jobs (if you've ever been to a Rokket Sisters gig you'll understand why!). Can you work out which instrument each plays, and her regular job?

1. Jody is the lead guitarist and Lucy is the bass guitarist with the group. Jody isn't the woman who works as a bus driver during the day.

2. The woman who works as a waitress for her living plays rhythm guitar with The Rokket Sisters. Her elder sister Linda is the group's drummer.

3. Carrie works as a barmaid in a local wine bar.

4. Neither Linda nor Jody is employed as a teacher.

	Instrument					Day job				
	Bass guitar	Drums	Keyboards	Lead guitar	Rhythm guitar	Barmaid	Bus driver	Company rep	Teacher	Waitress
Carrie										
Jody										
Judy										
Linda										
Lucy										
Barmaid										
Bus driver										
Company rep										
Teacher										
Waitress										

Member	Instrument	Day job

WEDDING SHOT

102 Uncle Jim has just received a set of photographs taken at his niece's wedding. Poor Jim is totally perplexed as to the identity of each of the people in a group shot, as the only face he recognises is his own! Can you help him work out who each individual is, where he or she is from and the age of each person in the group?

1   The guest from Etheridge is older than the person from Blackrock but either three or four years younger than Archie.

2   Maude is from Accringtown and is younger than the person (not Archie) from Mannstown, but older than Ethel.

3   Bill is four years older than Thomas.

	Town					Age				
	Accringtown	Blackrock	Etheridge	Mannstown	Trowville	41	45	54	57	58
Archie										
Bill										
Ethel										
Maude										
Thomas										
41										
45										
54										
57										
58										

Name	From	Age

NIGHTS OUT

The small town of Puggleton has five public bars. All have been losing trade recently after the closure of Ridley's Reliable Rubber Rings, the town's main employer, put many people out of work. So each public bar has decided to attract a bigger share of what custom there is by holding a special entertainment night once a week. What sort of entertainment is each offering and on which night?

1 The quiz night at The Plough is proving very popular with local people.

2 The entertainment at The Ferret takes place two nights earlier in the week than the karaoke night which, in turn, is earlier in the week than the quiz night.

3 The folk band regularly plays the night before the darts match which takes place earlier in the week than the entertainment laid on at The Fox.

4 The entertainment night at the Black Swan is earlier in the week than that at the King's Head.

	Entertainment					Night				
	Darts match	Folk band	Karaoke	Quiz night	Skittles	Tuesday	Thursday	Friday	Saturday	Sunday
Black Swan										
Kings Head										
The Ferret										
The Fox										
The Plough										
Tuesday										
Thursday										
Friday										
Saturday										
Sunday										

Public bar	Entertainment	Night

Mountain Biking

104 Four mountain-bikers decided to meet at Topps Hill and have a race to the top and back via a trail they had marked out. What was the order of finish for each biker, the time each took to reach the top, and the make of bike each rider owns? The time taken to reach the top didn't necessarily have an effect on a rider's finishing position, as some men made the descent quicker than others.

1 Eddie finished one place ahead of the man who owns the JetStream bike.

2 The man who rides a LightningOne isn't Mike, who finished somewhere behind the rider of the ArrowFlite cycle, who took sixteen minutes and five seconds to get to the top of the hill.

3 The man whose time was sixteen minutes and ten seconds is Tommy, who finished further behind than Mike.

4 Carl finished two places ahead of the man (not Mike) who took fifteen minutes and twenty-five seconds to reach the top of the hill.

	Order				Time				Bike			
	1st	2nd	3rd	4th	15m 25s	15m 45s	16m 05s	16m 10s	ArrowFlite	FlameStreak	JetStream	LightningOne
Carl												
Eddie												
Mike												
Tommy												
ArrowFlite												
FlameStreak												
JetStream												
LightningOne												
15m 25s												
15m 45s												
16m 05s												
16m 10s												

Name	Order	Time	Bike

SCHOOL TRIPS

The four children of the Thompson family all attend the local school, St Custard's Elementary. All four arrived home last week waving invitation forms for this year's various school exchange trips. Put on your thinking cap and work out each child's age, the destination they will be going to this year, and the starting date of the trip.

1 The pupil travelling to Wales on the last day of July is three years younger than Anna.

2 The trip to France will start on 21st July.

3 David (who isn't going to France) is older than the child who sets off in August.

4 William isn't the youngest of the four children.

5 Zoe is going to Belgium. She is either one year older or one year younger than William.

	Age				Destination				Date			
	10	11	13	14	Belgium	France	Ireland	Wales	21st July	24th July	31st July	13th August
Anna												
David												
William												
Zoe												
21st July												
24th July												
31st July												
13th August												
Belgium												
France												
Ireland												
Wales												

Child	Age	Destination	Date

111

WRITING LINES

106 Five children each misbehaved at school last week and received a detention as a result, the detention taking the form of a number of lines to be written. On which day did each child's punishment take place, and how many lines did he or she write?

1 The child who received a detention on Thursday had to write 60 more lines than Gordon.

2 Cheryl was told to write 30 fewer lines than Adam, whose detention was two days later in the week than Cheryl's.

3 Katie's detention was later in the week than Edward's, but the day before that of the child told to write 140 lines.

4 The child who wrote the most lines received a detention on Wednesday of last week.

	Monday	Tuesday	Wednesday	Thursday	Friday	50 lines	80 lines	110 lines	140 lines	170 lines
Adam										
Cheryl										
Edward										
Gordon										
Katie										
50 lines										
80 lines										
110 lines										
140 lines										
170 lines										

Child	Day	Lines

TOP OF THEIR GAME

Five experienced mountaineers have finalised plans for the first ascents of some of the world's highest peaks. Can you work out which mountain each will attempt and the country in which each is located? Every peak was named after its discoverer, so there are no language-related clues for you to cling to!

1. The peak named after Sir Christopher Kermet isn't in Argentina.

2. Of Bergmann and the man who intends to scale Fallov Peak, one is travelling to Chile and the other is travelling to Russia.

3. Of the mountaineer who will travel to Argentina and the one who will scale Widow's Peak, one is Montagnier and the other is Klamberer.

4. Of the man surnamed Skaler and the mountaineer travelling to Peru, one will be scaling Fallov Peak, and the other will climb Neverest.

5. Of the men planning to climb Pico Rodriguez and Kermet, one is Klamberer and the other is travelling to Russia.

		Mountain				Country				
	Fallov Peak	Kermet	Neverest	Pico Rodriguez	Widow's Peak	Argentina	Chile	Nepal	Peru	Russia
Bergmann										
Klamberer										
Montagnier										
Skaler										
Tumbla										
Argentina										
Chile										
Nepal										
Peru										
Russia										

Climber	Mountain	Country

WRITE ON

108 Four friends have each written a novel and hope that they'll be successful with their approaches to four different publishers. Can you work out each author's book title, the genre of the book and the publisher to whom it was sent?

1 Booke & Clubb received the comedy manuscript.

2 *Zenith Down* is a story of romance. It wasn't penned by Bryn, who sent his work to Boddis & Ripp.

3 The adventure story set in Africa is not entitled *Window Five.*

4 Nerys is the author of *Whirl's End.*

5 The science fiction story was written by Andrew, but not sent to Paige & Turner.

	Arches	Whirl's End	Window Five	Zenith Down	Adventure	Comedy	Romance	Sci-fi	Boddis & Ripp	Booke & Clubb	Paige & Turner	ParraGraff
Andrew												
Bryn												
Miranda												
Nerys												
Boddis & Ripp												
Booke & Clubb												
Paige & Turner												
ParraGraff												
Adventure												
Comedy												
Romance												
Sci-fi												

Name	Title	Genre	Publisher

YOUNG ARTISTS

Four children are currently sitting at easels numbered 1-4 in the art class at school. Each is painting a different picture. Can you identify each budding artist in terms of his or her surname, the subject of each child's painting and the number of the easel before which he or she is sitting?

1   The child surnamed Aster is painting a tree and is in front of an easel with a number two higher than that of Holly's easel.

2   The child surnamed Mitchell (who isn't painting a car) is at an easel with a number one lower than that of the child painting ducks.

3   One of the children is painting his or her mother, and is seated at an easel with a number one higher than that being used by Ricky, but one lower than that of the child (not Sara) with the surname Walters.

	Surname				Subject				Easel No			
	Aster	Goring	Mitchell	Walters	Car	Ducks	Mother	Tree	1	2	3	4
Colin												
Holly												
Ricky												
Sara												
Easel No 1												
Easel No 2												
Easel No 3												
Easel No 4												
Car												
Ducks												
Mother												
Tree												

Subject

Painter	Surname	Subject	Easel No

Springing Up

110 Five neighbours planted various numbers of crocus and daffodil bulbs in their gardens last autumn. This spring, they were delighted to see the colourful show the plants made. How many crocus and daffodil flowers did each see in his or her garden?

1 Mr Mason saw fewer crocuses in his garden than the number seen by Miss Stoker, but more than the number of crocuses in Ms Willis' garden.

2 Ms Willis saw fewer daffodils than Mr Havelock, who saw fewer daffodils than Miss Stoker.

3 The gardener who saw the most crocuses had four fewer daffodils than the number in Mr Mason's garden.

4 The number of crocuses in Mr Havelock's garden was the same as the number of daffodils in Mrs Carter's garden.

	Crocuses					Daffodils				
	39	40	43	44	45	40	44	46	50	52
Mrs Carter										
Mr Mason										
Mr Havelock										
Miss Stoker										
Ms Willis										
40 daffodils					
44 daffodils					
46 daffodils					
50 daffodils					
52 daffodils					

Gardener	Crocuses	Daffodils

Busy Saturday Night

Puggleton police station has had a busy Saturday night, with five call-outs received before midnight. Can you use your logical sleuthing skills to work out which crime scene was attended by each officer and the time of the call-out?

1   PC McNab (who didn't visit the scene of the burglary) was called out at 10.55pm last Saturday.

2   PC Dixon's call-out was the one before that of the officer who attended the burglary crime scene. PC Dixon didn't deal with the mugging.

3   PC Chase interviewed the people who had witnessed the bike theft, although by the time he reached the scene, the thief had pedalled away. PC Chase's call-out was earlier than PC Cooper's.

4   The call-out to the incident involving the theft of a car was dealt with by PC Peel.

		Crime					Time				
		Bar fight	Bike theft	Burglary	Car theft	Mugging	8.25pm	9.05pm	10.10pm	10.55pm	11.50pm
Officer	Chase										
	Cooper										
	Dixon										
	McNab										
	Peel										
	8.25pm										
	9.05pm										
	10.10pm										
	10.55pm										
	11.50pm										

Officer	Crime	Time

Rainy Afternoon

112 It's the start of the school summer holiday, it's raining and the Board children, stuck indoors are… well, bored. To keep them occupied, Mum gave each a small chore to do, then rewarded her son or daughter with a small treat and a comic to read. That solved Monday's problem – only another six weeks to go! What was each of the Board children's chore, treat and comic?

1 Annie (who wasn't asked to fold clothes) chose to read *Hooray!*. Neither she nor the child who read *Dash* was given a packet of potato chips.

2 David (who fed the family's pets) had a packet of peanuts, but didn't read *Dash*.

3 The child who read *Zippo* also did some vacuuming for Mrs Board.

4 Vicky's treat was a bar of chocolate.

	Chore				Treat				Comic			
	Feed pets	Fold clothes	Vacuuming	Washing up	Chocolate bar	Lollipop	Peanuts	Potato chips	Dash	Hooray!	Whee!	Zippo
Annie												
David												
Peter												
Vicky												
Dash												
Hooray!												
Whee!												
Zippo												
Chocolate bar												
Lollipop												
Peanuts												
Potato chips												

Child	Chore	Treat	Comic

A Farmer's Work
is Never Done

Fred the Farmer is ever a busy man, and apart from his usual farm work, tending the animals, planting and harvesting crops, etc, he has to take on outside work to help pay the bills. On different days of the week, Fred has regular small jobs in local villages. Harvest the clues and find out the name of the village in which Fred works on each day, what he does and how much he receives for his labour.

1   Fred works in Fieldham three days later in the week (and is paid $12 less) than the day on which he undertakes fencing work.

2   He works as a gardener in Hilldown later in the week than the day on which he receives $47 for his labours.

3   Every Friday, Fred travels to the village of Vale, but not to cut grass. On the day he cuts grass, Fred earns five dollars less than he gets for helping a local veterinary surgeon.

	Village				Work				Pay			
	Fieldham	Hilldown	Vale	Woodley	Cutting grass	Fencing	Gardening	Helping vet	$35	$40	$47	$52
Monday												
Tuesday												
Thursday												
Friday												
Pay $35												
$40												
$47												
$52												
Cutting grass												
Fencing												
Gardening												
Helping vet												

Day	Village	Work	Pay

MORE OF FRED THE FARMER

114 Fred the Farmer, despite all that he has to do on a regular basis, also has to find time next year to carry out some fairly big projects. Fred's worked out a programme to deal with these. Can you work out the month in which he plans to do each project and how long Fred has allowed himself for the job?

1 Fred intends to spend two more days digging ditches than the time he will spend on the job he has earmarked for April.

2 The barn is due to be erected in June. He has allocated two days longer for this task than for the one he intends to do the month after he has dug ditches.

3 Fred has allowed himself fewer days to fell trees than to build walls. He intends to build walls earlier than October.

4 He estimates that it will take precisely seven days to dig the pond.

		March	April	June	September	October	4	7	9	10	12
Project	Build walls										
	Dig ditches										
	Dig pond										
	Erect barn										
	Fell trees										
Days	4										
	7										
	9										
	10										
	12										

Project	Month	Days

120

FARMER'S DAUGHTERS

You remember Fred the Farmer? Of course you do! Well, this year he's got the additional headache and expense involved in marrying off his five daughters (five, how did Fred find the time...?!). What is each daughter's age, and what is the name of her prospective bridegroom?

1   Daisy is three years younger than David's fiancée, who is younger than Poppy.

2   Richard's fiancée is one year younger than Rosie, who isn't engaged to be married to Gerald.

3   Lily is six years older than Tansy.

4   John's fiancée is younger than Kenneth's intended bride, who isn't Poppy.

		Age					Groom				
		19	20	22	25	26	David	Gerald	John	Kenneth	Richard
Bride	Daisy										
	Lily										
	Poppy										
	Rosie										
	Tansy										
Groom	David										
	Gerald										
	John										
	Kenneth										
	Richard										

Bride	**Age**	**Groom**

SPLIT PERSONALITIES

116 Billy has taken photographs of four of his neighbours, cutting each into four pieces (head, body, legs and feet) and then reassembling them in such a way that each 'new' picture contains pieces of four 'old' ones. How have the pictures been reassembled?

1 Mr Holt's legs are in the same picture as the head of a woman.

2 Mr Lane's head is in the same picture as the feet of the woman whose head is in the same picture as Mr Lane's legs.

3 Mrs Lane's feet and Mr Holt's body are in two different pictures.

		Body				**Legs**				**Feet**			
		Mr Holt	Mrs Holt	Mr Lane	Mrs Lane	Mr Holt	Mrs Holt	Mr Lane	Mrs Lane	Mr Holt	Mrs Holt	Mr Lane	Mrs Lane
Head	Mr Holt												
	Mrs Holt												
	Mr Lane												
	Mrs Lane												
Feet	Mr Holt												
	Mrs Holt												
	Mr Lane												
	Mrs Lane												
Legs	Mr Holt												
	Mrs Holt												
	Mr Lane												
	Mrs Lane												

Head	Body	Legs	Feet

Playing Cards

The women in this puzzle are playing a game of cards and each has three in her hand: one heart, one diamond and one spade. Can you discover which three cards are in each woman's hand? (NB – A=ace, J=jack, Q=queen and K=king; and in the game ace=1, jack=11, queen=12, king=13 and the values of the other cards are as per their numbers.)

1   The woman with the jack of hearts is holding a diamond with a value one higher than that of the diamond in Geri's hand.

2   The woman with the nine of diamonds has a heart with a lower value than that of her spade, which has a higher value than that of Dawn's spade.

3   Ellen's heart has a value two lower than that of the diamond held by the woman (not Ellen or Geri) with the ace of spades.

4   Frances is holding a diamond with a value either one higher or one lower than that of the diamond held by Dawn.

5   Geri's spade has a higher value than that held by Frances.

	Heart				Diamond				Spade			
	5	6	J	Q	7	8	9	K	A	5	7	9
Dawn												
Ellen												
Frances												
Geri												
Spade A								
Spade 5								
Spade 7								
Spade 9								
Diamond 7				
Diamond 8				
Diamond 9				
Diamond K				

Player	Heart	Diamond	Spade

BUILDING SITE

118 It's lunch-break at the construction site of the Bluebottle Building in Bloxburg, East Dakota, and a group of artisans (all non-US citizens) are talking about where they come from. Use your skills to build on the information in the clues below, to find out each man's trade and country of origin.

1 Simon (who isn't from Mexico or Venezuela) is a bricklayer.

2 Joseph (who isn't a carpenter) is from either Mexico or Nicaragua.

3 Michael (who isn't an electrician) isn't the man from Jamaica who is employed as a plumber at the construction site.

4 The electrician is either from Venezuela or he's Anthony, who comes from Canada.

	Trade					From				
	Bricklayer	Carpenter	Electrician	Glazier	Plumber	Canada	Jamaica	Mexico	Nicaragua	Venezuela
Anthony										
Joseph										
Michael										
Samuel										
Simon										
Canada										
Jamaica										
Mexico										
Nicaragua										
Venezuela										

Name	Trade	From

WIZARD SHOW

It's Open Day at Bogwort's School for Young Wizards and the star pupils are showing off their (as yet) none-too-expert skills to their parents. Unfortunately, things have gone horribly wrong and five of the parents have been turned into things that they shouldn't have been turned into. Which parent was transformed by a careless pupil, and into what?

1   Of Plutonia and the person turned into a teapot, one was transformed by Adolph and the other was transformed by Mort.

2   Of Algol and the parent who was subjected to Uriah's badly-worded spell, one became a bat and the other became a duck (but not due to Manfred's carelessness).

3   Of the parent who suffered as a result of Mort's bad spell and the one who turned into a griffin, one was Merfyn and the other was Wanda.

4   Of Wanda and the parent changed into a fairy, one was affected by Herman's spell and the other wasn't!

| | \multicolumn{5}{c}{**Parent**} | \multicolumn{5}{c}{**Turned into**} |
	Algol	Merfyn	Plutonia	Uranius	Wanda	Bat	Duck	Griffin	Fairy	Teapot
Adolph										
Herman										
Manfred										
Mort										
Uriah										
Bat										
Duck										
Griffin										
Fairy										
Teapot										

Turned into (row label for Bat/Duck/Griffin/Fairy/Teapot)

Pupil	Parent	Turned into

WHEREFORE ART THOU?

120 Thespians R Us, one of the lesser-known theatrical agencies, has recently supplied several actors to star in plays by William Shakespeare in towns across the UK. However, due to chaotic management, the agency has lost track of which actor is where, and in which production and role. Can you help them to trace the whereabouts of their actors?

1 Ian Burton is neither the man playing Montjoy in Henry V, nor the man (not playing Montjoy) who is appearing in the production being staged in Westington.

2 Osric is a character in Hamlet. He is being played neither by Jack Lawes nor by the man currently in Bromford, who is Jack Lawes's cousin.

3 Lew Smith has the role of Edgar, but not in Macbeth. Nor is Lew Smith in Westington.

4 The man playing the role of Seyton isn't in Westington or Eastbank.

5 The play attracting record audiences at the theatre in Bromford isn't Macbeth.

	Play				Part				Town			
	Hamlet	Henry V	King Lear	Macbeth	Edgar	Montjoy	Osric	Seyton	Bromford	Crawwood	Eastbank	Westington
Derek Fox												
Ian Burton												
Jack Lawes												
Lew Smith												
Bromford												
Crawwood												
Eastbank												
Westington												
Edgar												
Montjoy												
Osric												
Seyton												

Actor	Play	Part	Town

Lost Cars

Yesterday, the car parks manager at the vast St Spenda's Shopping Centre was called by four distraught couples who couldn't remember where they had parked. As usual, the only advice he could give was that they should wait until the car parks emptied at closing time. What is the make of each couple's vehicle, and in which of the four areas (named after colours) and numbered space did they find it?

1   One car was eventually located in space number 16 in the blue area.

2   The Hondera found in the green area was in a space with a lower number than that in which Jack and Jo eventually found their car.

3   Jeff and Mary found their car in the red area. They don't own the Royola.

4   John and Mia own the car seen in space number 38.

5   Jack and Jo weren't looking for either the Royola or the Nickan.

	Car				Area				Space No			
	Fordson	Hondera	Nickan	Royola	Blue	Green	Red	Yellow	16	25	38	82
Jack and Jo												
Jeff and Mary												
Jim and Tina												
John and Mia												
Space No 16												
Space No 25												
Space No 38												
Space No 82												
Car park Blue												
Car park Green												
Car park Red												
Car park Yellow												

Couple	Car	Area	Space No

127

THE WRONG SANDWICHES

122 Wally, the office junior, has been sent to the sandwich shop with a list of requirements for his senior colleagues. However, the aptly-named Wally managed to lose the list on the way (some ten yards distance!) so he bet on memory – and lost. Who ordered what and what did they get instead?

1 The person who asked for a tuna sandwich received a salad sandwich instead. The one who wanted a salmon sandwich ended up eating a chicken sandwich.

2 Suzi (who asked Wally to get her a pastrami sandwich) didn't end up with the egg and cress sandwich.

3 Tim ate the roast beef sandwich that Wally had bought for him.

4 Neither Philip nor Tim ordered the salami sandwich.

5 Angela didn't get the egg and cress or salad sandwich.

	Wanted					Got				
	Bacon	Pastrami	Salami	Salmon	Tuna	Chicken	Egg/cress	Ham	Roast beef	Salad
Angela										
Gary										
Philip										
Suzi										
Tim										
Chicken										
Egg/cress										
Ham										
Roast beef										
Salad										

Name	Wanted	Got

MUSIC LOVERS

Five friends are regular attendees at London's Promenade Concerts. They normally go as a group but as there are certain composers that only one of them likes, on some occasions they go alone. Make a concerted effort to find out which composer each friend likes that none of the others do, and the date on which he or she went to the Proms alone.

123

1   The person (not Barney) who is a fan of Shostakovich went to the Proms alone ten days later than George, who is keen on the works of Schoenberg.

2   The Shostakovich fan went to the Proms alone on a later date than Rodney did so; and Rodney went to the Proms alone on a later date than Leila.

3   Penny (who didn't attend the Proms alone five days later than the Wagner fan) went alone five days before the person who particularly likes the music of Elgar.

	Composer					Date				
	Elgar	Schoenberg	Shostakovich	Stravinsky	Wagner	20th July	25th July	30th July	4th August	9th August
Barney										
George										
Leila										
Penny										
Rodney										
20th July										
25th July										
30th July										
4th August										
9th August										

Prommer	Composer	Date

On Their Way Home

124 Four criminals, originally from the UK, have been arrested whilst enjoying their ill-gotten gains in overseas havens. As a result, they're due to be extradited very soon, and British detectives are making plans to meet and greet them when they arrive back in the UK. What crime was committed by each villain, from which country is each due to be extradited, and on a flight to which airport?

1 The man accused of drug running isn't returning to the UK from Spain.

2 The one surnamed Blaggs isn't the kidnapper. The man who committed a bank robbery isn't surnamed Pincher.

3 The jewel thief will be met at Glasgow airport on his return to the UK.

4 Pincher (who isn't accused of kidnapping) will be flown back to Manchester airport.

5 One of the villains will be flown to Gatwick airport from Italy; his surname isn't Nicks.

6 Blaggs (who isn't the jewel thief) is being extradited from France.

	Crime				Country				UK arrival			
	Bank robbery	Drug running	Jewellery theft	Kidnapping	France	Greece	Italy	Spain	Gatwick	Glasgow	Heathrow	Manchester
Blaggs												
Nicks												
Pincher												
Scamma												
Gatwick												
Glasgow												
Heathrow												
Manchester												
France												
Greece												
Italy												
Spain												

Villain	Crime	Country	UK arrival

RELIGIOUS WARS

The land of Pirn (situated somewhere vaguely east of Atlantis, if you have to know!) suffers from terrible wars based on religious divisions which are aligned with Pirn's four provinces. Can you find the name of the religion in each province, together with the name of each leader, and the name of the religion's deity?

1 Bam is not the god revered in the province of Ducota. Nor has the Archbishop Sharen ever visited Ducota: he leads the religion in another province.

2 The Zemist god is Bom. The religion worshipping him is led by Cevin, but not in Buvairya.

3 The people of Ducota are not believers in either Zemism or Zomism.

4 Almost the entire population of the province of Yawkshya worships Bim.

5 Kyli is the leader of the Zimist religion, and has no patience with those who worship other gods, such as Bam or Bem.

		Religion				Leader				Deity			
		Zamism	Zemism	Zimism	Zomism	Cevin	Daren	Kyli	Sharen	Bam	Bem	Bim	Bom
Province	Buvairya												
	Ducota												
	Nawmundi												
	Yawkshya												
Deity	Bam												
	Bem												
	Bim												
	Bom												
Leader	Cevin												
	Daren												
	Kyli												
	Sharen												

Province	Religion	Leader	Deity

OLD WRECKS

126 The local scrap-yard has, amongst a huge variety of all things metal, several really old cars; models not seen on the roads for many a year. Rather than destroy them, the yard's owner, Rusty McCann, has decided (somewhat optimistically) to try to sell them as collectors' items. In which year was each car manufactured, and what price is Rusty asking for it?

1 Rusty is asking less for the Herald than for the car manufactured three years earlier than the Herald, but more for the Herald than the car manufactured one year earlier than the Minx.

2 The car on sale at the highest price was manufactured six years earlier than the cheapest of the five vehicles Rusty is trying to sell.

3 The Zephyr was manufactured in 1962. It is on sale for a higher price than the car manufactured in 1963.

4 The Rapier is being offered for sale at a higher price than the car manufactured one year later than the Hunter.

5 The Minx isn't for sale at $200.

		1962	1963	1965	1968	1969	$180	$200	$250	$275	$290
Car	Herald										
	Hunter										
	Minx										
	Rapier										
	Zephyr										
Price	$180										
	$200										
	$250										
	$275										
	$290										

Car	Year	Price

SKITTLED

The Cross Foxes skittles competition is at the end of its current season and tonight has seen an uproarious and closely fought Grand Final (with much superb ale quaffed!). In addition to the glory of winning a place, the top five scorers got to choose their favourite drink from the bar. Can you work out each one's final total score and the victory drink he or she chose?

1   Of the top five scorers: one is Jimmy; one got the lowest final total; one drank bitter beer; one is Suzanne; and one chose to drink gin and tonic (and got a higher score than Jimmy's).

2   Of the top five scorers: one drank cognac; one is Derek; one drank lager; one got the highest total score; and one is Fred, whose score was lower than Jimmy's.

3   Of the top five scorers: one is Derek; one got a final score of 1066; one drank lager; one is Jimmy; and one is Wendy, whose score was higher than that of at least one other player.

	Final total					Tipple				
	989	1005	1066	1091	1113	Bitter beer	Cognac	Gin and tonic	Lager	Scotch whisky
Derek										
Fred										
Jimmy										
Suzanne										
Wendy										
Bitter beer										
Cognac										
Gin and tonic										
Lager										
Scotch whisky										

Player	Final Total	Tipple

A FAMILY MATTER

128 Each of the four families in this puzzle consists of a husband, wife, son and daughter whose names begin with four different letters of the alphabet. Study the clues to discover who is related to whom.

1 Frankie's daughter isn't Jessica and his son isn't Gordon.
2 Josephine's son isn't Ian and her daughter isn't Fenella.
3 Ivana's husband isn't Graham and her son isn't Jimmy.

		Wife				Son				Daughter			
		Freda	Geraldine	Ivana	Josephine	Felix	Gordon	Ian	Jimmy	Fenella	Gracie	Iona	Jessica
Husband	Frankie												
	Graham												
	Ivor												
	Jude												
Daughter	Fenella												
	Gracie												
	Iona												
	Jessica												
Son	Felix												
	Gordon												
	Ian												
	Jimmy												

Husband	Wife	Son	Daughter

134

LIFE STORIES

Each of the four men in this puzzle was born, got married and died on three different days of the week, although obviously in different years. No man was born, married or died on the same day as any other, so work out the details from the clues below.

1 The day on which Alex married is one day later in the week than the day which he was born.

2 The day on which Bob died is the same as the day of the week on which Sean was born.

3 The man who was born on a Friday died on a Thursday.

4 The day on which Sean married is one day earlier in the week than that on which Max died, but one day later in the week than the day on which Max was born.

		Born				Married				Died			
		Monday	Tuesday	Wednesday	Friday	Monday	Tuesday	Thursday	Friday	Tuesday	Wednesday	Thursday	Friday
	Alex												
	Bob												
	Max												
	Sean												
Died	Tuesday												
	Wednesday												
	Thursday												
	Friday												
Married	Monday												
	Tuesday												
	Thursday												
	Friday												

Name	Born	Married	Died

WHERE DO THEY LIVE?

130 Five friends live in neighbouring houses, as you can see from the map below. Discover the name of the person at each residence, and the length of time in years that each has lived there.

1 No-one has lived in a house for the same number of years as the number of his or her house.

2 Norman has lived in his house for one year longer than the person who lives due west of him.

3 Harry has lived in his house for two years longer than Jane has lived in her house.

4 Jane has lived in her house for longer than Gordon has lived in his house, which is due south of Harry's house.

5 Rosie's house is further south than that of the person who has lived in a house for four years.

	Name					Years				
	Gordon	Harry	Jane	Norman	Rosie	2	3	4	5	6
No 1										
No 2										
No 3										
No 4										
No 5										
2 years										
3 years										
4 years										
5 years										
6 years										

N
W E
S

1   2

3

4   5

House No	Name	Years

APPLES AND PEARS

Five men harvested various numbers of apples and pears from their small orchards yesterday afternoon. How many did each man pick?

131

1   The man who picked the smallest quantity of apples didn't also pick the largest quantity of pears. Only one man picked exactly ten more apples than pears.

2   Harry picked more apples than Brian.

3   Arthur picked 20 more apples than pears. He also picked more pears than Wesley, who picked more apples than Arthur.

4   John (who didn't pick the highest number of pears) didn't pick exactly three more pears than Wesley.

5   One of the five men harvested 30 apples and 23 pears.

		Apples					Pears				
		25	30	35	40	45	15	18	20	23	25
	Arthur										
	Brian										
	Harry										
	John										
	Wesley										
Pears	15										
	18										
	20										
	23										
	25										

Name	Apples	Pears

SPACE SHOTS

132 Russian space scientists have recently had some success with various missions. Your aim is to match the lead scientist to the name of the mission over which he or she was in charge, its target and the percentage of accuracy achieved in each case with regard to its landing site and the experiments carried out there.

1 Professor Brusilov's mission achieved an accuracy one per cent lower than that of Mission Onega, which travelled to Mercury.

2 Mission Ladoga (which wasn't to Mars) achieved an accuracy two per cent higher than the mission (not Baikal) overseen by Doctor Nevsky.

3 Doctor Simonov's mission wasn't the one that achieved the highest degree of accuracy. The planet targeted by Doctor Simonov's mission has a shorter name (in English, at least) than the planet which Mission Orel was despatched.

	Mission				Target				Accuracy			
	Baikal	Ladoga	Onega	Orel	Jupiter	Mars	Mercury	Venus	1%	3%	4%	5%
Brusilov												
Lazarev												
Nevsky												
Simonov												
Accuracy 1%												
3%												
4%												
5%												
Jupiter								
Mars								
Mercury								
Venus								

Name	Mission	Target	Accuracy

POSTAL DELIVERIES

Paul the postman has just delivered one item to each of the houses you see in the picture below. Can you work out who lives in each house, his or her surname and the item each received?

1　The person surnamed Wyatt didn't receive the letter. The letter was delivered to the house next to and west of Nigel's, which is next to and west of that belonging to the person surnamed Bourne.

2　Karen lives next door to Larry, whose surname isn't Finch.

3　The person who received a birthday card lives closer to Melissa than to the person surnamed Moore.

4　The person surnamed Wyatt lives further east than the person who received a postcard, but lives further west than the person who received a catalogue.

	Occupant				Surname				Item			
	Karen	Larry	Melissa	Nigel	Bourne	Finch	Moore	Wyatt	Birthday card	Catalogue	Letter	Postcard
No 1												
No 3												
No 5												
No 7												
Birthday card												
Catalogue												
Letter												
Postcard												
Bourne												
Finch												
Moore												
Wyatt												

WEST ⇦　**EAST** ⇨

No 1　No 3　No 5　No 7

House No	Occupant	Surname	Item

Dog's Dinner

134 New brands of dog food appear on the supermarket shelves all the time and recently five owners decided to try some on their pet pooches. Can you sniff out which dog each owns, and which brand of food it was given?

1 The name of Joan's dog is one letter longer than the name of the dog given Rollova to eat.

2 The owner who bought Barko has a name three letters longer than that of Rex's owner. Rover's owner didn't try feeding Barko.

3 Quentin's dog has a name one letter shorter than the name of Sally-Anne's dog, but one letter longer than that of the dog whose owner bought Walkis.

4 Fido was tried on Diggo, which he liked very much.

	Dog					Food				
	Archie	Fido	Mitzi	Rex	Rover	Barko	Diggo	Rollova	Waggo	Walkis
Bill										
Joan										
Quentin										
Roberta										
Sally-Anne										
Barko										
Diggo										
Rollova										
Waggo										
Walkis										

Owner	Dog	Food

CONFERENCE

'The Future of the Memo in Office Politics' is the title of this year's annual conference of Messer & Gabel, the world's foremost producers of plastic cutlery, and the delegates are congregated at the Schadenfreude Hotel and Conference Centre in Berlin. Five delegates are due to give presentations. What is the surname of each speaker and at what time is his or her presentation due to start?

135

1   Helmut's presentation will begin either ninety minutes earlier or ninety minutes later than that of the person surnamed Krenz, whose presentation will begin later than Anna's, which isn't scheduled for 0800 hours.

2   Sofie's presentation will begin either one hour earlier or one hour later than that of the speaker surnamed Strauss. Sofie's surname isn't Schlinder.

3   The delegate surnamed Schlinder will begin speaking either ninety minutes earlier or ninety minutes later than Bernhard, whose presentation will begin more than one hour before that given by the delegate surnamed Weber.

	Krenz	Popper	Schlinder	Strauss	Weber	0700 hours	0800 hours	0930 hours	1100 hours	1145 hours
Anna										
Bernhard										
Helmut										
Josef										
Sofie										
0700 hours										
0800 hours										
0930 hours										
1100 hours										
1145 hours										

Speaker	Surname	Time

141

Shiver Me Timbers!

136 Four pirate ships are heading towards the Caribbean after pillaging on the high seas. What is the name of each captain's ship, its cargo and destination?

1 If Captain Stern's ship is bound for Cuba, then the *Siren* has a cargo of silver; otherwise, Captain Crowe's has a cargo of rum and the *Siren* is bound for Trinidad.

2 If the *Walrus* is bound for Barbados, then Captain Stern's ship is the *Golden Fox*; otherwise Captain Dedman's ship is the *Walrus* and Captain Stern's ship is heading for Cuba.

3 If the *Siren* is carrying anything other than gems, then Captain Stern commands the *Walrus*; otherwise Captain Crowe commands the *Swordfish* and Captain Stern's ship has a hold full of gold.

	Ship				Cargo				Desti-nation			
	Golden Fox	Siren	Swordfish	Walrus	Gems	Gold	Rum	Silver	Antigua	Barbados	Cuba	Trinidad
Crowe												
Dedman												
Planck												
Stern												
Destination Antigua												
Barbados												
Cuba												
Trinidad												
Cargo Gems												
Gold												
Rum												
Silver												

Captain	Ship	Cargo	Destination

BROTHERS AND SISTERS

Four boys who are very close friends each have one sister. Can you discover the names of each brother-sister pair, together with their ages?

1   Tracey is two years older than Richard.
2   Jake is two years older than Micky.
3   Micky is two years older than his sister.
4   Heather is two years older than Kathy.
5   Chris is older than her brother.
6   Dave and his sister are both younger than Chris's brother.

	Sister				His age				Her age			
	Chris	Heather	Kathy	Tracey	12	13	14	16	10	12	14	15
Dave												
Jake												
Micky												
Richard												
Her age 10												
12												
14												
15												
His age 12												
13												
14												
16												

Brother	Sister	His age	Her age

RAFFLE PRIZES

138 A great many tickets were sold in a recent raffle in aid of charity and five lucky people each won a prize. What did each person win and on which different day last week did he or she collect a prize?

1 The necklace was collected earlier in the week than the radio, which was collected the day before Charles went to pick up his prize.

2 Steve collected his prize later in the week than someone picked up the cuckoo clock, which was later in the week than the day on which someone else picked up a prize.

3 The book was collected earlier in the week than the day on which Miranda was handed her prize.

4 Betty collected her prize either the day before or the day after someone collected the television.

	Prize					Day				
	Book	Clock	Necklace	Radio	Television	Monday	Tuesday	Wednesday	Thursday	Friday
Betty										
Charles										
Frederick										
Miranda										
Steve										
Monday					
Tuesday					
Wednesday					
Thursday					
Friday					

Winner	Prize	Day

FAIRY STORY

Five little girls all attended a fancy dress party, dressed as fairies. However, each girl returned home minus one of her accessories. How old is each girl, and what did she lose at the party?

139

1 Bella (who lost one of her pink slippers) is one year older than the girl who lost her silver wig.

2 Lucy (who lost one of her sparkly wings) is younger than Clarissa, but older than the girl who lost her (equally sparkly) tiara.

3 Miranda is younger than the girl who mislaid her magic wand, but older than Susan, who didn't lose her tiara.

	Age					Lost				
	4	5	6	7	8	Magic wand	Silver wig	Slipper	Tiara	Wing
Bella										
Clarissa										
Lucy										
Miranda										
Susan										
Magic wand										
Silver wig										
Slipper										
Tiara										
Wing										

Girl	Age	Lost

SPEILING SPELEOLOGISTS

140 Four cavers are sitting at a hotel bar, exchanging tall tales of previous exploits, each trying to top the other for stories of courage, etc, etc. Each caver tells of his close shave with death. In which cave did each man almost meet an untimely end, what depth did he manage to reach and what was the reason for his retreat?

1 Rod has never explored either the Darkole or Forling cave. The man who almost met his death in the Forling cave was at a greater depth than the man who was subjected to an attack by bats.

2 Karl almost drowned when the cave he was in flooded. He reached a depth either 70 feet more of 70 feet less than the man who went into the Dedropp cave. Mitch's descent wasn't 150 feet more than Karl's.

3 Alfred reached a greater depth than the man in Buryam cave, although Alfred didn't descend to 600 feet.

4 The man who went down 500 feet didn't do so in the Darkole cave, which was where one caver was almost fatally overcome by exhaustion.

	Cave				Depth				Reason			
	Buryam	Darkole	Dedropp	Forling	380 feet	450 feet	500 feet	600 feet	Bat attack	Exhaustion	Flooding	Rockfall
Alfred												
Karl												
Mitch												
Rod												
Bat attack												
Exhaustion												
Flooding												
Rockfall												
380 feet												
450 feet												
500 feet												
600 feet												

Caver	Cave	Depth	Reason

NATURAL CRAFTS

On four days last week, different teachers took classes in various arts and crafts, as well as taking the children on a nature trip, to gather wild food. Can you discover the day on which each teacher gave a class, together with the type of craft and wild food associated with his or her lesson?

141

1   Mr Cotter's class took place the day before the woodwork lesson.
2   Mr Player (who didn't teach the children spinning) took a class two days before the children gathered nuts from the trees in the wood.
3   Miss Jones gave a lesson in basket-making, but didn't gather fungi on her nature trip.
4   The lesson given by Miss Jones took place earlier in the week than the one during which the children picked wild berries.
5   The children gathered leaves and roots on the same day as they enjoyed the woodwork lesson.

	Day				Craft				Wild food			
	Monday	Wednesday	Thursday	Friday	Basket-making	Pottery	Spinning	Woodwork	Berries	Fungi	Leaves and roots	Nuts
Mr Cotter												
Miss Jones												
Mr Player												
Mrs Samson												
Berries												
Fungi												
Leaves/roots												
Nuts												
Basket-making												
Pottery												
Spinning												
Woodwork												

Teacher	Day	Craft	Wild food

147

SPOILING THE KIDS

142 Uncle Rich is over from California to visit his adored nephews and nieces in London. Yesterday he took the children on a shopping trip and treated them lavishly, somewhat to the consternation of their parents! What did Rich buy for each child, and how much did he spend?

1 Rich spent £40 more on an iPod than he did on Caitlin's gift, which was either £10 more or £10 less than Barney's present.

2 The games console cost £40 less than the hi-fi which Uncle Rich bought for one of his nephews.

3 The scooter cost either £5 more or £5 less than Caroline's present.

	Item					Amount				
	Games console	Hi-fi	iPod	Scooter	Watch	£110	£120	£125	£150	£160
Barney										
Caitlin										
Caroline										
Sally										
Toby										
£110					
£120					
£125					
£150					
£160					

Child	Item	Amount

SERVICE PLEASE

The developers are just about to complete works at Tottering Towers apartment block. However, some of their services subcontractors are behind schedule and this factor could inconvenience several of the families who are due to move in. Consider the clues and find out which family is due to move into each apartment and the lack of which service is affecting their move.

143

1   The family affected by the gas supplier being unable to fit appliances is due to move into an apartment with a number three lower than that purchased by the Evans family.

2   The people surnamed Jones (who cannot move in until internet access has been provided) have bought an apartment with a number four higher than that affected by the subcontractor who hasn't yet laid in the television cables.

3   The phone company is affecting one family's move into an apartment with a number one lower than that purchased by the Williams family.

4   The Roberts family is not waiting to move into apartment 3.

		Evans	Hughes	Jones	Roberts	Williams	Electricity	Gas	Internet	Phone	Television
Apartment	3										
	6										
	7										
	9										
	10										
Service	Electricity										
	Gas										
	Internet										
	Phone										
	Television										

Apartment	Family	Service

SPLIT PERSONALITIES

144 Joan has taken photographs of four members of her family, cutting each into four pieces (head, body, legs and feet) and then reassembling them in such a way that each 'new' picture contains pieces of four 'old' ones. How have the pictures been reassembled?

1 Joan's father's body and her sister's legs are in two different pictures.
2 Joan's brother's legs are now attached to her father's feet.
3 Joan's father's head and her brother's body are in two different pictures.

		Body				Legs				Feet			
		Brother	Father	Mother	Sister	Brother	Father	Mother	Sister	Brother	Father	Mother	Sister
Head	Brother												
	Father												
	Mother												
	Sister												
Feet	Brother												
	Father												
	Mother												
	Sister												
Legs	Brother												
	Father												
	Mother												
	Sister												

Head	Body	Legs	Feet

Playing Cards

The people in this puzzle are playing a game of cards and each has three in his or her hand: one heart, one club and one diamond. Can you discover which three cards are in each person's hand? (NB – A=ace, J=jack, Q=queen and K=king; and in the game ace=1, jack=11, queen=12, king=13 and the values of the other cards are as per their numbers.)

1 The player with the queen of clubs has a heart with a lower value than that of the heart held by the person with the eight of diamonds.

2 The player with the eight of diamonds has a club with a value two lower than that of the club held by the person with the ace of hearts.

3 Louisa has a diamond with a value three lower than that of the diamond held by the person with the eight of clubs.

4 Frank's heart has a value three higher than that of his diamond.

5 Martin's heart has a value three lower than that of Jeanne's club, which has a value two lower than that of Frank's club.

	Heart				Club				Diamond			
	A	9	J	K	4	6	8	Q	3	6	8	J
Frank												
Jeanne												
Louisa												
Martin												
Diamond 3												
6												
8												
J												
Club 4												
6												
8												
Q												

Player	Heart	Club	Diamond

151

PETS IN WAITING

146 Five people are in the waiting room of Poorly Pets veterinary surgery, having brought in their sick animals to see the vet, Mrs Unwel. Find out the name of each person's pet and the kind of animal it is.

1   Lucky is neither the cat nor the kitten.

2   Neither Mrs Bird nor Mr Katz owns a kitten or a puppy, nor is the kitten called Rosie.

3   Neither Mr Parott nor Miss Bull owns Daisy, and Daisy is neither the dog nor the rabbit.

4   The woman who owns the rabbit hasn't called her pet Lucky.

5   Mr Parott's pet is neither Sam nor Fluff, and Fluff isn't the kitten.

6   Neither Mr Katz nor Mrs Bird owns a cat, and neither Mr Parott nor Miss Bull is the owner of the puppy.

	Daisy	Fluff	Lucky	Sam	Rosie	Cat	Dog	Kitten	Puppy	Rabbit
Mrs Bird				.						
Miss Bull										
Mrs Clore										
Mr Katz										
Mr Parott										
Cat										
Dog										
Kitten										
Puppy										
Rabbit										

Owner	Pet's name	Animal

STAMP SWAPS

Five schoolboys who are avid philatelists regularly swap stamps with one another. Today, each boy traded a stamp from one country for a stamp from a different country. Can you use the clues to discover what each gave and got?

1 No boy either gave or got a stamp from a country the initial letter of which is the same as that of his name.

2 Frankie swapped his stamp from Estonia, but not for a stamp from Denmark.

3 The boy who gave a stamp from Denmark received one from Greece.

4 The boy who gave a stamp from Greece isn't Eddie.

5 The boy who gave a stamp from Finland didn't get one from Denmark.

6 Gordon didn't give anyone a stamp from Finland, nor did he get a stamp from Denmark.

	Gave					Got				
	Chile	Denmark	Estonia	Finland	Greece	Chile	Denmark	Estonia	Finland	Greece
Chris										
Dave										
Eddie										
Frankie										
Gordon										
Chile					
Denmark					
Estonia					
Finland					
Greece					

Collector	Gave	Got

IT'S SHOWTIME!

148 Nightclub owner Seymour Kustamas is holding a 'Festive Gala Night' at the Taupe Dragon NiteSpot and has booked four top-class cabaret acts to delight the patrons. Can you work out each star's act, its scheduled start time and the fee that's been agreed?

1 The comedian (not necessarily a man) is scheduled to appear thirty minutes earlier or thirty minutes later than Mr Wundaful, who has agreed a fee of either $20 higher or $20 lower than that arranged with the person who will appear last.

2 The juggler will perform either one hour earlier or one hour later than the singer, who has negotiated a higher fee than Sherri Glass will be paid, but a lower fee than Max Power.

3 Rokki Shaw will receive either $10 more or $10 less than the psychic.

	Act				Time				Fee			
	Comedian	Juggler	Psychic	Singer	9.00pm	9.30pm	10.30pm	11.45pm	$125	$140	$150	$170
Max Power												
Mr Wundaful												
Rokki Shaw												
Sherri Glass												
$125												
$140												
$150												
$170												
9.00pm												
9.30pm												
10.30pm												
11.45pm												

Name	Act	Time	Fee

154

STOCK SALE

Bryncir livestock market is the local auction centre for many farmers and smallholders. Last month four men hooked up their trailers and took a number of animals to Bryncir, hoping for good prices. What kind of animal did each farmer take, how many animals did he transport, and on which date of the month did he visit the market?

149

1 The bullocks were taken to Bryncir the week after the animals (not heifers) were transported by Eric but the week before the man who took the highest number of animals.

2 The man who went on the 15th took fewer animals than Michael.

3 The man who took ten animals went to the market either the week before or the week after the pigs were taken.

4 The man (not Alan) who took five animals went to market two weeks before the man who took fifteen animals.

	Animals				Number				Date			
	Bullocks	Heifers	Pigs	Sheep	5	10	15	20	1st	8th	15th	22nd
Alan												
Edgar												
Eric												
Michael												
1st												
8th												
15th												
22nd												
5												
10												
15												
20												

Farmer	Animals	Number	Date

IN THE SWIM

150 Five girls had a competition amongst themselves, to see who was fastest in swimming a length at the local bathing pool. Swim through these clues to discover the order in which each finished, together with the colour of her bathing costume.

1 The girl in the yellow costume finished somewhere ahead of Esther.

2 The girl in the pale blue costume finished two places ahead of Harriet.

3 Andrea finished more than one place ahead of the girl in the black costume, but further behind than the one in the pink costume (who is Caroline's cousin).

4 Jill (whose costume isn't mauve) didn't win the race.

	First	Second	Third	Fourth	Fifth	Black	Blue	Mauve	Pink	Yellow
Andrea										
Caroline										
Esther										
Harriet										
Jill										
Black										
Blue										
Mauve										
Pink										
Yellow										

Girl	Order	Costume

BATHING BELLES

Five young women are sunning themselves on the beach and attracting attention from a lot of young men! Each woman is wearing a striped bikini, and your task is to look at the clues to discover the colour of each woman's bikini, as well as that of its stripes.

1   The woman whose bikini has red stripes isn't Jessica, whose bikini is neither gold nor turquoise.

2   Lauren's bikini is pale blue. Noelle (whose bikini isn't pink) is wearing a bikini with green stripes.

3   The stripes on the pink bikini aren't yellow.

4   The gold bikini with brown stripes isn't being worn by Myra.

5   Either the blue bikini or the turquoise bikini has black stripes.

	Bikini					Stripes				
	Blue	Gold	Pink	Turquoise	White	Black	Brown	Green	Red	Yellow
Jessica										
Kathy										
Lauren										
Myra										
Noelle										
Black					
Brown					
Green					
Red					
Yellow					

Stripes

Woman	Bikini	Stripes

NUTS AND LEAVES

152 Four children each brought quantities of nuts and leaves into Miss Fall's nature class this morning. Can you discover not only how many nuts and leaves each child brought in, but also the 'other' (less welcome) find he or she decided to show Miss Fall and the rest of the class?

1 The child who brought along a rather hairy brown spider (luckily it was in a sealed jar) brought fewer nuts and more leaves than Ronald.

2 The slimy slug was brought in by the child who brought one fewer nut and two more leaves than Colin.

3 Alison's contribution to the nature class was the rotting toadstool, together with one fewer nut than was brought in by the child who brought along the slug.

4 Tina brought more than four nuts to the nature class.

	Nuts				Leaves				'Other'			
	4	5	6	7	8	9	10	11	Frog	Slug	Spider	Toadstool
Alison												
Colin												
Ronald												
Tina												
Frog								
Slug								
Spider								
Toadstool								
Leaves 8				
9				
10				
11				

Child	Nuts	Leaves	'Other'

SORE THROAT REMEDIES

After making and receiving telephone calls all afternoon, four women found they'd talked themselves hoarse! Each made herself a soothing drink from hot water and one other ingredient, after which she was able to carry on chatting into the evening. How many calls did each woman make and receive, and what did she put in her drink?

153

1 Judy received two more calls than the woman who drank peppermint and hot water, who isn't Miriam.

2 The woman who drank honey and hot water made one fewer call than the woman who received the highest number of calls.

3 The woman who made the highest number of calls drank a mixture of ginger and hot water. She didn't receive the lowest number of calls.

4 Lola made one more call than the woman who received six calls, but Lola made one fewer call than the woman who drank lemon juice and hot water.

	Made				Received				Drink			
	4	5	6	7	5	6	7	8	Ginger	Honey	Lemon	Peppermint
Judy												
Karen												
Lola												
Miriam												
Ginger												
Honey												
Lemon												
Peppermint												
Received 5												
6												
7												
8												

Woman	Made	Received	Drink

FRIENDLY DEBATE

154 Every year five old college friends take their summer vacation together. This year, however, they can't agree where and when to go, and today they are debating the matter over lunch at La Maison Canteloupe burger bar. Where does each friend want to go, and in which month?

1 Yolanda isn't the woman who has suggested going to Mexico two months later than the holiday date put forward by Nia.

2 None of the friends wants to go to London in September.

3 The date suggested for the trip to California is one month earlier than that put forward by Amanda, who has no desire to visit Rome.

4 Catherine has suggested a date one month later than that preferred by Helen, who recommends that the five friends spend their holiday in New England.

	Destination					Month				
	California	London	Mexico	New England	Rome	April	May	June	August	September
Amanda										
Catherine										
Helen										
Nia										
Yolanda										
April					
May					
June					
August					
September					

Name	Destination	Month

160

SEA STORIES

When Mrs Quinn's five young boys returned after a day spent on their father's fishing boat, they were eager to tell her how many sharks and whales they had seen! Mrs Quinn thought their stories were rather doubtful, but there was no denying that the boys had had fun. How many sharks and whales did each of her sons say he had seen?

155

1   Carl said he'd seen three more whales than sharks, and one more whale than the boy who told his mother that he had seen six sharks.

2   Phil told Mrs Quinn that he saw fewer sharks (but three more whales) than Martin.

3   Joe didn't say that he'd seen the highest or lowest numbers of either sharks or whales, although he did tell his mother that he'd seen more sharks than Martin.

	Sharks					Whales				
	2	3	4	5	6	2	4	5	6	7
Carl										
Hal										
Joe										
Martin										
Phil										
Whales 2										
4										
5										
6										
7										

Boy	Sharks	Whales

HIGH WAY

156 This year, several people have tried to beat the record for walking the entire length of the arduous Twisty Dankle Ridge (the name's origins are lost in the mists of time, apparently) a high-level, boulder-strewn route popular with hikers. On which day did each hiker set off, what kind of weather condition almost thwarted his attempt and how much time did he take to complete the course?

1 The man whose attempt was almost thwarted by persistent heavy rain walked four days earlier than Graham, who took either 20 minutes longer or 20 minutes less time to complete the course than the man affected by gale force winds.

2 The man who walked on Saturday took either ten minutes longer or ten minutes less time to complete the course than Bertram, who was almost forced to abandon his walk due to the ice that covered Twisty Dankle Ridge.

3 Malcolm didn't make the hike on Sunday, although he did walk Twisty Dankle Ridge later in the week than Bertram.

4 The man who took seven hours and ten minutes to walk the course isn't Donald. Donald's walk didn't take place three days later than Malcolm's walk.

	Tuesday	Wednesday	Saturday	Sunday	Gales	Ice	Rain	Sleet	6 hours 45 mins	7 hours 10 mins	7 hours 30 mins	7 hours 40 mins
Bertram												
Donald												
Graham												
Malcolm												
6 hours 45 mins												
7 hours 10 mins												
7 hours 30 mins												
7 hours 40 mins												
Gales												
Ice												
Rain												
Sleet												

Hiker	Day	Weather	Time

PAULA'S PARTY

Paula had intended to have a small get-together with four friends last Saturday night, but made the mistake of telling them they could bring someone with them. This was misinterpreted, and each person brought several others along, as well as (luckily) a contribution to the party. At what time did each guest arrive, how many people did he or she come with, and what did he or she bring along?

157

1   The person who contributed the sandwiches brought along one fewer guest than Bob.

2   The person who brought cakes arrived a quarter of an hour earlier than the person (not Bob) who brought five extra people to Paula's party, but a quarter of an hour later than Andy.

3   The person who brought wine also brought seven other people.

4   The person who brought four extra guests was the first to arrive.

5   Neither Michelle nor Andy brought beer to Paula's party.

	Arrived				Extra guests				Brought			
	7.00pm	7.15pm	7.30pm	7.45pm	4	5	6	7	Beer	Cakes	Sandwiches	Wine
Andy												
Bob												
Lynne												
Michelle												
Beer												
Cakes												
Sandwiches												
Wine												
4 people												
5 people												
6 people												
7 people												

Guest	Arrived	Extras	Brought

SECONDHAND DEALS

158 Five people looking to buy secondhand cars were in a bar discussing what they wanted when the barman overheard them and directed them to five other people, who were looking to sell those cars and who were also (coincidentally) in the bar at the same time! They all struck deals, but can you discover the name of the person buying and selling each car?

1   If Mrs Croft is buying the Ardi, then Mr Barnes is buying the Vauxer; otherwise Mr Worth is buying the Ardi, and Mr Smith is selling the Vauxer.

2   If Mrs White is selling the Foat, then Mrs Dean is buying the Mavda; otherwise Ms North is selling the Foat, and Mrs Dean is buying the Hondo.

3   If Mrs Dean is buying a car from Mr Smith, then Mr Young is buying the Mavda; otherwise Mrs Dean is buying a car from Mr Butcher, and Mr Barnes is buying the Mavda.

4   If Mr Worth is buying a car from Miss French, then Mrs Croft is buying the Foat; otherwise Mr Butcher is selling the Foat and Mr Worth isn't buying a car from Miss French.

		Mr Barnes	Mrs Croft	Mrs Dean	Mr Worth	Mr Young	Mr Butcher	Miss French	Ms North	Mr Smith	Mrs White
		Buyer					**Seller**				
Car	Ardi										
	Foat										
	Hondo										
	Mavda										
	Vauxer										
Seller	Mr Butcher										
	Miss French										
	Ms North										
	Mr Smith										
	Mrs White										

Car	Buyer	Seller

CROSS-CHANNEL

Five international transport companies are each sending a consignment from the UK to other countries in Europe. From which and to which ports are each freight company's loads travelling?

1   Either the Ed Hobart consignment or the Weelz consignment is leaving from Portsmouth; and either the truck leaving from Portsmouth or the one owned by QuikSend is going to Calais.

2   Either the truck leaving from Ramsgate or the one leaving from Newhaven is heading for Calais; and either the truck leaving from Ramsgate or the one owned by Weelz is going to Ostend.

3   Either the truck leaving from Portsmouth or the one going to Le Havre is owned by Parsel.

4   The Ed Hobart consignment is leaving from either Plymouth or Dover; and the QuikSend consignment is leaving from either Plymouth or Ramsgate.

5   Neither the truck leaving from Newhaven nor the one leaving from Plymouth is going to Zeebrugge. Nor is Zeebrugge the destination of the Ed Hobart consignment.

	From					To				
	Dover	Newhaven	Plymouth	Portsmouth	Ramsgate	Calais	Dunkirk	Le Havre	Ostend	Zeebrugge
Ed Hobart										
Parsel										
QuikSend										
Van Truk										
Weelz										
Calais										
Dunkirk										
Le Havre										
Ostend										
Zeebrugge										

To

Company	From	To

SIBLINGS' PETS

160 The children in this puzzle all have various numbers of cats and dogs as pets. Discover not only the brother-sister pairs, but also the number of cats and dogs they have between them.

1 Brian and his sister have exactly the same number of cats as they do dogs.
2 Cheryl and her brother have more dogs than cats.
3 Gary and his sister have more cats than dogs.
4 Lavinia and her brother have two more dogs than Melanie and her brother.
5 Sharon and her brother have two more dogs than Patrick and his sister.
6 Desmond and his sister have more cats than Gary and his sister.

	Cheryl	Lavinia	Melanie	Sharon	4	5	6	8	2	4	6	7
Sister					**Cats**				**Dogs**			
Brian												
Desmond												
Gary												
Patrick												
Dogs 2												
4												
6												
7												
Cats 4												
5												
6												
8												

Brother	Sister	Cats	Dogs

COUNTY CHAMPIONS

Four neighbours each entered two different vegetables in this year's County Agricultural Show. Every man won first prize for one of his exhibits, and second prize for another. Can you judge from the clues which vegetable won a prize for each man, together with his exhibit in another category, for which (sadly) he did not win a prize?

161

1   The man who entered his homemade cheese won second prize for the type of vegetable for which Arthur won first prize.

2   Raoul's magnificent carrots won a first prize.

3   The man whose carrots were awarded second prize isn't Eric, who also entered fruit into one of the categories at this year's County Show.

4   The man who entered his ducks' eggs was awarded first prize for his peas, but didn't get a prize for his potatoes. His neighbour Sam also didn't get a prize for his potatoes.

	First				Second				Other			
	Carrots	Onions	Peas	Potatoes	Carrots	Onions	Peas	Potatoes	Cheese	Eggs	Flowers	Fruit
Arthur												
Eric												
Raoul												
Sam												
Cheese												
Eggs												
Flowers												
Fruit												
Carrots												
Onions												
Peas												
Potatoes												

Entrant	First	Second	Other

CYCLE TOUR

162 Cathy and Bill have just returned from a county cycling holiday. They covered a different number of miles each day, taking in the views as they travelled from town to town. Can you discover how far they cycled each day, as well as the town in which they spent the night before moving on again the next morning?

1   One trip took Cathy and Bill from Mountford to Bearwood, a distance twice as far as the journey they made to West Point.

2   The trip to West Point was made two days before they went to Elm Hill, but later in the week than the longest journey.

3   They didn't travel as far on the day they went to Sandy Bay as the distance they cycled on Friday. Friday's journey wasn't as far as the one cycled by Cathy and Bill on Tuesday.

	Miles					To (town)				
	10	15	20	30	35	Bearwood	Elm Hill	Mountford	Sandy Bay	West Point
Monday										
Tuesday										
Wednesday										
Thursday										
Friday										
Bearwood										
Elm Hill										
Mountford										
Sandy Bay										
West Point										

Day	Miles	Town

Hats and Scarves

Five women are at a bus stop, waiting for a bus to take them home. Each is wearing a hat and scarf in two different colours, both of which start with different letters to the initial letter of their names. What two-colours are their hats and scarves?

163

1. Pam's hat is the same colour as Rhoda's scarf.
2. The woman with a pink scarf has a hat the colour of which begins with the same letter as the name of the woman wearing the red scarf.
3. The woman with a green hat has a name that begins with the same letter as the colour of the scarf worn by the woman with the red hat.
4. The woman with a black hat is wearing an orange scarf.

	Hat					Scarf				
	Black	Green	Orange	Pink	Red	Black	Green	Orange	Pink	Red
Brenda										
Greta										
Olga										
Pam										
Rhoda										
Scarf Black										
Green										
Orange										
Pink										
Red										

Name	Hat	Scarf

INSIDE JOB

164 Ellonerth General Hospital has discovered that during recent surgical operations, surgeons accidentally left items inside four of its patients. Can you carry out your own procedure to discover what operation each patient underwent, which surgeon performed it, and what item was left in each case?

1 Mr Delver accidentally dropped his iPod into one poor patient.

2 Mr Cutham didn't perform a liver operation. The operation on a lung wasn't carried out on Mrs Ferguson, in whom the car keys were later found.

3 Mr Morrison had an operation on his duodenum.

4 Mrs Johnson's operation was carried out by Mr Sewham.

5 Mr Payne carried out the lung operation, but didn't accidentally leave his wristwatch in his patient.

	Operation				Surgeon				Item left			
	Appendix	Duodenum	Liver	Lung	Mr Cutham	Mr Delver	Mr Payne	Mr Sewham	Car keys	iPod	Wallet	Wristwatch
Mr Anderson												
Mrs Ferguson												
Mrs Johnson												
Mr Morrison												
Item left Car keys												
iPod												
Wallet												
Wristwatch												
Surgeon Mr Cutham												
Mr Delver												
Mr Payne												
Mr Sewham												

Patient	Operation	Surgeon	Item left

MATCHING PAIRS

Four children played a very simple card game of matching pairs, where each had to pick up two cards that were of the same suit. Every child won one game, enjoying it immensely. No child picked up a card of the same value as that chosen by any other child. Can you discover which two cards each chose, and their matching suit?

165

1   The four children are: the child who picked up a seven; the child who picked up a five; Nathan; and the one who picked up a pair of hearts, neither of which was a two.

2   The four children are: Paul; the child who picked up a two; the child who picked up a four; and the one who picked up a pair of diamonds.

3   The four children are: the child who picked up a five; Rowena; Laura; and the child who picked up a pair of clubs, neither of which was a nine.

4   The four children are: the child who picked up an eight; the child who picked up a nine; Rowena; and the one who picked up a pair of spades.

	Suit				Lowest value				Highest value			
	Hearts	Clubs	Diamonds	Spades	2	3	4	5	6	7	8	9
Laura												
Nathan												
Paul												
Rowena												
Highest 6								
7								
8								
9								
Lowest 2								
3								
4								
5								

Child	Suit	Lowest	Highest

STONEWALL

166 Peter and Paul are professional stone wall builders in northwest Wales. They are currently building a new wall high up in Snowdonia but the changeable weather and variable conditions are making progress extremely erratic. Can you work out how many hours work they managed to achieve on each day, and the length of wall they built?

1 The longest stretch of wall was built in less time than it took to construct the wall 16 feet in length, but more time than it took to construct the shortest section of wall.

2 The shortest stretch of wall was completed two days later than the day on which Peter and Paul managed to put in a full eight hours work.

3 The men worked for two hours longer on Monday than on the day when they built a section of wall three feet longer than the one they constructed on Monday.

4 The section of wall measuring 18 feet in length was built earlier in the week than (but not the day before) the shortest section of wall.

5 More hours were worked on Tuesday than on Saturday.

	Hours					Length				
	3	5	6	7	8	12 feet	15 feet	16 feet	18 feet	20 feet
Monday										
Tuesday										
Thursday										
Friday										
Saturday										
12 feet										
15 feet										
16 feet										
18 feet										
20 feet										

Day	Hours	Length

TRAVELLERS

The five people in this puzzle each visited two different towns last week. Anyone may have visited two towns on the same day, so travel through these clues to discover the day on which they visited each town.

1 Carl went to Eastlake two days after Betsy did so. He went to Westlake two days before Lenny went there.

2 Lenny went to Eastlake three days before he visited Westlake.

3 The person who went to Eastlake on Thursday went to Westlake on Monday.

4 Andrew went to Westlake later in the week than the day on which Michelle went to Eastlake.

	Eastlake					Westlake				
	Monday	Tuesday	Wednesday	Thursday	Friday	Monday	Tuesday	Wednesday	Thursday	Friday
Andrew										
Betsy										
Carl										
Lenny										
Michelle										
Westlake Monday					
Tuesday					
Wednesday					
Thursday					
Friday					

Name	Eastlake	Westlake

Traffic Lights

168 Traffic Lights are small, chocolate-covered treats for children. They come in tubes and are of three different colours. The four siblings below have eaten some already, but (before they consume any more) can you work out how many of each colour remain in each child's tube?

1. No child has exactly the same number of sweets in one colour as he or she has in other colours. In other words, each child has three different quantities of red, orange and green sweets.

2. Josie has one more orange sweet than the child who has the fewest red sweets.

3. Jude has more orange sweets than his brother.

4. Josie has one more green sweet than the child who has seven red sweets.

5. Jenny has one fewer red sweet than the child who has five orange sweets.

		Red				Orange				Green			
		4	5	7	8	3	5	6	7	6	7	8	9
	Jenny												
	Jim												
	Josie												
	Jude												
Green	6												
	7												
	8												
	9												
Orange	3												
	5												
	6												
	7												

Child	Red	Orange	Green

Timber!

Roote & Branch Tree Surgeons are today taking down four large trees in a local garden. R&B's lads have each bet a small amount of money on who can finish his tree first. What tree did each choose to fell, what was its height, and how long did it take each man to complete the task?

169

1   Mr Barker's tree took a quarter of an hour longer to fell than the beech, which wasn't as tall as the tree felled by Mr Barker.

2   The yew tree was either four feet taller or four feet shorter than the tree felled by Mr Hughes, which didn't take as long to bring down as the yew tree.

3   The ash tree was either five feet taller or five feet shorter than the tree which took the shortest time to fell. Mr Wood didn't bring down the ash tree.

4   The tallest tree wasn't the willow, although the willow was taller than the beech tree.

5   The tree felled by Mr Barker wasn't as tall as the ash, which didn't take five minutes longer to fell than the beech tree.

	Ash	Beech	Willow	Yew	57 feet	61 feet	64 feet	66 feet	2 hours 15 mins	2 hours 20 mins	2 hours 30 mins	2 hours 45 mins
Mr Barker												
Mr Hughes												
Mr Sawyer												
Mr Wood												
2 hours 15 mins												
2 hours 20 mins												
2 hours 30 mins												
2 hours 45 mins												
57 feet												
61 feet												
64 feet												
66 feet												

Name	Tree	Height	Time

BOOKS

170 There are five books lined up on the shelf you see below, each with a different subject and a different number of pages. Can you identify them all, given these clues?

1 The book on music is next to and right of the book with 144 pages, which is of a different height to the music book. The gardening book has sixteen fewer pages than the music book.

2 The gardening book is next to and between two books of different sizes: the one with the most pages and the one on cooking.

3 The book with the fewest pages is next to and left of the book on art.

4 Book D has 176 pages.

	Subject					No of pages				
	Art	Cooking	Gardening	Mountains	Music	128	144	160	176	192
Book A										
Book B										
Book C										
Book D										
Book E										
128 pages					
144 pages					
160 pages					
176 pages					
192 pages					

LEFT ⇦   **RIGHT** ⇨

A   B   C   D   E

Book	Subject	No of pages

WEEKDAY WEDDINGS

The Reverend Lovejoy married five couples on different days last week. Can you work out the name of the bride and groom he joined together in holy matrimony on each day, given that the initials of each couple are two different letters?

1   Myra and Matthew married more than one day apart. Myra's husband isn't Vernon.

2   Monday's bride wasn't Simone, whose wedding was earlier in the week than Dean's.

3   Matthew's wife isn't Fiona. Nor did Fiona marry Vernon.

4   Veronica's husband isn't Freddy or Matthew.

5   Dawn married the day after Fiona, who married two days before Shane.

	Bride					Groom				
	Dawn	Fiona	Myra	Simone	Veronica	Dean	Freddy	Matthew	Shane	Vernon
Monday										
Tuesday										
Wednesday										
Thursday										
Friday										
Dean										
Freddy										
Matthew										
Shane										
Vernon										

Wedding day	Bride	Groom

A FAMILY MATTER

172 Each of the four families in this puzzle consists of a husband, wife, son and daughter whose names begin with four different letters of the alphabet. Can you work out who is related to whom?

1 Neither Wesley nor Dawn is a child of Rachel.

2 Hannah's father isn't William.

3 William's wife isn't Diane.

4 Roy's sister isn't Hannah.

5 Wendy isn't David's mother.

6 Hannah's brother has a name that begins with the same letter as that of a woman who isn't married to Horace.

		Wife				Son				Daughter			
		Diane	Hilary	Rachel	Wendy	David	Harry	Roy	Wesley	Dawn	Hannah	Rosie	Willow
Husband	Des												
	Horace												
	Richard													
	William													
Daughter	Dawn												
	Hannah												
	Rosie												
	Willow												
Son	David												
	Harry												
	Roy												
	Wesley												

Husband	Wife	Son	Daughter

LIFE AFTER FAME

Four former TV celebrities, now past their peak, have developed new careers out of the spotlight. Can you discover the type of programme in which each regularly appeared, together with the year in which he retired and his current job?

1   The man who used to present a weekly documentary programme retired one year later than the celebrity now working as a teacher, but the year before Fred Fisher (who didn't appear in a soap opera).

2   Bob Barnet (who now works as a clerk) retired the year before the man who was one of the leading actors in a soap opera broadcast three times a week.

3   The man who achieved fame as a sports presenter now works as a plumber, having retired one year later than Keith King.

	Programme				Retired				Job			
	Documentary	Quiz	Soap opera	Sport	2008	2009	2010	2011	Clerk	Journalist	Plumber	Teacher
Bob Barnet												
Fred Fisher												
Keith King												
Mike Mole												
Clerk												
Journalist												
Plumber												
Teacher												
2008												
2009												
2010												
2011												

Celebrity	Programme	Retired	Job

DAD'S TAXI

174 Five girls each asked their father to take them to different places yesterday afternoon. Luckily for him, they asked at the same time, so he was able to take them all in one journey, albeit a rather lengthy one! Where was each girl going, and in what order was she dropped off at her destination?

1 The girl taken to her friend's house was dropped off immediately after Juliette, who was dropped off later than the girl going to the swimming pool, who wasn't the first to leave the car.

2 Madge got out of the car earlier than the girl (not Juliette) who asked to be taken to the library.

3 Katy left the car immediately before the girl who was dropped off at the cinema, but later than Imelda.

4 Leonie didn't visit a friend yesterday afternoon.

	Going to					Order				
	Cinema	Friend	Library	Shops	Swimming pool	First	Second	Third	Fourth	Fifth
Imelda										
Juliette										
Katy										
Leonie										
Madge										
First										
Second										
Third										
Fourth										
Fifth										

Girl	Going to	Order

ALL CHANGE

Five people in neighbouring houses all repainted their front doors last month. Each chose a different colour to that which they'd had previously, so use the clues to find out the colours of the doors before and after painting.

1   The number of the house that used to have a black front door is one higher than that of the house that once had a blue front door, but one lower than that of the house that now has a red front door.

2   The door that used to be blue wasn't repainted green.

3   The door that was red wasn't at No 5, although it was at a house with a lower number than the one that is now black.

4   The numbers of the houses where the doors were once and are now green are not consecutive. The green door wasn't once white, and the white door wasn't once green. The white door wasn't once blue, and the blue door wasn't once white.

	Was					Is now				
	Black	Blue	Green	Red	White	Black	Blue	Green	Red	White
No 5										
No 6										
No 7										
No 8										
No 9										
Black					
Blue					
Green					
Red					
White					

Is now

House No	Was	Is now

SPLIT PERSONALITIES

176 Peter has taken photographs of four members of his family, cutting each into four pieces (head, body, legs and feet) and then reassembling them in such a way that each 'new' picture contains pieces of four 'old' ones. How have the pictures been reassembled?

1 Peter's father's body, his grandma's head and his uncle's feet are in three different pictures.

2 Peter's sister's body is now attached to his uncle's head.

		Body				Legs				Feet			
		Father	Grandma	Sister	Uncle	Father	Grandma	Sister	Uncle	Father	Grandma	Sister	Uncle
Head	Father												
	Grandma												
	Sister												
	Uncle												
Feet	Father												
	Grandma												
	Sister												
	Uncle												
Legs	Father												
	Grandma												
	Sister												
	Uncle												

Head	Body	Legs	Feet

PLAYING CARDS

The men in this puzzle are playing a game of cards and each has
three in his hand: one club, one diamond and one spade. Can you
discover which three cards are in each man's hand? (NB – A=ace,
J=jack, Q=queen and K=king; and in the game ace=1, jack=11,
queen=12, king=13 and the values of the other cards are as per their
numbers.)

177

1   The man with the ace of diamonds has a spade with a value three lower than
    that of the spade held by Keith, whose diamond has a lower value than that of
    the diamond held by Dave.

2   Dave's club has a value two higher than that of the club held by the man with
    the king of spades.

3   Henry's club has a higher value than that of the club held by George.

4   George's diamond has the same value as one of the cards held by Dave.

5   The man with the queen of diamonds is holding a spade with a higher value
    than that of Henry's club.

		Club				Diamond				Spade			
		2	4	6	J	A	6	8	Q	2	5	8	K
	Dave												
	George												
	Henry												
	Keith												
Spade	2												
	5												
	8												
	K												
Diamond	A												
	6												
	8												
	Q												

Player	Club	Diamond	Spade

GET WELL SOON

178 When Ian was ill last week, five of his friends called to see him at different times on different days, each bringing him a small gift to cheer him up a bit. At what time and on which day did each of Ian's friends visit?

1   Harry called in to see Ian the day before the person who came at 3.15pm.

2   Wednesday's visitor came at a time either thirty minutes earlier or thirty minutes later than the time of Tim's visit.

3   Ian's last visitor of the week was Bill, who came at either 3.00pm or 3.30pm.

4   George didn't visit Ian at 2.30pm on any day. The person who called on Tuesday didn't arrive at 4.00pm.

5   The person who called on Thursday did so at a time either fifteen minutes earlier or fifteen minutes later than the visiting time of Friday's caller.

	Time					Day				
	2.30pm	3.00pm	3.15pm	3.30pm	4.00pm	Tuesday	Wednesday	Thursday	Friday	Saturday
Bill										
Brenda										
George										
Harry										
Tim										
Tuesday										
Wednesday										
Thursday										
Friday										
Saturday										

Friend	Time	Day

HEATING PROBLEM

Five neighbours choose to heat their homes using different fuels.
Discover where each person lives (the map below shows their houses:
two in Snug Street and three in Warm Way) together with the type of
fuel he or she uses.

1   The five neighbours are: the person who lives at No 1; Greg; the person who lives directly north of the neighbour who burns wood to heat his or her home; the person (not Claire) who heats his or her home with electricity; and the one who lives directly east of the person who uses electricity.

2   Four of the neighbours are: the person who uses coal as a fuel; Alan; the person who lives in the house directly west of Alan's; and the person (not the one who uses electricity to heat his or her home) who lives directly west of the person who uses coal.

3   Three of the neighbours are: Deborah; the person who uses gas to heat his or her home; and the person who lives directly north of the one who uses gas.

	House No					Fuel				
	1	2	3	4	5	Coal	Electricity	Gas	Oil	Wood
Alan										
Claire										
Deborah										
Edgar										
Greg										
Coal										
Electricity										
Gas										
Oil										
Wood										

N W E S

SNUG STREET — 3, 5

WARM WAY — 2, 1, 4

Neighbour	House No	Fuel

WHAT A COINCIDENCE

180 Four women have just discovered an amazing coincidence: each has had surnames in common with the other women, although none is related or has been married to the same man! Which name was given at birth, what name did she take when she married her first husband, and what name did she take after divorcing him and marrying her second husband?

1 Each woman has had three different surnames to date.

2 The surname which June was given at birth is the same as that taken by Gloria when she married her first husband.

3 Sheila was given the surname Smith at birth.

4 Gloria's current surname is White. The surname she was given at birth is the same as the current surname of the woman who was given the surname Jones at birth.

	Born				First husband				Current husband			
	Baker	Jones	Smith	White	Baker	Jones	Smith	White	Baker	Jones	Smith	White
Alice												
Gloria												
June													
Sheila													
Current Baker												
Current Jones												
Current Smith												
Current White												
First Baker								
First Jones								
First Smith								
First White								

Name	Born	First	Current

DATES

Four friends were all born on different dates in different months of different years. Discover the facts relating to each person.

181

1. Ronald is two years younger than the friend whose birthday falls the month before Theo's.

2. The man born in 1982 celebrates his birthday two months later than that of the friend whose birthday falls later in its month than the date of Ronald's birthday.

3. The man whose birthday is on 14th April is taller than Theo.

4. The youngest man's birthday is earlier in the year than that of Charles, whose birthday is earlier in the year than that of the man who was born on the tenth of the month.

	Date				Month				Year			
	10th	12th	14th	16th	January	February	March	April	1981	1982	1983	1984
Charles												
Harry												
Ronald												
Theo												
1981												
1982												
1983												
1984												
January												
February												
March												
April												

Friend	Date	Month	Year

SLUGS AND SNAILS

182 Fed up with the constant attack on their vegetable plots, but not wishing to kill the pests, five neighbours collected various quantities of slugs and snails from their gardens last night, and took them to a local wooded area, where they could do less harm: at least, less harm to lettuces and cabbages! How many did each person collect?

1 Antony collected two more snails than the person who collected eight slugs.

2 Felicity collected two more slugs than the person who collected five snails.

3 Michael collected two more snails than the number of slugs collected by Pete.

4 Claire collected a different number of snails than the number of slugs collected by Antony.

5 The number of slugs and snails collected by Claire amounted to more than fifteen.

	Slugs					Snails				
	5	6	7	8	9	4	5	6	7	8
Antony										
Claire										
Felicity										
Michael										
Pete										
4 snails					
5 snails					
6 snails					
7 snails					
8 snails					

Name	Slugs	Snails

KITTENS

Five young girls each received a kitten for a birthday present and every girl is taking very good care of it. How old is each girl, and what is the name of her kitten?

1 Sally is younger than the girl who has called her kitten Katie, but older than the girl (not Rose) who has called her kitten Sammy.

2 Sooty belongs to the ten-year-old girl.

3 The girl who has called her kitten Lucky is one year younger than Lynne.

4 The kitten named Sammy doesn't belong to Pamela, who is two years younger than Cindy.

	Age					Kitten				
	7	8	10	11	12	Katie	Lucky	Moppet	Sammy	Sooty
Cindy										
Lynne										
Pamela										
Rose										
Sally										
Katie					
Lucky					
Moppet					
Sammy					
Sooty					

Girl	Age	Kitten

OCTOGENARIANS' OFFSPRING

184 Four women in their eighties were discussing their families the other day. Each woman has a different number of children, grandchildren and great-grandchildren, so that (for example) the woman who has five children hasn't five grandchildren or five great-grandchildren. How many offspring has each octogenarian?

1 Diane has more children than the number of great-grandchildren Barbara has.

2 Barbara has one fewer child than Cynthia, who has both more grandchildren than Diane and two more great-grandchildren than Edna.

3 The woman with three children has two more grandchildren than the woman who has six great-grandchildren.

	Children				Grand-children				Great grand-children			
	3	4	5	6	4	5	6	7	3	5	6	8
Barbara												
Cynthia												
Diane												
Edna												
Great grand-children 3												
5												
6												
8												
G'children 4												
5												
6												
7												

Woman	Children	G'children	Gt g'children

LOST AND FOUND

Four people lost and found items on different days last week, Monday to Sunday. Each person found something lost by one of the others, on the same day as it was lost, so use the clues to discover the details.

1. Scott lost his wallet and was delighted to get it back, as it contained quite a lot of money.
2. The book was lost two days later than the item lost by Doreen, but earlier in the week than the item that Doreen found.
3. Jeremy lost something two days earlier than the set of keys was found by Liz.

	Lost by				Found by				Day			
	Doreen	Jeremy	Liz	Scott	Doreen	Jeremy	Liz	Scott	Monday	Wednesday	Friday	Sunday
Book												
Keys												
Mobile phone												
Wallet												
Monday												
Wednesday												
Friday												
Sunday												
Found by Doreen												
Jeremy												
Liz												
Scott												

Item	Lost by	Found by	Day

BROTHERLY LOVES

186 Five brothers have each proposed marriage to their girlfriends, and each has been accepted. Who is every man's fiancée and in which month next year will they marry?

1 Lara and her fiancé will marry before Penny and her fiancé, but later in the year than Ross and his intended bride Mandy.

2 Joe didn't propose marriage to Denise, whose wedding day will be in September of next year.

3 Hannah is engaged to Eddie. Their wedding will take place earlier in the year than that of Joe and his fiancée, but later in the year than that of Kevin and his intended bride.

	Fiancée					Wedding				
	Denise	Hannah	Lara	Mandy	Penny	May	June	July	August	September
Bob										
Eddie										
Joe										
Kevin										
Ross										
May					
June					
July					
August					
September					

Brother	Fiancée	Wedding

NONAGENARIANS

Five residents of the Bide-a-While care home for the elderly celebrated birthdays last month. Each is in his or her nineties, so use the clues to discover their full names and ages.

1 Two of the women have a difference of one year in their ages. The other (third) woman is one year older than one of the men and one year younger than another of the men.

2 The resident aged 96 isn't Edith, who is older than Kenneth who, in turn, is older than the person surnamed Dawkins.

3 Doris (whose surname isn't Dawkins) is one year younger than the resident surnamed Barton.

4 The resident surnamed Mallett is one year older than Margaret.

5 The surname of the youngest person is neither Dawkins nor Price.

	Surname					Age				
	Barton	Dawkins	Ford	Mallett	Price	93	94	95	96	97
Doris										
Edith										
Gregory										
Kenneth										
Margaret										
93										
94										
95										
96										
97										

Name	Surname	Age

FRUIT MACHINE

188 Keith is fed up with wasting his time and gambling his money on slot fruit machines – but decided to have a few 'last tries' before he gave it up for good! Four times he put money into the machine and pulled the handle, and on each occasion three different symbols appeared, one in each of the left, middle and right viewing panels of the machine. Can you discover what they were?

1 The symbol in the right panel on Keith's first try was the same as the one in the left panel on his second try. The symbol in the middle panel on the first try was different from that in the right panel on Keith's second try.

2 The symbol in the right panel on Keith's fourth try was the same as the symbol in the left panel on his third try.

3 The symbol in the middle panel on Keith's first try was the same as the symbol in the right panel which appeared at the same time as the symbol of a lemon showed in the left panel.

4 On one of his tries (not the fourth), Keith saw a bar in the left frame and an orange in the middle frame.

5 The melon appeared earlier than at least one of the two symbols of oranges.

		Left				Middle				Right			
		Bar	Bell	Lemon	Orange	Cherry	Melon	Orange	Plum	Bar	Bell	Cherry	Lemon
	First try												
	Second try												
	Third try												
	Fourth try												
Right	Bar												
	Bell												
	Cherry												
	Lemon												
Middle	Cherry												
	Melon												
	Orange												
	Plum												

Try	Left	Middle	Right

DORA'S DIARIES

When tidying her desk recently, Dora discovered four old diaries from years past, that she'd received as presents. They might have made for interesting reading, had Dora kept up her intention of writing them every day, but although she started well, her interest waned and, after a few weeks, they remained untouched. What colour is the diary for each year, who gave it to Dora, and what is the different number of pages filled in each case?

1 Every date has a single page in all of Dora's diaries.

2 Dora filled seven more pages into the blue diary given to her by her aunt than she filled in the oldest diary.

3 The red diary is older than the one given to Dora by her father, but newer than the diary Dora kept for eight weeks.

4 The black diary was a gift from a man and the 2004 diary (not the one she kept for nine weeks) was a gift from a woman.

5 More pages were written in the diary from Dora's brother than in the green diary, which wasn't a gift from her sister. The diary kept for the shortest time wasn't given by Dora's sister.

	Colour				From				Pages filled			
	Black	Blue	Green	Red	Aunt	Brother	Father	Sister	42	49	56	63
2002												
2003												
2004												
2005												
42 pages												
49 pages												
56 pages												
63 pages												
From Aunt												
Brother												
Father												
Sister												

Year	Colour	From	Pages

FOR SALE

190 The local newsagency charges a small fee for placing postcards in its shop window, advertising secondhand goods for sale. Currently there are five such advertisements in the window (depicted below), all placed by different people. Who placed each postcard, and what is he or she selling?

1 The postcard placed by Miss Tarrant is lower than that advertising the clock, but higher than the advertisement placed by Mr Palmer.

2 The postcard giving details of the motorbike is higher than the one placed by Mr Mitchell, which is next to and between the one advertising the lawnmower and the one placed by Miss Tarrant.

3 Mr Palmer's advertisement (not on postcard E) is next to the one placed by Mr Fox, which is lower than the one giving details of the table for sale.

HIGHEST

A
B
C
D
E

LOWEST

	Seller					Item				
	Mr Fox	Mrs Greaves	Mr Mitchell	Mr Palmer	Miss Tarrant	Bed	Clock	Lawnmower	Motorbike	Table
Card A										
Card B										
Card C										
Card D										
Card E										
Bed										
Clock										
Lawnmower										
Motorbike										
Table										

Postcard	Seller	Item

196

CUSHIONS

Each of the cushions on the sofa depicted below is of a different colour and has a different pattern. Can you work out every cushion's colour and pattern, given the clues below?

1   Cushion E isn't the green one, which is further right than the mauve cushion.

2   The cushion with a zigzag pattern is further left than the striped cushion.

3   The black, square-patterned cushion is next to the yellow one.

4   There is one cushion between the white cushion and that with a diamond pattern, which is next to and left of the cushion decorated with a pattern of circles, which is further right than the white cushion.

	Colour					Pattern				
---	Black	Green	Mauve	Yellow	White	Circles	Diamonds	Squares	Stripes	Zigzags
Cushion A										
Cushion B										
Cushion C										
Cushion D										
Cushion E										
Circles										
Diamonds										
Squares										
Stripes										
Zigzags										

LEFT ⇦   **RIGHT** ⇨

A B C D E

Cushion	Colour	Pattern

197

Toy Yachts

192 Four boys are at the boating lake in the park. Each was given a yacht for his birthday, so sail through the clues to find out who owns each yacht depicted below, its colour and the age of its owner.

1 The blue yacht belongs to a boy who is either three years older or three years younger than Ian.

2 Adam's yacht is further left than the yacht belonging to Thomas which, in turn, is further left than that owned by the boy who is two years younger than Adam.

3 The white yacht belongs to Larry and is further left than that owned by the boy who is one year older than the owner of the green yacht.

	Boy				Colour				Boy's age			
	Adam	Ian	Larry	Thomas	Blue	Green	Red	White	5	6	7	9
Yacht A												
Yacht B												
Yacht C												
Yacht D												
5												
6												
7												
9												
Blue								
Green								
Red								
White								

LEFT ⇐   **RIGHT** ⇒

A   B   C   D

Yacht	Boy	Colour	Boy's age

UFOs

Mr Brown lives in an apartment overlooking the backs of the houses depicted below. It's not a nice neighbourhood, as they have a strange way of discarding unwanted items: they throw them into other people's gardens! Mr Brown sees it all... Where does each person live, on which night did he or she threw something, and what is the number of the house in the garden of which it landed?

1　The person who lives at No 3 threw something to the east. This was two nights later than an object landed in the garden of No 3.

2　The person who lives at No 7 threw something the night after an object was thrown by Mr James.

3　Mrs Hale lives directly next door to and between two men, both of whom threw something to the east.

4　Mr Penny threw a half used can of paint into a woman's garden on Friday night.

	Lives at No				Night				Landed at No			
	1	3	5	7	Monday	Tuesday	Wednesday	Friday	1	3	5	7
Mrs Hale												
Mr James												
Mrs Lang												
Mr Penny												
No 1												
No 3												
No 5												
No 7												
Monday												
Tuesday												
Wednesday												
Friday												

Landed at

WEST ⇦　　**EAST** ⇨

No 1　No 3　No 5　No 7

Occupant	Lives at	Night	Landed at

SANGRIA AIRLINES REGRETS ...

194 Last week, some of Sangria Airlines' flights were affected by a combination of industrial action, snow, the wrong kind of snow, computer malfunction, technical disfunction, legal injunctions and other 'operational difficulties'. What was the destination airport of each numbered flight, and to which airport was it diverted?

1 Flight No 276 was diverted to the airport at which flight No 147 should have landed.

2 The original destination airport of flight No 276 was Newfort.

3 Flight No 799 was diverted to the airport at which flight No 509 should have landed. Flight No 509 was diverted to Morneton.

4 Flight No 255 was diverted to Rayford.

5 The flight originally bound for Berryham was diverted to the airport that was the original destination of the plane that was diverted to Berryham.

	Destination					Diverted to				
	Berryham	Morneton	Rayford	Newfort	Westwick	Berryham	Morneton	Rayford	Newfort	Westwick
Flight No 147										
Flight No 255										
Flight No 276										
Flight No 509										
Flight No 799										
Berryham										
Morneton										
Rayford										
Newfort										
Westwick										

Diverted to (left side label for bottom rows)

Flight No	Destination	Diverted to

Handy To Know

Andy Mann the handyman is a godsend to the people who live in the remote village of Eyup; he carries out work for the community and is very affordable. Last week, Andy completed jobs for five customers. Can you find out what job he did for each customer, and how much Andy charged for the work?

195

1. The price charged for repairs made to a large shed in someone's yard was more than the amount paid by Mr Hughes, which was $25 less than the amount Andy charged Mr Thomas.

2. The amount charged by Andy for the new door was higher than the price paid by Mrs Roberts.

3. Mrs Roberts' bill was either $25 higher or $25 lower than the price paid by Mr Williams. Mrs Roberts' bill was also either $25 higher or $25 lower than the amount Andy charged for the fencing, which wasn't the job he did for Mr Williams.

4. Andy charged more for the concreting than for Mr Williams' job, Mr Williams paid more for Andy's labours than was paid by Mr Thomas.

	\multicolumn{5}{c}{**Job**}	\multicolumn{5}{c}{**Cost**}
	Chimney pots	Concreting	Fencing	New door	Shed repairs	$100	$125	$150	$175	$200
Mr Hughes										
Mrs Parry										
Mrs Roberts										
Mr Thomas										
Mr Williams										
$100					
$125					
$150					
$175					
$200					

Customer	Job	Cost

BIRTHDAY GIFTS

196 Four women whose birthdays were last week each received a gift from their husbands. What is the name of each woman's husband, what gift did she receive, and on which day was her birthday?

1 Philip is either married to the woman whose birthday was on Tuesday or he's the man who gave the watch to a woman whose birthday isn't on Tuesday.

2 Graham's wife celebrated her birthday earlier in the week than that of the woman (not Olivia) who was given a pearl necklace. Olivia's husband is neither Graham nor Dave.

3 Maxine's birthday was earlier in the week than that of the woman given a huge basket of flowers for her birthday, which wasn't on Saturday.

4 Laura (whose husband isn't Dave) didn't celebrate her birthday on Thursday.

5 Nancy's birthday was the day after that of the woman who received a bottle of perfume from her husband, who isn't Graham.

	Husband				Gift				Birthday			
	Dave	Graham	Martin	Philip	Flowers	Necklace	Perfume	Watch	Tuesday	Wednesday	Thursday	Saturday
Laura												
Maxine												
Nancy												
Olivia												
Tuesday												
Wednesday												
Thursday												
Saturday												
Flowers												
Necklace												
Perfume												
Watch												

Woman	Husband	Gift	Birthday

LATE AGAIN!

Four employees at Bowler's cricket bat factory are on a sticky wicket at the moment, as they are often late for their shifts. Today, the same four were late again, and the boss was interested to hear their excuses. Can you find out what time each employee was due to start, how many minutes late he was, and the excuse (car broke down; dog swallowed car key; heavy traffic; wife ill) he gave the boss?

197

1   The two people who have shifts that start in the afternoon were late by fifteen minutes more than the men who claimed that they were held up due to a car breakdown and heavy traffic.

2   The man who was held up by traffic was due to start his shift five hours earlier than the man who was eight minutes later than Jeff Ball, who said that his dog had swallowed his car keys.

3   Ted Stump's shift was due to start one hour earlier than Jeff Ball's.

4   Sam Fielder (who wasn't seven minutes late for his shift) wasn't due to start earlier than Fred Bale today.

	Due start				Late by				Excuse			
	8.00am	9.00am	1.00pm	2.00pm	7 minutes	15 minutes	22 minutes	30 minutes	Car	Dog	Traffic	Wife
Fred Bale												
Jeff Ball												
Sam Fielder												
Ted Stump												
Car												
Dog												
Traffic												
Wife												
7 minutes												
15 minutes												
22 minutes												
30 minutes												

Employee	Due start	Late by	Excuse

ROUND OF DRINKS

198 Five friends, each with a different drink, are seated around the table you see in the diagram below. Who is the occupant of each seat, and what is he or she drinking?

1   The person drinking mineral water is seated one place clockwise of Sally, who is not seated one place clockwise of Vanessa.

2   Donald (who is drinking cola) is seated one place anti-clockwise of the person drinking tea, who isn't in seat C on the plan below.

3   The person drinking coffee is seated one place clockwise of Alison, who is seated one place clockwise of the person drinking lemonade. None of these three people is in seat C on the plan below.

	Friend					Drink				
	Alison	Donald	Raymond	Sally	Vanessa	Cola	Coffee	Lemonade	Tea	Water
Seat A										
Seat B										
Seat C										
Seat D										
Seat E										
Cola					
Coffee					
Lemonade					
Tea					
Water					

Clockwise

Seat	Friend	Drink

STAYING AHEAD

The Cannie family are very good at managing their finances through careful budgeting and spending. Mr and Mrs Cannie rigorously put aside amounts in certain months in order to meet substantial outgoings that occur just once a year. For what expense did they set aside money in each of the listed months, and how much did they put away each time?

1 The amount for life insurance 1 (Mrs Cannie's) was put aside three months earlier than the amount for life insurance 2 (Mr Cannie's), and the two expenses differed by $50.

2 The Cannie's home insurance money amounted to more than that put aside in July, but less than they saved towards the car insurance.

3 The amount set aside for car insurance was $100 more than the money they had set aside six months after they saved towards their home insurance.

4 Mr and Mrs Cannie didn't save towards their car insurance within three months of putting aside money for their home insurance.

	Expense					Amount				
	Car insurance	Car service	Home insurance	Life insurance 1	Life insurance 2	$200	$230	$300	$350	$400
February										
May										
July											
August											
November											
$200					
$230					
$300					
$350					
$400					

Month	Expense	Amount

FORMULA 6

200 Formula 6 motor racing is for amateur drivers who own their own vehicles (usually secondhand). The recent big race at the little-known Silver Hatch circuit was a great day out for both drivers and fans, with much fine champagne wasted on the podium. Can you find the places of each of the first four drivers to complete the race, the car each drove, and their starting positions?

1   Herrero (who didn't drive the Boyota) finished one place behind the driver of the Blue Cow, whose starting position was one lower than Schmidt's.

2   The driver of the Laurent finished one place behind the driver of the Boyota, whose starting position was one lower than that of one of the other three drivers. Smith didn't drive the Boyota.

3   The driver who finished third started in a position with a higher number than Forgeron's.

	Place				Car				Position			
	1st	2nd	3rd	4th	Blue Cow	Boyota	Laurent	Motus	2	3	6	7
Forgeron												
Herrero												
Schmidt												
Smith												
Position 2												
Position 3												
Position 6												
Position 7												
Blue Cow												
Boyota												
Laurent												
Motus												

Driver	Place	Car	Position

SOLUTIONS

No 1

The woman who has 5 children isn't the waitress (clue 1), accountant (clue 2) or journalist (4), so she's the teacher. The journalist has 3 children (4), so the waitress has 2 children (1) and Lorna has 4. By elimination, Lorna is an accountant. She lives at either No 1 or No 2 (2), as does Joanne (3). Thus Sophie lives at No 3 (1) and the waitress lives at No 4. By elimination, she's Angela. Sophie is the teacher (2), so Joanne is the journalist. Joanne lives at No 1 (3), so Lorna lives at No 2.

Thus:

No 1 - Joanne - journalist - 3 children;
No 2 - Lorna - accountant - 4 children;
No 3 - Sophie - teacher - 5 children;
No 4 - Angela - waitress - 2 children.

No 2

Adrian lives in Paris (clue 1) and Ambrose lives in Madrid (clue 4). Alistair is the artist (3). The author who lives in Rome isn't Arnold (2), so Arthur. The analyst isn't Adrian (1) or Arnold (2), so Ambrose. The architect isn't Arnold (5), so Adrian. Arnold is the accountant. He doesn't live in Lisbon (5), so in Munich. Alistair lives in Lisbon.

Thus:

Adrian - Paris - architect;
Alistair - Lisbon - artist;
Ambrose - Madrid - analyst;
Arnold - Munich - accountant;
Arthur - Rome - author.

No 3

Barbara's bed cover is turquoise (clue 5). Chris isn't using squares (clue 1), so her bed cover isn't lilac (6). Nor is it cream (3) or pink (5), so lemon. Her shapes aren't diamonds (2), pentagons (3) or triangles (4), so circles. Barbara's aren't diamonds (2), pentagons (3) or squares (6), so triangles. The woman stitching squares isn't Mary (1) or Ellen (6), so Stephanie. Stephanie's bed cover is lilac (6). The pink bed cover isn't Mary's (1), so Ellen's. Mary's is cream, so her shapes are pentagons (3) and Ellen's are diamonds.

Thus:

Barbara - turquoise - triangles;
Chris - lemon - circles;
Ellen - pink - diamonds;
Mary - cream - pentagons;
Stephanie - lilac - squares.

No 4

Ralph is the salesman (clue 2). Michael isn't the accountant or the manager (4), so he's the clerk. The accountant who drank whisky/ginger isn't Tim (3), so Peter. Tim is the manager, whose surname is Goring (4). Peter's surname is Fletcher (1). Ralph's isn't Davis (2), so Johnston. Michael is Mr Davis, who (2) drank gin/tonic. Tim drank rum/cola (3), so Ralph drank brandy/soda.

Thus:

Michael - Davis - clerk - gin/tonic;
Peter - Fletcher - accountant - whisky/ginger;
Ralph - Johnston - salesman - brandy/soda;
Tim - Goring - manager - rum/cola.

No 5

David's girlfriend is Barbara (clue 3). Shirley received assorted chocolates and roses (clue 2). Her boyfriend isn't Ian (1) or Gordon (2), so Michael. Ian sent milk chocolates and tulips (1). His girlfriend isn't Pamela (1), so Jenny. Pamela's boyfriend is Gordon. Barbara didn't get the lilies (3), so asters. Pamela received lilies. The white chocolates weren't sent to Barbara (4), so to Pamela. Barbara received dark chocolates.

SOLUTIONS

Thus:
Barbara - dark - asters - David;
Jenny - milk - tulips - Ian;
Pamela - white - lilies - Gordon;
Shirley - assorted - roses - Michael.

No 6

Remember throughout that no boy has 17 cars (grid). Pierre has 15 cars and the boy surnamed Williams has 20 (clue 2), so Dean has 18 cars and the boy surnamed Cross has 19 (clue 1). Tony thus has 20 cars and Alan has 19 (4). Frank has 16 cars. Pierre's surname is Robson and Frank's is Hart (3), so Dean's surname is Porter.

Thus:
Alan - Cross - 19 cars;
Dean - Porter - 18 cars;
Frank - Hart - 16 cars;
Pierre - Robson - 15 cars;
Tony - Williams - 20 cars.

No 7

Bobby whose favourite plaything is the rubber ball (clue 5) isn't the collie (clue 1), Alsatian (2), poodle (3) or whippet (4), so he's a dachshund. The whippet who plays with the rubber ring isn't Sammy (4), Spot (2) or Patch (3), so Zeus. Spot is the Alsatian (2) and Patch is the poodle (3), so Sammy is the collie, who (1) plays with the rag doll. Spot's favourite plaything isn't the rubber bone (2), so the teddy bear. The rubber bone is Patch's toy.

Thus:
Bobby - dachshund - rubber ball;
Patch - poodle - rubber bone;
Sammy - collie - rag doll;
Spot - Alsatian - teddy bear;
Zeus - whippet - rubber ring.

No 8

The man dressed as a gorilla was at the bus station (clue 1). Henry who was at the town hall didn't dress as a pirate or a punk rocker (clue 3), so as Dracula.

The one dressed as a pirate wasn't at the library (2), so the supermarket, thus (4) he's Samuel. The man at the bus station wasn't Clive (1), so Peter. Clive was thus at the library, dressed as a punk rocker. He didn't raise $35 (2), so $40 (1) and Peter (gorilla, above) raised $47. Samuel (pirate, above) raised $35 (2), so Henry raised $42.

Thus:
Clive - library - punk rocker - $40;
Henry - town hall - Dracula - $42;
Peter - bus station - gorilla - $47;
Samuel - supermarket - pirate - $35.

No 9

Apple pie was served on the 23rd (clue 4), so bread and butter pudding was served on the 2nd (clue 1) and roast pork on the 16th. By elimination, chicken and rice pudding were served together (2) on the 9th, so Mr and Mrs Smith's son's favourite pudding is apple pie. Spotted dick was served on the 16th. Roast beef is the favourite of Mr and Mrs Smith's daughter (3), thus it was served on the 2nd. Lamb was served on the 23rd. Mrs Smith's favourite wasn't served on the 9th (3), so the 16th. Mr Smith's favourite was served on the 9th.

Thus:
2nd - beef - bread and butter - daughter;
9th - chicken - rice - Mr Smith;
16th - pork - spotted dick - Mrs Smith;
23rd - lamb - apple pie - son.

No 10

Brian's lesson is at 10.30am (clue 3), so the flute lesson is at 9.30am (clue 2), William's is at 10.00am, and Lucy's is at 11.00am. Frank is learning piano (5), thus his lesson is at 11.30am, so Tina's is at 9.30am. Brian is learning clarinet (1). William (10.00am lesson, above) isn't learning saxophone (4), so violin. Lucy is learning to play the saxophone.

208

SOLUTIONS

Thus:
Brian - clarinet - 10.30am;
Frank - piano - 11.30am;
Lucy - saxophone - 11.00am;
Tina - flute - 9.30am;
William - violin - 10.00am.

No 11

Stanley used gooseberries (clue 3). The MAN (clue 4) who used soda and blackcurrants isn't Terence, so Harry. The drink of cold tea and pineapple wasn't made by Diane (1) or Louise (2), so by Terence. Louise used cola but not strawberries (2), so banana. Diane thus used strawberries. She didn't use milk (2), so lemonade. Stanley used milk.

Thus:
Diane - lemonade - strawberries;
Harry - soda water - blackcurrants;
Louise - cola - banana;
Stanley - milk - gooseberries;
Terence - cold tea - pineapple.

No 12

No business has 13 staff (grid), so the legal business has 11 staff (clue 2) and Susan's company has 12. The millinery business thus has 14 staff (clue 3) and Francesca's has 15. It isn't the publishing company (1), so it's the accountancy firm. The publishing company has 12 staff. The accountancy firm isn't on the second floor (4), so the third (1). Susan (publishing company, above) and Martin are on either the second and/ or fourth floors (1), so Richard is on the first. Susan is on the second floor (2), so Martin is on the fourth. The legal firm (11 staff, above) isn't on the first floor (4), so the fourth. Richard owns the millinery business.

Thus:
Francesca - third - accountancy - 15 staff;
Martin - fourth - legal - 11 staff;
Richard - first - millinery - 14 staff;
Susan - second - publishing - 12 staff.

No 13

No-one spent 1¾ hours in the sea (grid). The woman who spent 2 hours in the sea didn't bring a bucket and spade (clue 1), umbrella or surfboard (clue 3), so a beachball. The one who spent one hour in the sea didn't bring a bucket and spade (1), so she brought the umbrella (3) and the woman who spent 1¼ hours in the sea brought the surfboard. The woman who brought the bucket and spade thus spent 1½ hours in the sea, so (1) the woman in the sea for 2 hours had a pink towel. Cora was in the sea for one hour (2) and the woman with the orange towel was in the sea for 1½ hours. Dora was in the sea for 1¼ hours (1). Flora spent 1½ hours in the sea (4) and Dora's towel was brown. Thus Nora spent 2 hours in the sea, and Cora's towel was scarlet.

Thus:
Cora - umbrella - scarlet - 1 hour;
Dora - surfboard - brown - 1¼ hours;
Flora - bucket/spade - orange - 1½ hours;
Nora - beachball - pink - 2 hours.

No 14

The country scene card was from Jenny's brother (clue 2). The river scene card scented with honeysuckle wasn't from her mother (clue 4), grandfather (1) or grandmother (3), so from her father. The lavender-scented card from her grandmother didn't feature butterflies or kittens (3), so mountains. The pine-scented card from her grandfather didn't feature butterflies (1), so kittens. The card with a picture of butterflies was thus from Jenny's mother. The patchouli-scented card wasn't from her brother (2), so her mother. Jenny's brother gave the rose-scented card.

SOLUTIONS

Thus:
Brother - country scene - roses;
Father - river scene - honeysuckle;
Grandfather - kittens - pine;
Grandmother - mountains - lavender;
Mother - butterflies - patchouli.

No 15

The peridots are in stainless steel (clue 1) and the agates are in gold (clue 4). The ring is made of titanium (3). The necklace has garnets and isn't of silver (2), so platinum. The peridots aren't in the earrings (1) or bracelet (5), so the brooch. The bracelet isn't gold (4), so silver. The earrings are gold. The bracelet doesn't contain amethysts (5), so jade. The amethysts are in the ring.
Thus:
Bracelet - silver - jade;
Brooch - stainless steel - peridots;
Earrings - gold - agates;
Necklace - platinum - garnets;
Ring - titanium - amethysts.

No 16

James is married to Melissa (clue 2) and Neil is married to Penny (clue 4). Opal is canoeing (1), thus her husband isn't Adam (3), so Philip. Adam is married to Nadine and (3) they're walking. Neil isn't diving (4), so horse-riding. James is diving. The couple in Portugal aren't canoeing, diving or horse-riding (4), so walking. James isn't in Italy or Scotland (2), so France. Opal isn't in Italy (1), so Scotland. Neil is in Italy.
Thus:
Adam - Nadine - Portugal - walking;
James - Melissa - France - diving;
Neil - Penny - Italy - horse-riding;
Philip - Opal - Scotland - canoeing.

No 17

Patricia has either 2 or 3 children (clue 2). She isn't married to the plumber (clue 1), the electrician (2) or the doctor (who has 4 or 5 children, 3),

so Patricia's husband is the chef. Thus Jeff has 2 children (4) and Patricia has 3. Vera has 2 children (3). Jeff isn't the electrician (2) or the doctor (3), so the plumber. Kevin has 3 children (1). Gordon isn't the doctor (3), so he's the electrician. Rupert is the doctor. Gordon has 5 children (2), so Rupert has 4. His wife isn't Willow (5), so Tamsin. Gordon's wife is Willow.
Thus:
Gordon - Willow - 5 children - electrician;
Jeff - Vera - 2 children - plumber;
Kevin - Patricia - 3 children - chef;
Rupert - Tamsin - 4 children - doctor.

No 18

The person who planted a tree on Monday isn't Miss Bishop or Ms Fisher (clue 1), Mr Evans or Mrs Dean (clue 3), so Mr Coutts, who (2) planted the pear tree. Miss Bishop planted an apple tree (1) and Mrs Dean planted a damson tree (3). Ms Fisher didn't plant the greengage tree (1), so the cherry tree, on Saturday (4). Mr Evans planted the greengage tree. No-one planted a tree on Thursday (grid), so Mr Evans planted a tree on Tuesday (3) and Mrs Dean planted hers on Wednesday. Miss Bishop planted a tree on Friday.
Thus:
Miss Bishop - apple - Friday;
Mr Coutts - pear - Monday;
Mrs Dean - damson - Wednesday;
Mr Evans - greengage - Tuesday;
Ms Fisher - cherry - Saturday.

No 19

Verna is frightened of the dark (clue 2) and Yolande fears snakes (clue 5). Toni who uses herbal tea (4) isn't frightened of spiders (1) or heights (3), so flying. Sharon's fear isn't of heights (3), so spiders, thus (1) she's the woman undergoing hypnotherapy. The woman who uses prayer to combat her fear of heights (3) is thus Rachel. The support group isn't used by Verna (2), so by Yolande. Verna practises yoga.

Thus:

Rachel - heights - prayer;
Sharon - spiders - hypnotherapy;
Toni - flying - herbal tea;
Verna - dark - yoga;
Yolande - snakes - support group.

No 20

Remember throughout that each 'new' picture is made of pieces of four 'old' ones. Aunt Claire's head isn't with Aunt Anne's body (clue 1). So Uncle John's legs and Aunt Anne's body (clue 2) are with Uncle Bill's head and (by elimination) Aunt Claire's feet. Uncle John's feet aren't with the head of Aunt Anne (3), so Aunt Claire. Thus Aunt Claire's head is with Uncle Bill's body and Aunt Anne's legs. By elimination, Uncle John's head is with Aunt Claire's body, Uncle Bill's legs and Aunt Anne's feet. Aunt Anne's head is with Uncle John's body, Aunt Claire's legs and Uncle Bill's feet.

Thus (head - body - legs - feet):

Aunt Anne - Uncle John - Aunt Claire - Uncle Bill;
Aunt Claire - Uncle Bill - Aunt Anne - Uncle John;
Uncle Bill - Aunt Anne - Uncle John - Aunt Claire;
Uncle John - Aunt Claire - Uncle Bill - Aunt Anne.

No 21

Margaret hasn't the 2 of diamonds (clue 2), so she hasn't the 7 of spades (clue 4). Thus Margaret has the 6 of spades (1) and Teresa has the 8 of clubs. Jacqueline hasn't the 7 of spades (3), so she hasn't the 2 of diamonds (4). Thus Jacqueline has the ace of diamonds (3). The woman with the 2 of diamonds and 7 of spades hasn't the 8 of clubs (4), so Elizabeth has the 2 of diamonds and 7 of spades. She hasn't the 9 of clubs (4) or the queen of clubs (5), so the jack. Margaret has the queen of clubs and (2) king of diamonds. Jacqueline has the 9 of clubs. Teresa has the queen of diamonds. She hasn't the jack of spades (5), so Jacqueline has the jack and Teresa has the king of spades.

Thus (club - diamond - spade):

Elizabeth - jack - 2 - 7;
Jacqueline - 9 - ace - jack;
Margaret - queen - king - 6;
Teresa - 8 - queen - king.

No 22

The week 3 soup was made with Kelvedon Wonder peas (clue 4). The week 5 soup contained mint but not Ambassador peas (clue 1), Hurst Greenshaft peas (2) or Onward peas (3), so Little Marvel peas. Parsley was used in week 4 (4). The week 1 soup wasn't made with carrots (2) or garlic (3), so potatoes and (2) Hurst Greenshaft peas. Onward peas were used in week 2 (3) and garlic in week 3. Carrots were used in week 2 and Ambassador peas in week 4.

Thus:

Week 1 - Hurst Greenshaft - potatoes;
Week 2 - Onward - carrots;
Week 3 - Kelvedon Wonder - garlic;
Week 4 - Ambassador - parsley;
Week 5 - Little Marvel - mint.

No 23

Terence prefers game shows (clue 4). The person who prefers cartoons isn't Linda or Robert (clue 2) or David (3), so Suzanne. No-one's favourite programme is on at 8.30pm (grid), so the cartoons aren't on at 9.00pm (2). Thus the cartoons will be broadcast at 8.00pm (1) and Linda's favourite is on at 7.00pm. The documentary will be shown at 7.30pm (2) and

viewed by David (3), and the wildlife programme will be shown at 9.30pm. By elimination, Robert's favourites are wildlife programmes and Linda's are soap operas. The game show will be broadcast at 9.00pm.
Thus:
David - documentary - 7.30pm;
Linda - soap opera - 7.00pm;
Robert - wildlife - 9.30pm;
Suzanne - cartoons - 8.00pm;
Terence - game show - 9.00pm.

No 24
The man who received the jumper has a birthday in November (clue 1) and John's birthday is in September (clue 3). Judy's husband Steven didn't receive the jumper (5). His birthday isn't in February (3), so July. Peter's isn't in November (1), so February. Thus Peter is married to Harriet (3). By elimination, Malcolm's birthday is in November. Dorothy made a bookcase (4), so Malcolm is married to Beryl. Dorothy's husband is thus John. Judy (whose husband's birthday is in July, above) didn't make the mug (2), so the paperweight. The mug was made by Harriet.
Thus:
Beryl - jumper - Malcolm - November;
Dorothy - bookcase - John - September;
Harriet - mug - Peter - February;
Judy - paperweight - Steven - July.

No 25
Remember throughout that each child has three different quantities (intro). The child with 5 red plus 2 green pens isn't Neil (clue 2), Sharon or Lucy (clue 1), so Jamie. Sharon has 3 green pens (1). Neil hasn't 5 green pens (2), so 4. Lucy has 5 green pens. The child with 5 black pens isn't Jamie or Lucy (intro) or Neil (2), so Sharon. Lucy has 4 black

pens (3). The child with 4 red pens isn't Lucy or Neil (intro), so Sharon. Jamie (2 green pens, above) hasn't 2 black pens (intro), so 3. Neil has 2 black pens. Neil hasn't 2 red pens (intro), so 3. Lucy has 2 red pens.
Thus (black - green - red):
Jamie - 3 - 2 - 5;
Lucy - 4 - 5 - 2;
Neil - 2 - 4 - 3;
Sharon - 5 - 3 - 4.

No 26
Samuel becomes a yeti (clue 4). Philip is affected when the moon is three-quarters full (clue 2). Abigail isn't affected by a quarter moon, full moon or no moon (3), so by a half moon. The character who turns into a werewolf when there is no moon isn't Neil (1), so Caroline. By elimination, the one who becomes a goblin when the moon is in its first quarter (3) is Neil. Philip doesn't change into a vampire (2), so a troll. Abigail becomes a vampire. Samuel is transformed when the moon is full.
Thus:
Abigail - vampire - half;
Caroline - werewolf - no moon;
Neil - goblin - quarter;
Philip - troll - three-quarters;
Samuel - yeti - full.

No 27
Mitch keeps Sussex chickens (clue 1). Clarice who sold 50 dozen doesn't keep Dorkings (clue 2), Australorps (1) or Leghorns (3), so Welsummer chickens. The person who sold 90 dozen eggs isn't Mitch (1) or Bill (3), so Juliette sold 90 dozen (4) and George sold 80 dozen. Juliette doesn't keep Australorps (1) or Leghorns (3), so Dorkings. Bill doesn't keep Leghorns (3), so Australorps. George keeps Leghorns. Bill sold 70 dozen eggs (1) and Mitch sold 60 dozen.

SOLUTIONS

Thus:
Bill - Australorp - 70 dozen;
Clarice - Welsummer - 50 dozen;
George - Leghorn - 80 dozen;
Juliette - Dorking - 90 dozen;
Mitch - Sussex - 60 dozen.

No 28

The person who wants chicken nuggets is second in the queue (clue 1). The person who wants cola is third (clue 2), thus the one who wants a hamburger is first. Dean who wants fried fish is thus third (3) and the person who wants lemonade is second. By elimination, the person who is fourth will order a cheeseburger, but not with a milkshake (4), so coffee. The person who wants a milkshake is first. He/she isn't Catherine (1) or Moira (4), so Fred. Catherine isn't second (1), so fourth. Moira is second in the queue.

Thus:
Catherine - cheeseburger - coffee - fourth;
Dean - fried fish - cola - third;
Fred - hamburger - milkshake - first;
Moira - chicken nuggets - lemonade - second.

No 29

Tanya's father's name is Lee (clue 5), so the man named Jo (clue 2) is her brother, who entered a painting competition (2) and won a TV appearance (4). Tanya's father won a car and doesn't excel at sculpture (5) or photography (3), so pottery. The person who excels at photography and won a holiday isn't her mother (3), so her sister. Thus her mother excels at sculpture and won money. Tanya's mother is Pat (1), so her sister is Chris.

Thus:
Brother - Jo - painting - TV appearance;
Father - Lee - pottery - car;
Mother - Pat - sculpture - money;
Sister - Chris - photography - holiday.

No 30

Gayle's sister's present is in gold paper (clue 2) and her mother's is in silver paper (clue 4). The book is wrapped in green paper (1) and isn't for her grandfather (3) or her uncle (5), so her aunt. Her grandfather's watch isn't in purple paper (3), so red. Thus her uncle's present is in purple paper. Her uncle will get gloves (5). The scarf isn't wrapped in gold paper (2), so silver. The gold parcel contains a pen.

Thus:
Green - book - aunt;
Gold - pen - sister;
Purple - gloves - uncle;
Silver - scarf - mother;
Red - watch - grandfather.

No 31

Stuart will erect the tent (clue 4) and Thomas has a green sleeping bag (clue 5). The boy with the brown sleeping bag who will cook supper isn't Zach (1) or Jim (3), so Robbie. Jim won't be fetching wood (3), so his sleeping bag isn't black (4). Jim's sleeping bag isn't orange (3), so red. He won't be fetching water (2), so he will light a fire. Thomas won't be fetching water (5), so he will fetch wood and Zach will fetch water. Stuart has a black sleeping bag (4). Zach's sleeping bag is orange.

Thus:
Jim - light a fire - red;
Robbie - cook supper - brown;
Stuart - erect the tent - black;
Thomas - fetch wood - green;
Zach - fetch water - orange.

No 32

The woman who believes she died in 1742 isn't Naomi (clue 1), Karen (clue 2) or Marcia (4), so Lesley. Marcia thinks she was a milkmaid (4). Karen thinks she died in either 1820 or 1859 (2), so Lesley's character wasn't a seamstress. Nor was she a queen (3), so Lesley thinks she was a servant girl. The woman who thinks she was Maud died in 1820 (1) and Naomi's character died in 1781. Karen wasn't a seamstress (2), so a queen. Naomi thinks she was a seamstress. Karen thus thinks she died in 1820 (2) and the woman who was Joan died in 1742 (Lesley, above). By elimination, Marcia's character died in 1859. Naomi believes she was Alice (3). Marcia believes she was called Catherine.

Thus:
Karen - Maud - queen - 1820;
Lesley - Joan - servant girl - 1742;
Marcia - Catherine - milkmaid - 1859;
Naomi - Alice - seamstress - 1781.

No 33
Pippa chose tuna filling (clue 4) and Polly's surname is Pelling (clue 5). Ms Purser who chose salad isn't Penny (3), so Pauline. Penny chose chilli sauce (3), but not ham (1), so baked beans. Polly thus chose ham. Penny's surname isn't Phillips (2), so Parsons. Pippa is Ms Phillips. Polly chose cheese sauce (1). Tomato sauce wasn't chosen by Pauline (3), so Pippa. Pauline chose mayonnaise.

Thus:
Pauline - Purser - salad - mayonnaise;
Penny - Parsons - baked beans - chilli;
Pippa - Phillips - tuna - tomato;
Polly - Pelling - ham - cheese.

No 34
Remember throughout that no child is aged 5 or 9 (grid). The 4-year-old (youngest) isn't William (clue 1), Ellen or Simon (clue 2), so Greta is 4 (3) and Chris is 7. Simon is thus 8 (2). Greta's card is next to and left of Chris's (2), which is next to and left of Simon's (4). The child who gave card A (furthest left) isn't William (1) or Ellen (who gave either B or E, 2). So Greta gave A, Chris gave B and Simon gave C. Ellen

thus gave E (2), so William gave card D. William is 6 (1), so Ellen is 10 years old.

Thus:
Card A - Greta - 4 years old;
Card B - Chris - 7 years old;
Card C - Simon - 8 years old;
Card D - William - 6 years old;
Card E - Ellen - 10 years old.

No 35
The woman who married Angus in April isn't Angela or Avril (clue 1) or Andrea (clue 2). Thus Abigail married in April (3) and Alison married in July. Andrea married in June (2) and Arnold in May. Avril's husband is Alan (1). Andrea's isn't Anthony (2), so Adrian. By elimination, Alison's husband is Anthony, so Angela's is Arnold. Avril married in August.

Thus:
Abigail - Angus - April;
Alison - Anthony - July;
Andrea - Adrian - June;
Angela - Arnold - May;
Avril - Alan - August.

No 36
No girl is 13 years old (grid). The girl who prefers lily spray is either 14 or 15 years old (clue 1), as is the girl who prefers lavender (clue 3). The girl who prefers lemon isn't 12 (3), so she's 16 and the girl who prefers lavender is 15. The one who prefers lilac is thus 12, and the one who prefers lily is 14. The 12-year-old's bedroom is pink (1). The 16-year-old is either Lola or Lucy (4), so Leanne is 15 (1) and her bedroom isn't pink. Since no girl is 13, Leanne's bedroom isn't green (2). The white bedroom isn't Laura's or Leanne's (4), so Leanne's is blue. Laura's isn't green (2), so pink. The 14-year-old's is green (2), so the 16-year-old's bedroom is white. The green bedroom isn't Lola's (2), so Lucy's. Lola's bedroom is white.

Solutions

Thus (spray - bedroom):
Laura - 12 years old - lilac - pink;
Leanne - 15 years old - lavender - blue;
Lola - 16 years old - lemon - white;
Lucy - 14 years old - lily - green.

No 37
Bella's family feud involved cattle rustling (clue 2). Her surname isn't Hancock (clue 2) or Lowell (3). Bella's feud ended seven years before the Hancock family's feud (2). Eliza's surname wasn't Hancock (2), so Bella's wasn't Dayton (1). Thus Bella was Mrs Giles. Eliza wasn't Mrs Dayton (1), so Mrs Lowell. Thus her family's feud concerned horse theft (3). It was ended seven years later than Helen's (3), so Helen was Mrs Dayton (1). Her family didn't fight over mining rights (1), so a gambling debt. By elimination, Verity was Mrs Hancock whose family feud concerned mining rights. The woman who ended the 59-year feud wasn't Helen or Verity (1) or Bella (2), so Eliza. Thus Helen settled a feud after 52 years (1) and Verity settled a feud after 45 years. Bella settled a feud after 38 years.
Thus:
Bella - Giles - cattle rustling - 38 years;
Eliza - Lowell - horse theft - 59 years;
Helen - Dayton - gambling debt - 52 years;
Verity - Hancock - mining rights - 45 years.

No 38
Wendy's brother isn't William (clue 1), Richard or Terence (clue 3), so either Mark or Steven, neither of whom is surnamed Chester or Dale (2). Wendy's surname isn't Atkins or Brown (3), so Evans. Terence's surname isn't Atkins or Brown (3) or Chester (4), so Dale. Richard's isn't Atkins or Brown (3), so Chester. Terence Dale's sister isn't Tanya (1), Mary (2) or Sandra (4), so Ruth. Richard Chester's sister isn't Mary (2) or Sandra (4), so Tanya. Mary's brother isn't Mark (1) or Steven (2), so William. Sandra's brother isn't Steven (1), so Mark. Wendy's brother is Steven. Sandra's surname isn't Atkins (4), so Brown. William's surname is Atkins.
Thus:
Mark - Sandra - Brown;
Richard - Tanya - Chester;
Steven - Wendy - Evans;
Terence - Ruth - Dale;
William - Mary - Atkins.

No 39
Remember throughout that no child is 9 years old (grid). The 12-year-old isn't Gina or Lynne (clue 1), Timmy (clue 2) or Vincent (4), so Edward. The 11-year-old saw a cloud shaped like a wheelbarrow (3). The 8-year-old isn't Lynne (1), Timmy (2) or Vincent (4), so Gina. The 7-year-old isn't Lynne (1) or Timmy (2), so Vincent. Lynne is 11 (1) and Edward's cloud resembled a dog. Timmy is 10 years old, so Vincent's cloud looked like a castle (2). Gina's looked like a ship (4), so Timmy's resembled a pyramid.
Thus:
Edward - 12 years old - dog;
Gina - 8 years old - ship;
Lynne - 11 years old - wheelbarrow;
Timmy - 10 years old - pyramid;
Vincent - 7 years old - castle.

No 40
Remember throughout that each bear is wearing clothing in three different colours (intro). Bernie isn't wearing blue (clue 1), so has clothing in green, red and yellow, in some order. Pebble's hat is red and Candy's trousers are red (clue 3), so Bernie has a red coat. Sukie has blue trousers (1). Sukie's coat isn't green (2), so yellow. By elimination, Sukie's hat is green and Candy's is blue.

Solutions

So Bernie has a yellow hat and green trousers. Pebble has yellow trousers. Candy has a green coat. Pebble's is blue.

Thus (coat - hat - trousers):
Bernie - red - yellow - green;
Candy - green - blue - red;
Pebble - blue - red - yellow;
Sukie - yellow - green - blue.

No 41

Mr Dale (a man) who bought a stepladder (clue 2) is either Marc or Tony. The customer served fourth wasn't Tony (clue 1) or Marc (3), thus Mr Dale wasn't served fourth. The customer served fourth isn't surnamed Parker (1) or Bartlet (3), so Morton is the surname of either Pamela or Wilma, as is Parker (MRS, 1). Marc's surname isn't Bartlet (3), so Dale. Tony's surname is Bartlet. The customer served first isn't surnamed Parker (1) or Dale (3), so Bartlet. Tony didn't buy paint (1) or a saw (3), so nails. The person who bought paint isn't surnamed Parker (1), so Morton. Mrs Parker thus bought a saw. Marc was served before Mrs Parker (3), who was served before Ms Morton (1), so Mark was second and Mrs Parker was third. Pamela's surname isn't Parker (4), so Morton. Wilma is Mrs Parker.

Thus:
Marc - Dale - stepladder - second;
Pamela - Morton - paint - fourth;
Tony - Bartlet - nails - first;
Wilma - Parker - saw - third.

No 42

The 4-year-old chose modelling clay (clue 3). No child is 7 years old (grid), so Lucy who chose a bat and ball is 8 (clue 1) and the child who wanted a doll is 6. The one who wanted building bricks is thus 9 (2) and Peter is 5. By elimination, Peter chose the teddy bear, so (4) Rebecca is 6. Tammy isn't 4 (3), so she's 9. Martin is 4 years old.

Thus:
Lucy - 8 years old - bat and ball;
Martin - 4 years old - modelling clay;
Peter - 5 years old - teddy bear;
Rebecca - 6 years old - doll;
Tammy - 9 years old - building bricks.

No 43

Mr Chapman is at either table No 1 or table No 2 (clue 2). If Mr Phillips is at table No 1, then Mrs Rothman is at No 2 (4), leaving no room for Mr Chapman (above). The person at No 4 who has ordered coconut cake (1) isn't Mr Phillips or Mrs Rothman (4), so Mr Phillips is at table No 2 and Mrs Rothman is at table No 3. Mr Chapman is at No 1 (2) and Mrs Brown is at No 4. Mrs Lane is thus at No 5, so Mrs Rothman has ordered sponge cake (3). The chocolate cake is for table No 1 (5) and the cherry cake is for table No 2. The person at table No 5 has ordered fruit cake.

Thus:
Table No 1 - Mr Chapman - chocolate;
Table No 2 - Mr Phillips - cherry;
Table No 3 - Mrs Rothman - sponge;
Table No 4 - Mrs Brown - coconut;
Table No 5 - Mrs Lane - fruit.

No 44

The man with both the 3 of hearts and the 5 of clubs isn't Darren (clue 3), Alan or Clive (clue 1), so Robin. The man with the 4 of hearts isn't Alan or Clive (1), so Darren. Alan has the jack of hearts (1), Clive has the 7 of hearts, Clive has the 10 of clubs, and Alan has the 6 of clubs. Thus Darren has the queen of clubs. The man with the 9 of spades isn't Clive or Darren (2), so Alan has the 9 of spades (4) and Robin has the 5 of spades. Clive has the 3 of spades (2) and Darren has the ace of spades.

Thus (heart - club - spade):
Alan - jack - 6 - 9;
Clive - 7 - 10 - 3;
Darren - 4 - queen - ace;
Robin - 3 - 5 - 5.

No 45

Hilary's mother is Cheryl (clue 3). Anita's child isn't Florence (clue 5) or Benny (6), so Jimmy. Benny's favourite animals are chimpanzees (6). Thus his mother isn't Felicity (2), so Martina. Florence's mother is Felicity. Florence didn't prefer the lizards (2) or tigers (4), so the polar bears. Hilary didn't prefer the lizards (3), so the tigers. Jimmy's favourite animals are lizards. Hilary bought a mug (4). The child who bought a colouring book isn't Jimmy or Florence (1), so Benny. The pencil case wasn't bought by Florence (5), so by Jimmy. Florence bought postcards.

Thus:
Benny - Martina - chimpanzees - colouring book;
Florence - Felicity - polar bears - postcards;
Hilary - Cheryl - tigers - mug;
Jimmy - Anita - lizards - pencil case.

No 46

Diane made the figurine (clue 2) and Damian made the bowl (clue 3). The person who made the vase isn't Doris or Douglas (1), so Deirdre. Diane's finishing position was one higher than that of the person who made the plate (2), so the person who made the plate isn't Doris (3). Thus Douglas made the plate and Doris made the mug. Deirdre's finishing position was three higher than Doris's (1), which was one lower than Damian's (3), so Deirdre finished fifth, Doris was eighth and Damian was seventh. Diane was first (2) and Douglas was second.

Thus:
Damian - bowl - seventh;
Deirdre - vase - fifth;
Diane - figurine - first;
Doris - mug - eighth;
Douglas - plate - second.

No 47

The 7-day holiday wasn't in New Zealand (clue 1), France (clue 2), Jordan (3) or Mexico (4), so Italy. Patricia went to France (2). Mitch was away for either 10 or 14 days (1). He didn't go to New Zealand (1) or Jordan (3), so Mexico. His holiday was longer than Patricia's (4) which was longer than Florence's (2). So Mitch's holiday was 14 days, Patricia's 10 days and Florence's 7 days. Andrew was away for 18 days (3), so Eric was away for 21 days. Eric went to Jordan (3) and Andrew went to New Zealand.

Thus:
Andrew - 18 days - New Zealand;
Eric - 21 days - Jordan;
Florence - 7 days - Italy;
Mitch - 14 days - Mexico;
Patricia - 10 days - France.

No 48

The person who collected a cat on Friday isn't Lynne (clue 1), Nigel or Anne (clue 2), so Charles. Nigel adopted Katie (2). Cookie wasn't adopted by Lynne or Charles (1), so by Anne. Anne bought the blanket (1). The person who collected a cat on Tuesday isn't Anne (1) or Nigel (2), so Lynne. Thus Anne collected her cat on Wednesday (1), so Nigel collected his cat on Thursday. Lynne didn't buy the collar (1) or food bowl (2), so the toy mouse. Lynne's cat isn't Sooty (3), so Dizzy. Charles adopted Sooty. Nigel didn't buy the food bowl (2), so the collar. Charles bought the food bowl.

SOLUTIONS

Thus:
Anne - Cookie - blanket - Wednesday;
Charles - Sooty - food bowl - Friday;
Lynne - Dizzy - toy mouse - Tuesday;
Nigel - Katie - collar - Thursday.

No 49

Remember throughout that each 'new' picture is made of pieces of four 'old' ones (intro). Sue's head isn't in the same picture as Ben's legs (with Sue's feet, clue 1) or Lucy's legs (with Sue's body, clue 2), so Sue's head is with Richard's legs. They're not with Lucy's body (3), so Ben's; thus they're also with Lucy's feet. Lucy's legs are with Sue's body (2), so not with Lucy's head. Lucy's head is thus with Richard's body, so they're not with Richard's feet. Thus Richard's feet are with Ben's head. Richard's head isn't with Sue's feet (4), so Ben's feet. Ben's legs and Sue's feet (1) are thus with Lucy's head. By elimination, Sue's legs are with Lucy's body. They're not with Ben's feet (5), so Richard's feet (and Ben's head, above). Richard's head is with Sue's body.

Thus (head - body - legs - feet):
Ben - Lucy - Sue - Richard;
Lucy - Richard - Ben - Sue;
Richard - Sue - Lucy - Ben;
Sue - Ben - Richard - Lucy.

No 50

Suitcase E doesn't belong to Sean (clue 1), Linda or Paul (clue 2) or Ruth (3), so Mark. Sean's is D (1) and case C belongs to the person going to Switzerland. The owner of case A isn't going to South Africa (2), India (3) or China (4), so Denmark. The person going to China owns B (4). Sean isn't going to India (3), so South Africa. Mark is going to India. Ruth's case isn't A or B (4), so C. Linda's is B (2) and Paul's is A.

Thus:
Suitcase A - Paul - Denmark;
Suitcase B - Linda - China;
Suitcase C - Ruth - Switzerland;
Suitcase D - Sean - South Africa;
Suitcase E - Mark - India.

No 51

The charge of 6 silver coins wasn't made for crossing the Flowwin (clue 1), Crashen (clue 2), Dropyn (3) or Runnin River (4), so the Spurton. Frimbi's bridge didn't cross the Spurton (4). The price to cross the Crashen was 3 coins (2), so travellers crossing the Flowwin paid 4 coins (1) and Frimbi charged 5 coins. Thus neither Zwerg nor Dwivolt charged 6 coins (5). Hagrim's price wasn't 6 coins (1), so Blaggitt charged 6 coins and (3) it cost 5 coins to cross the Dropyn. Thus it cost 2 coins to cross the Runnin River. Hagrim's price wasn't 4 coins (1), so Dwivolt charged 4 coins (5) and Zwerg charged 3 coins. Hagrim's price was 2 silver coins.

Thus:
Blaggitt - Spurton - 6 coins;
Dwivolt - Flowwin - 4 coins;
Frimbi - Dropyn - 5 coins;
Hagrim - Runnin - 2 coins;
Zwerg - Crashen - 3 coins.

No 52

The person who borrowed 2 books doesn't prefer sci-fi (clue 1), romance (clue 2) or humour (3), so crime. His/her surname isn't Lawson (2), Stoner or Morgan (4), so Pugh. Thus 3 sci-fi books were borrowed (1) and Keith borrowed 4 books. Helen prefers humour (3), so Keith prefers romance. By elimination, Helen borrowed 5 books. Keith's surname isn't Pugh or Stoner (1) or Lawson (2), so Morgan. Helen's isn't Lawson (2), so Stoner. Thus the person surnamed Lawson is Janice (2) and Ivan's surname is Pugh. Janice borrowed 3 books.

SOLUTIONS

Thus:

Helen - Stoner - humour - 5 books;
Ivan - Pugh - crime - 2 books;
Janice - Lawson - sci-fi - 3 books;
Keith - Morgan - romance - 4 books.

No 53

Remember throughout that each family has members whose names begin with different letters (intro). Freda's son is Adam (clue 1) and her daughter isn't Carol, so her daughter is Jodie, and her husband is Colin. Amy and Christopher aren't the children of Jack (clue 2), so their father is Fred and their mother is Julia. By elimination, Alan's wife is Colette, so their daughter is Faye, thus their son is James. Jack's wife is Anna, their son is Ferdy and their daughter is Carol.

Thus (husband - wife - son - daughter):

Alan - Colette - James - Faye;
Colin - Freda - Adam - Jodie;
Fred - Julia - Christopher - Amy;
Jack - Anna - Ferdy - Carol.

No 54

Friday's visitor desires employment (clue 1) and Thursday's desires love (clue 5). Flora visited on Wednesday (4), so Cordelia who desires health (2) visited on Tuesday, and the girl who desires travel visited on Monday. Thus Dulcie visited on Monday (3) and Flora desires wealth. Friday's visitor wasn't Beth (1), so Edna. Beth visited Granny Cauldron on Thursday.

Thus:

Beth - Thursday - love;
Cordelia - Tuesday - health;
Dulcie - Monday - travel;
Edna - Friday - employment;
Flora - Wednesday - wealth.

No 55

The child surnamed Jarvis isn't Jane (clue 1), Raymond or Larry (clue 3), so either Danny or Tina. The child who

asked for 8 presents isn't Danny (2) or Tina (4), so the child surnamed Jarvis didn't ask for 8 presents. Thus the child surnamed Jarvis asked for 6 (3) and Raymond listed 3 presents. No child listed 5 presents (grid), so Jane listed 8 (4) and Tina listed 6. Danny asked for 7 (2) and Jane's surname is Thorpe. Larry listed 4 presents. Danny's surname isn't Day (1) or Lister (2), so Raven. Larry's surname isn't Lister (1), so Day. Raymond's surname is Lister.

Thus:

Danny - Raven - 7 presents;
Jane - Thorpe - 8 presents;
Larry - Day - 4 presents;
Raymond - Lister - 3 presents;
Tina - Jarvis - 6 presents.

No 56

Remember throughout that each girl's pyjamas and toothbrush are of two different colours (clue 1). Mary didn't drink cocoa, hot milk or cold milk (clue 2), so water. Milly's toothbrush is blue (5). Mandy's pyjamas are pink (5), so her toothbrush isn't pink. The girl with a pink toothbrush isn't Mary (3), so Molly. Mary's toothbrush isn't turquoise (4), so Mandy's is turquoise and Mary's is red. Mandy drank cold milk (4). Molly's pyjamas are red (3). Milly's toothbrush is blue, so her pyjamas are turquoise. Mary's pyjamas are blue. Milly drank cocoa (2), so Molly drank hot milk.

Thus (pyjamas - toothbrush):

Mandy - pink - turquoise - cold milk;
Mary - blue - red - water;
Milly - turquoise - blue - cocoa;
Molly - red - pink - hot milk.

No 57

Polly is from Rezel (clue 1). Bxcn who changed her name to Louise isn't from Breel or Degrex (clue 2), so Wargis. Bill isn't from Breel (3), so Degrex. Norman is from Breel. Norman's hair

SOLUTIONS

was violet (3). Lgrt had gold hair (4).
Norman's former name wasn't Nzdf (2),
so Grvl. Bill (from Degrex, above) wasn't
originally called Lgrt (4), so Nzdf.
Polly's original name was thus Lgrt.
Nzdf's hair wasn't green (3), so purple.
Bxcn's hair was green.

Thus:

Bxcn - Louise - Wargis - green;
Grvl - Norman - Breel - violet;
Lgrt - Polly - Rezel - gold;
Nzdf - Bill - Degrex - purple.

No 58

Terry blamed Brian for his unbrushed
teeth (clue 1). Brian isn't blue (clue 2),
buff (3), brown (4) or black (5),
so beige. Bobby is black and wasn't
responsible for the mud on the floor
(5), an unmade bed (3) or being late for
dinner (4), so spilt milk. The buff bear
was responsible for the unmade bed (3)
and the brown bear made Terry late for
dinner (4), so the blue bear was involved
in the incident concerning mud on the
floor. Billy is neither blue nor brown (2),
so buff. Bamber isn't brown (2), so blue.
Bernie is brown.

Thus:

Bamber - blue - mud on floor;
Bernie - brown - late for dinner;
Billy - buff - unmade bed;
Bobby - black - spilt milk;
Brian - beige - unbrushed teeth.

No 59

Remember throughout that no man
has been at Clore and Ball for 21 years
(grid). Robert is with the man who has
been there for 15 years (clue 2) and
Albert has been an employee for 25
years. Either Joe has been there for 17
years and George for 15 years (clue 4)
or Joe has been there for 19 years and
George 17 years. In other words, the
man who has been there for 17 years is
either Joe or George. Thus Eddie has
been there for 19 years (3) and Max will

be working with the man who has been
there for 17 years. The latter is thus Joe
(4), and George has been there for 15
years. Charlie has been there for 23
years. Noel will be working with Charlie
(1) and Liam with Albert. Pete will be
working with Eddie.

Thus:

Albert - 25 years - Liam;
Charlie - 23 years - Noel;
Eddie - 19 years - Pete;
George - 15 years - Robert;
Joe - 17 years - Max.

No 60

The person who solved 38 (fewest)
puzzles isn't Darren (clue 2), Ellen or
Pamela (clue 3), so Michael. The one
who solved 40 puzzles isn't Darren (2),
so Pamela solved 40 (3), Ellen solved 42
and Michael took 35 minutes to solve a
puzzle. Darren solved 44 puzzles. His
surname is Sharp (2) and Pamela's
is Vance. Thus Ellen took 55 minutes
to solve a puzzle (1) and is surnamed
Peterson, and Michael's surname is
Trotter. Pamela took 45 minutes (2) and
Darren took 25 minutes.

Thus:

Darren - Sharp - 44 puzzles - 25 minutes;
Ellen - Peterson - 42 puzzles -
    55 minutes;
Michael - Trotter - 38 puzzles -
    35 minutes;
Pamela - Vance - 40 puzzles - 45 minutes.

No 61

The woman whose flight left at 0930
hours isn't Nicola or Jean (clue 1) or Sue
(clue 3), so Angela. The flight at 1145
hours wasn't to Venezuela (1), Germany
(2) or Belgium (3), so New Zealand,
thus Nicola's flight wasn't to New
Zealand (1). Shane lives in Belgium (3).
Nicola and Colin don't live in Venezuela
(1), so Germany. Thus Micky's flight
was the next to leave after theirs (2). It
wasn't to Venezuela (1), so New Zealand.

SOLUTIONS

Ray lives in Venezuela. Nicola's flight was at 1100 hours (2). Jean's was at 1145 hours (1), so she lives in New Zealand. Sue doesn't live in Belgium (3), so Venezuela. Angela lives in Belgium. Sue's flight was at 1015 hours.

Thus:

Angela - Shane - Belgium - 0930 hours;
Jean - Micky - New Zealand - 1145 hours;
Nicola - Colin - Germany - 1100 hours;
Sue - Ray - Venezuela - 1015 hours.

No 62

Shelley is 25 (clue 1). The 22-year-old isn't Kate (clue 2) or Vera (3). Vera helped with the catering (3), so she isn't 28 (1). Thus Vera is 29 (3). Kate who helped with the invitations (2) isn't 28 (1), so 24. The 22-year-old helped with the location (2) and isn't Moira, so Deborah. Moira is 28. She made the decorations (1), so Shelley helped with the music.

Thus:

Deborah - 22 years old - location;
Kate - 24 years old - invitations;
Moira - 28 years old - decorations;
Shelley - 25 years old - music;
Vera - 29 years old - catering.

No 63

Box A isn't gold (clue 1), red (clue 2), purple or silver (4), so green and (3) box C contains candies. Box D is either purple or silver (4), so the red box is E (2), D is purple (4) and C is silver. B is thus gold and (1) contains stamps. Box A contains coins (2). The pens aren't in E (1), so D. Box E contains buttons.

Thus:

Box A - green - coins;
Box B - gold - stamps;
Box C - silver - candies;
Box D - purple - pens;
Box E - red - buttons.

No 64

Geraldine lives in apartment 1 (clue 1). Grant painted his walls grey (clue 4). Apartment 3 has cream walls and isn't home to Henry (2), so Heather. Apartment 2 has a new carpet (3), so Grant lives in apartment 2 (4) and apartment 4 has a new television. By elimination, Henry lives in apartment 4. The new curtains aren't in apartment 3 (5), so apartment 1. Apartment 3 has a new light fitting. The walls in apartment 1 aren't white (1), so beige. Apartment 4 has white walls.

Thus:

Apartment 1 - Geraldine - beige - curtains;
Apartment 2 - Grant - grey - carpet;
Apartment 3 - Heather - cream - light fitting;
Apartment 4 - Henry - white - television.

No 65

Warren's party was on Friday (clue 3). Monday's party wasn't Pippa's (clue 1) or Candice's (4), so Larry's and (2) 12 guests were invited to Wednesday's party. The child who invited 12 isn't Pippa (5), so Candice. Pippa's party was on Tuesday. Larry's surname is Fisher (1). The child who invited 10 guests isn't Warren (3) or Pippa (5), so Larry. Thus Candice's surname is Best (3) and Warren invited 6 guests. Pippa invited 5 guests. Warren's surname is Parry (4), so Pippa's is Flynn.

Thus:

Candice - Best - 12 guests - Wednesday;
Larry - Fisher - 10 guests - Monday;
Pippa - Flynn - 5 guests - Tuesday;
Warren - Parry - 6 guests - Friday.

No 66

Patrick didn't write 19 pages (clue 3), so 18 pages (clue 1) and Naomi wrote 15. Pauline wrote 17 pages and Joseph wrote 19 (2), so Maurice wrote 16 pages. Patrick (18 pages, above) didn't hand in his essay on Monday or Tuesday (2), so Joseph (19 pages, above) is the 'tallest child' and handed in his essay on either Thursday or Friday (3). Maurice also handed in his work on either Thursday or Friday (1), so Patrick did so on Wednesday. Pauline handed in her essay on Monday (2), so Naomi handed in hers on Tuesday (1) and Maurice handed in his on Friday. Joseph's essay was handed in on Thursday.

Thus:
Joseph - 19 pages - Thursday;
Maurice - 16 pages - Friday;
Naomi - 15 pages - Tuesday;
Patrick - 18 pages - Wednesday;
Pauline - 17 pages - Monday.

No 67

Thyme was planted on Monday (clue 3), so parsley was planted in pot E on Tuesday (clue 2) and pot B was planted on Saturday (1). Chives aren't in pot B (1) and dill wasn't planted on Saturday. Thus pot B contains garden mint. Pot A doesn't contain chives (1) or thyme (3), so dill. No pot was planted on Thursday (grid), so the dill was planted on Wednesday (1) and (since B was planted on Saturday, above) pot D contains chives. By elimination, pot C contains thyme. Pot D was planted on Friday.

Thus:
Pot A - dill - Wednesday;
Pot B - garden mint - Saturday;
Pot C - thyme - Monday;
Pot D - chives - Friday;
Pot E - parsley - Tuesday.

No 68

No-one has 3 willows (clue 1), 3 elms (clue 2) or 3 oaks (3), so there are 3 ash trees. No-one has 8 elms (2) or 8 oaks (3), so there are 8 willows and (1) Rachel has 3 trees. Ralph has 8 trees (2) and there are 10 elms. Thus there are 5 oaks. Rodney doesn't have elms (2), so oaks. Ruth has elm trees.

She doesn't live at No 6 (1), so she lives at No 5 (2) and Rodney lives at No 7. Ralph (willows, above) lives at No 6 (1), so Rachel lives at No 8.

Thus:
No 5 - Ruth - 10 - elm trees;
No 6 - Ralph - 8 - willow trees;
No 7 - Rodney - 5 - oak trees;
No 8 - Rachel - 3 - ash trees.

No 69

The person who called at 11.00am didn't have a response time of 4 minutes (clue 3). No-one called at 10.15am (grid), so the 4-minute response time was to the 10.30am call (clue 1) and the monitor problem was reported at 10.00am. The 7-minute response time wasn't regarding a monitor (1), keyboard (2) or mouse (3), so a memory stick. Neil had a keyboard problem (2). The person who called at 10.00am (monitor problem, above) isn't Martha (1) or Karen (2), so Antony. Karen didn't have a mouse problem (2), so a memory stick problem. Martha had a mouse problem. The memory stick response time was 7 minutes (above), so Neil's was 6 minutes (2). Antony's wasn't 4 minutes (1), so 5 minutes. Martha's was 4 minutes. Karen rang at 10.45am (2), so Neil rang at 11.00am.

Thus:
Antony - 10.00am - monitor - 5 minutes;
Karen - 10.45am - memory stick - 7 minutes;
Martha - 10.30am - mouse - 4 minutes;
Neil - 11.00am - keyboard - 6 minutes.

No 70

Monday's route wasn't A (clue 1), D or E (clue 3), so B was taken on Monday (2), the 13-minute journey on Tuesday and C was taken on Wednesday. Tuesday's route wasn't A (1) or E (3), so D. Thus route A wasn't taken on Thursday (1), so Friday. Route E was taken on Thursday. Route C took 15 minutes (1). Route B

SOLUTIONS

took 11 minutes (3). Route E didn't take 12 minutes (4), so 14 minutes. Route A took 12 minutes.

Thus:

Route A - Friday - 12 minutes;
Route B - Monday - 11 minutes;
Route C - Wednesday - 15 minutes;
Route D - Tuesday - 13 minutes;
Route E - Thursday - 14 minutes.

No 71

Remember throughout that no man's name begins with the same letter as his surname (intro). Nancy's surname is Stanford (clue 3). Mrs Walker isn't Glenda or Rosemary (1) or Fiona (2), so Lydia. Lydia's husband isn't William (intro), Hal, Lee or Sean (4), so Chris. Sean's surname is Connor (4). Glenda's husband isn't Sean (2) and Fiona's surname isn't Connor. Thus Rosemary is married to Sean. Glenda's husband isn't William or Lee (2), so he's Hal and Fiona's surname is Holmes. Thus Glenda's surname is Lacey. Nancy's husband is Lee (3), so Fiona's is William.

Thus:

Fiona - William - Holmes;
Glenda - Hal - Lacey;
Lydia - Chris - Walker;
Nancy - Lee - Stanford;
Rosemary - Sean - Connor.

No 72

The call made by Mrs Gates wasn't at 8.30pm (clue 2). No guest rang at 9.00pm (grid), so neither Mr Jackson nor Mr Sands made the 8.30pm call (clue 3). Thus Miss Milton made the call at 8.30pm. The WOMAN in room 267 (1) is thus Mrs Gates, and (4) the WOMAN in room 309 is Miss Milton. The man in room 134 didn't call at 9.30pm (4), so at 10.30pm. Thus he's Mr Sands (3) and Mr Jackson rang at 10.00pm. Mr Jackson was in room 282 Mrs Gates called at 9.30pm, so Miss Milton wanted towels (1). Mrs Gates

wanted a blanket (2) and Mr Sands wanted coffee (3). Mr Jackson wanted a pillow.

Thus:

Mrs Gates - blanket - room 267 - 9.30pm;
Mr Jackson - pillow - room 282 - 10.00pm;
Miss Milton - towels - room 309 - 8.30pm;
Mr Sands - coffee - room 134 - 10.30pm.

No 73

Jenny's apron took four weeks to make (clue 5). Cara's apron had a buttercup (clue 3). The girl who made an apron with a daisy took 3 weeks to make it (1). She isn't Tracey (2), so Alice. Cara's didn't take 6 weeks to make (3), so 5 weeks. Tracey's took 6 weeks. Jenny's apron doesn't have a primrose (5), so a poppy. Tracey stitched the primrose. Tracey's apron is blue (2), so Cara's isn't pink (4). The pink apron wasn't made by Jenny (5), so Alice's is pink and (4) Jenny's is green. Cara's apron is orange.

Thus:

Alice - pink - daisy - 3 weeks;
Cara - orange - buttercup - 5 weeks;
Jenny - green - poppy - 4 weeks;
Tracey - blue - primrose - 6 weeks.

No 74

Remember throughout that each woman did two different tasks (intro). Cora was gardening this morning (clue 2). The woman who was cleaning this morning and shopping this afternoon isn't Donna or Georgina (clue 1) or Naomi (4), so Patricia. Donna was cleaning this afternoon (1). Cora wasn't baking this afternoon (2), so ironing. Naomi's morning job wasn't ironing (2) or shopping (4), so baking. By elimination, she was gardening this afternoon and Georgina was baking. Georgina wasn't ironing this morning (3), so shopping. Donna was ironing this morning.

SOLUTIONS

Thus (morning - afternoon):
Cora - gardening - ironing;
Donna - ironing - cleaning;
Georgina - shopping - baking;
Naomi - baking - gardening;
Patricia - cleaning - shopping.

No 75

Sally's basket is brown (clue 4). Edward collected 11 eggs (clue 1). His basket isn't black (1), red (2) or green (3), so blue; thus (4) Sally collected 15 eggs. Paul collected 17 eggs (2) and the child with the red basket collected 21. Paul's basket is green (3). Helen didn't collect 21 eggs (5), so her basket is black and she collected 19 eggs. John's basket is red.
Thus:
Edward - blue - 11 eggs;
Helen - black - 19 eggs;
John - red - 21 eggs;
Paul - green - 17 eggs;
Sally - brown - 15 eggs.

No 76

The man who is 5 feet 8 inches tall isn't Ralph (clue 2), Rupert or Rory (4), so Richard. No man weighs 175 pounds (grid), so Ralph weighs either 160 or 170 pounds (1), as does Richard (3). Thus Ralph isn't 5 feet 9 inches tall (2). The man who is 5 feet 9 inches tall isn't Rory (4), so Rupert. The man with brown hair isn't Rupert, Richard or Rory (5), so Ralph. Richard weighs 10 pounds less than the man with red hair (3), so Richard doesn't weigh 10 pounds less than Ralph. Thus Ralph weighs 160 pounds and Richard weighs 170 pounds. The man with red hair weighs 180 pounds (3). Richard has blond hair (1). By elimination, the man with black hair weighs 165 pounds. Rupert's hair isn't red (3), so black. Rory has red hair.

Ralph is 5 feet 11 inches tall (2), so Rory is 5 feet 10 inches tall.
Thus:
Ralph - brown - 5 feet 11 inches - 160 pounds;
Richard - blond - 5 feet 8 inches - 170 pounds;
Rory - red - 5 feet 10 inches - 180 pounds;
Rupert - black - 5 feet 9 inches - 165 pounds.

No 77

Bad Bill raided either 8 or 9 ships (clue 1), as had Dirty Dan (clue 2). Thus neither captained the *Golden Doe* (2). The *Golden Doe's* captain hadn't raided 6 ships (2), so 7 and Dirty Dan's ship had raided 9. Bad Bill's ship had raided 8 ships. The *Golden Doe* hadn't a crew of 28 or 29 (1), so 30 (2) and the captain who had raided 6 ships had 31 crew. Bad Bill had a crew of 29 (1), so Dirty Dan had a crew of 28 and sailed the *Barbaric*. Bad Bill's ship was the *Swordfish* (3) and Terrible Tom had 31 crew. Horrible Harry had a crew of 30. The *Katrina* was captained by Terrible Tom.
Thus:
Bad Bill - *Swordfish* - 29 crew - 8 ships;
Dirty Dan - *Barbaric* - 28 crew - 9 ships;
Horrible Harry - *Golden Doe* - 30 crew - 7 ships;
Terrible Tom - *Katrina* - 31 crew - 6 ships.

No 78

Molly's husband is Rory (clue 1) and Megan's is Raymond (clue 2). Mandy's husband isn't Robert or Richard (3), so Rupert. They don't live at No 6 (2), so they're at No 1 (3) and Richard is at No 3. Megan and Raymond are at No 6 (2). Rory isn't at No 8 (1), so No 2. Robert is at No 8. Moira lives at No 3 (1) and Muriel at No 8.

Solutions

Thus:
No 1 - Rupert - Mandy;
No 2 - Rory - Molly;
No 3 - Richard - Moira;
No 6 - Raymond - Megan;
No 8 - Robert - Muriel.

No 79

The 11.15am appointment was with the doctor (clue 3), so (from the listed times) Louise saw her optician at 10.30am (clue 1) and the 9.45am appointment was on Thursday. Friday's appointment wasn't at 11.15am (3), 9.15am or 10.30am (4), so 11.45am. Monday's appointment with the hairdresser (2) was thus at 9.15am. Tuesday's was at 10.30am (4), so the 11.15am appointment was on Wednesday. The chiropodist was seen on Thursday (3), so Friday's appointment was with the dentist.
Thus:
Chiropodist - 9.45am - Thursday;
Dentist - 11.45am - Friday;
Doctor - 11.15am - Wednesday;
Hairdresser - 9.15am - Monday;
Optician - 10.30am - Tuesday.

No 80

Remember throughout that each 'new' picture is made of pieces of four 'old' ones (intro). Mr White's feet and Miss Owen's body are in the same picture (clue 3). They're not with Mrs Rose's legs (with Miss Owen's feet, clue 2), so they're with Mr Potter's legs and (by elimination) Mrs Rose's head. Mr White's body isn't with Miss Owen's head (with Mr White's legs, 1), so it's with Mr Potter's head, thus Mr Potter's feet are with Mrs Rose's body. They're not with Miss Owen's legs (4), so they're with Mr White's legs and Miss Owen's head. Mr Potter's body is thus with Mr White's head. By elimination, Miss

Owen's legs are with Mrs Rose's feet. Mrs Rose's legs aren't with Mr White's body (5), so they're with Mr Potter's body. Thus Mr White's body is with Miss Owen's legs.
Thus (head - body - legs - feet):
Miss Owen - Mrs Rose - Mr White - Mr Potter;
Mr Potter - Mr White - Miss Owen - Mrs Rose;
Mrs Rose - Miss Owen - Mr Potter - Mr White;
Mr White - Mr Potter - Mrs Rose - Miss Owen.

No 81

The player with the ace of hearts isn't James (clue 1), Ruby (clue 2) or Maria (3), so Kevin. The person with the 3 of diamonds isn't James (2) or Kevin (4). Ruby has either the 6 or 10 of clubs (2). Thus the person with the 3 of diamonds and either the 4 or 8 of clubs (1) is Maria. So Maria has the 8 of clubs (3) and Kevin (ace of hearts, above) has the 6 of clubs. Thus Ruby has the 10 of clubs and James has the 4 of clubs. James has the 8 of hearts (1). Ruby has the queen of hearts (2), so Maria has the 4 of hearts. James has the king of diamonds (2). Ruby has the 6 of diamonds (4) and Kevin has the jack of diamonds.
Thus (heart - club - diamond):
James - 8 - 4 - king;
Kevin - ace - 6 - jack;
Maria - 4 - 8 - 3;
Ruby - queen - 10 - 6.

No 82

The woman who eats apples didn't smoke 16 or 18 cigarettes per day (clue 4), so she isn't Vera (clue 2). Nor is she Claire (2), Sonja (3) or Brenda (4), so Nadine eats apples. The woman who smoked 18 cigarettes isn't Vera (2), Sonja (3) or Brenda (4), so Claire who (2) chews peppermints. Vera smoked 16 per day (2). The woman who smoked

10 isn't Nadine (1) or Brenda (4), so Sonja. Thus the woman who smoked 14 per day chews gum (3). By elimination, she's Brenda. Nadine smoked 12 per day, so (1) Sonja chews toffees. Vera eats peanuts.

Thus:

Brenda - 14 per day - gum;
Claire - 18 per day - peppermints;
Nadine - 12 per day - apples;
Sonja - 10 per day - toffees;
Vera - 16 per day - peanuts.

No 83

The bow on present E isn't yellow (clue 1), scarlet (clue 2), pink (3) or blue (4), so purple. The bow on the present of books is blue (2). The one on the cosmetics isn't yellow or purple (1) or scarlet (2), so pink. The bow on present A isn't yellow (1), blue (2) or pink (3), so scarlet. The one on present B isn't yellow (1) or blue (2), so pink. Present C has a yellow bow (1), so the bow on D is blue. The ornament is in present E (1). Present A contains perfume (3), so the coffee set is in present C.

Thus:

Present A - perfume - scarlet;
Present B - cosmetics - pink;
Present C - coffee set - yellow;
Present D - books - blue;
Present E - ornament - purple.

No 84

Fred hasn't 10 grandchildren (clue 2), so he has 5 and George has 4 (clue 1). Ann has 8 grandchildren (4). Bob hasn't 8 (3), so 10. Tony has 8 grandchildren. George's grandchild was born in July (1). Bob's wasn't born in March (3). No child was born in June (grid), so Bob's was born in May (2) and Fred's in March. Tony's grandchild was born in April. George's wife is Susan (3). Fred's isn't Rosie (2), so Jane. Bob's wife is Rosie.

Thus:

Bob - Rosie - 10 grandchildren - May;
Fred - Jane - 5 grandchildren - March;
George - Susan - 4 grandchildren - July;
Tony - Ann - 8 grandchildren - April.

No 85

Bob went to Gunnerford (clue 1). The man who went east to Battlebury wasn't Johnnie or Tommy (clue 3), so Albert. The tanks were found by the man who went south (2). The man who went to Trenchbridge found the missile launcher (4). He didn't travel north (4), so west. Bob didn't travel north (1), so south. The man who went to Sapper's Wood travelled north. The ammo dump wasn't in the east (5), so the north. Thus Albert found the field guns. Tommy didn't go west (6), so north. Johnnie travelled west.

Thus:

Albert - east - Battlebury - field guns;
Bob - south - Gunnerford - tanks;
Johnnie - west - Trenchbridge -
    missile launcher;
Tommy - north - Sapper's Wood -
    ammo dump.

No 86

Lyndsey's favourite is Gary (clue 1) and Poppy's is the keyboard player (clue 2). Ashley is the vocalist (4). Holly's favourite is Leroy, who isn't the bass guitarist or lead guitarist (3), so the drummer. Gary isn't the lead guitarist (1), so the bass guitarist. Ashley isn't the favourite of Catherine (4), so Madeline. Catherine's favourite is the lead guitarist. Errol isn't the keyboard player (2), so the lead guitarist. Poppy's idol is Ben.

Thus:

Catherine - Errol - lead guitarist;
Holly - Leroy - drummer;
Lyndsey - Gary - bass guitarist;
Madeline - Ashley - vocalist;
Poppy - Ben - keyboard player.

Solutions

No 87

Arthur found the portrait (clue 3). The candelabra wasn't found by Boris or Caitlin (clue 2) or Martin (4), so Gloria. The item worth $7,000 wasn't found by Boris or Gloria (2), Arthur (3) or Martin (4), so by Caitlin. It isn't the chair (1) or figurine (2), so the tapestry. Boris' item is worth $6,000 (2) and the candelabra is worth $5,000. The figurine isn't worth $6,000 (3), so Boris found the chair. Martin found the figurine. Arthur's item is worth $3,000 (3) and the figurine is worth $4,000.

Thus:

Arthur - portrait - $3,000;
Boris - chair - $6,000;
Caitlin - tapestry - $7,000;
Gloria - candelabra - $5,000;
Martin - figurine - $4,000.

No 88

Remember throughout that each family has members whose names begin with four different letters (intro). Thus Melissa's father isn't Malcolm, so Nancy's mother isn't Marian (clue 2). Marian's daughter isn't Joelle (clue 1), so Marian's daughter is Gemma. John's son is Gerry (1) and his wife isn't Marian, so Norma; thus their daughter is Melissa. Nancy's mother is Jennifer (2). By elimination, Marian's husband is Nigel, and their son is Joe. Mitch's father is Geoff, whose wife is Jennifer. Malcolm's wife is Glenda, their son is Neil, and their daughter is Joelle.

Thus (husband - wife - son - daughter):

Geoff - Jennifer - Mitch - Nancy;
John - Norma - Gerry - Melissa;
Malcolm - Glenda - Neil - Joelle;
Nigel - Marian - Joe - Gemma.

No 89

Nicholas saw the romance (clue 1) and Brian saw the western (clue 4). *The Question* is the murder mystery (2). It wasn't seen by Vernon (2), so Vernon saw the science fiction film and Rupert saw *The Question*. Josie saw *Aunt Agatha* (1) and Verity saw *Gordon's Goal* (3). Rupert's girlfriend isn't Sarah (2), so Marcia. Verity's boyfriend isn't Nicholas or Brian (3), so Vernon. Nicholas' girlfriend isn't Josie (1), so Sarah and (by elimination) they saw *Heaven Scent*. Brian's girlfriend is Josie.

Thus:

Brian - Josie - *Aunt Agatha* - western;
Nicholas - Sarah - *Heaven Scent* - romance;
Rupert - Marcia - *The Question* - murder mystery;
Vernon - Verity - *Gordon's Goal* - science fiction.

No 90

One pond has 3 koi carp and 2 tench (clue 4). Thus Norman has 3 tench and 6 koi carp (clue 2). Lynne hasn't 2 tench (2), so 4 (1) and Tricia has 6 tench. Lynne hasn't 4 koi carp (3) or 2 koi carp (5), so 5 koi carp. Tricia has 4 koi carp (1) and Barry has 2 koi carp. John has 3 koi carp (and 2 tench, 4). Barry has 5 tench.

Thus (koi carp - tench):

Barry - 2 - 5;
John - 3 - 2;
Lynne - 5 - 4;
Norman - 6 - 3;
Tricia - 4 - 6.

No 91

The man who won $180 isn't Seth (clue 2), Saul or Simon (clue 5), so Stan (3) and Steve who backed West Hope won $160. Saul didn't win $120 (5), so he won $140 and Simon won $120. Seth thus won $100 and backed Good Will (4). Stan backed Sunrise (5). Saul didn't back Minaret (1), so Bay Laurel. Simon backed Minaret.

SOLUTIONS

Thus:
Saul - Bay Laurel - $140;
Seth - Good Will - $100;
Simon - Minaret - $120;
Stan - Sunrise - $180;
Steve - West Hope - $160.

No 92

Tim's wife is Tina (clue 3). Marie's baby is due in July (clue 1) and her husband bought a doll's house. Ben's baby isn't due in July (2) and he didn't buy a train set. Ross bought a teddy bear (4), so Ben bought a bicycle. Marie's husband is thus Jack. Tim bought a train set. Kirsty's baby is due in June (5), thus her husband isn't Ben (2), so Ross. Ben is Jenny's husband. Jenny's baby is due in March (2) and Tina's is due in April.
Thus:
Jenny - Ben - March - bicycle;
Kirsty - Ross - June - teddy bear;
Marie - Jack - July - doll's house;
Tina - Tim - April - train set.

No 93

December's trip was to Poland (clue 2). Belinda doesn't live in Poland, Italy or Portugal (clue 3), so Mexico. Trevor's sister lives in Portugal (1) and his aunt lives in Italy (4). His grandmother doesn't live in Poland (2), so Mexico. His cousin thus lives in Poland. January's trip wasn't to see his sister (1) or aunt (4), so his grandmother. Trevor visited Gloria earlier than he saw his sister (1), so he visited Gloria in April and his sister in August. By elimination, Gloria is his aunt. His cousin isn't Isabel (5), so Katrina. Isabel is Trevor's sister.
Thus:
Belinda - grandmother - January - Mexico;
Gloria - aunt - April - Italy;
Isabel - sister - August - Portugal;
Katrina - cousin - December - Poland.

No 94

Mr Evans was held up by cattle (clue 3). The person held up due to an accident was thus Mr Church (clue 1). He wasn't delayed for 30 minutes (1), so for 25 minutes (4) and Miss O'Hare was held up for 10 minutes. Ms Dawlish's delay was 30 minutes (1). The breakdown didn't affect Miss O'Hare or Mr McNab (3), so Ms Dawlish. Thus Mr Evans wasn't held up for 20 minutes (2), so 15 minutes. The 20-minute delay due to a caravan (2) was thus Mr McNab's. Miss O'Hare was held up by roadworks.
Thus:
Mr Church - accident - 25 minutes;
Ms Dawlish - breakdown - 30 minutes;
Mr Evans - cattle - 15 minutes;
Mr McNab - caravan - 20 minutes;
Miss O'Hare - roadworks - 10 minutes.

No 95

Miss Young's car isn't Car 5 (clue 2), so it's Car 4 (clue 3) and Car 1 is black. A man owns Car 2 (2), so Mrs Scott owns Car 1 (1). Mr Warner owns Car 5 (2). Car 2 isn't Mr Porter's (1), so Mr Berry's. Mr Porter owns Car 3. Car 2 is red (2). Car 3 isn't green (1) or blue (4), so white. It's owned by a man (Mr Porter, above), so Miss Young's car is blue (4). Car 5 is green.
Thus:
Car 1 - Mrs Scott - black;
Car 2 - Mr Berry - red;
Car 3 - Mr Porter - white;
Car 4 - Miss Young - blue;
Car 5 - Mr Warner - green.

No 96

Box B has a depth of either 26 cm or 27 cm (clue 1) as has box C (clue 2). The box 25 cm deep isn't D (3), so A. D has a depth of 29 cm, so a height of 28 cm (3). B's height is thus 29 cm (1) and its depth is 27 cm. C has a depth of 26 cm, so a width of 25 cm (2) and a height of 26 cm. Box A has a height

SOLUTIONS

of 30 cm. B has a width of 24 cm (1), so D has a width of 26 cm (3) and A has a width of 27 cm.

Thus (height - width - depth):
Box A - 30 cm - 27 cm - 25 cm;
Box B - 29 cm - 24 cm - 27 cm;
Box C - 26 cm - 25 cm - 26 cm;
Box D - 28 cm - 26 cm - 29 cm.

No 97

Nick's top subject is English (clue 3) and Jane's is geography (clue 4). Fiona's isn't mathematics (2), so science. Neil's top subject is mathematics. The Class 2 pupil was first (3). Fiona in Class 4 wasn't fifth (2), so she was fourth (1) and the Class 1 pupil was second. The Class 3 pupil was fifth. Neil is in Class 3 (2). Nick isn't in Class 2 (3), so Class 1. Jane is in Class 2.

Thus:
Fiona - Class 4 - fourth - science;
Jane - Class 2 - first - geography;
Neil - Class 3 - fifth - mathematics;
Nick - Class 1 - second - English.

No 98

Jonathan and Jennifer didn't sell 10 ornaments on Wednesday (clue 2), so 7 ornaments weren't sold on Friday (clue 4). Thus they sold 9 ornaments on Friday (2) and 9 collages plus 7 ornaments on Wednesday. They sold 4 collages on Tuesday (4). They sold 5 ornaments on Tuesday (3) and 8 collages on Monday. Ten ornaments were sold on Monday (4), so 6 were sold on Thursday. They didn't sell 7 collages on Thursday (1), so 5. They sold 7 collages on Friday.

Thus:
Monday - 8 collages - 10 ornaments;
Tuesday - 4 collages - 5 ornaments;
Wednesday - 9 collages - 7 ornaments;
Thursday - 5 collages - 6 ornaments;
Friday - 7 collages - 9 ornaments.

No 99

Dave is one place anticlockwise of Roger (clue 1), so isn't studying history or mathematics (clue 2). Dave's homework isn't drama or English (1), so geography. Thus in clue 2, Dave is the 'other' boy, who isn't in seats B or E; so Roger isn't in C or A. Roger isn't in B or D (1), so he's in E, the boy doing English is in A, John is in B, the boy doing drama is in C, and Dave is in D. Since he's the 'other' boy (2), Roger is doing history, Eddie is in A, John is studying mathematics, and Thomas is in C.

Thus:
Chair A - Eddie - English;
Chair B - John - mathematics;
Chair C - Thomas - drama;
Chair D - Dave - geography;
Chair E - Roger - history.

No 100

Remember throughout that each colour is in three differently-lettered cans and on three different shelves (intro). On the middle shelf, the blue paint is further right than both the red paint (clue 2) and the green paint (clue 3), so the blue paint is in either can C or can D, and the red paint isn't in can A (2). Thus the yellow paint on the middle shelf is in either C or D (1), as is the blue paint (above). So the red paint is in B (2) and the blue paint is in C. The yellow paint is thus in D, so the green paint is in A on the middle shelf. The paint in D on the top shelf isn't yellow (intro), blue or green (3), so red. Thus the blue paint is in B on the top shelf (2), the green paint is in C (3) and the yellow paint is in A. On the bottom shelf, the paint in A isn't yellow or green (in A on the top and middle shelves respectively) or red (1), so blue. The red paint isn't in D or B (red on the top and middle shelves), so C. The yellow paint

229

SOLUTIONS

(D on the middle shelf) is in B and the green paint is in D.
Thus (top - middle - bottom):
Can A - yellow - green - blue;
Can B - blue - red - yellow;
Can C - green - blue - red;
Can D - red - yellow - green.

No 101

Jody plays lead guitar and Lucy plays bass guitar (clue 1). The waitress who plays rhythm guitar isn't Linda (clue 2) or Carrie (3), so Judy. Linda plays the drums (2). Thus Carrie who works as a barmaid (3) plays keyboards. Jody doesn't work as a bus driver (1) or teacher (4), so she's a company rep. The teacher isn't Linda (4), so Lucy. Linda is a bus driver.
Thus:
Carrie - keyboards - barmaid;
Jody - lead guitar - company rep;
Judy - rhythm guitar - waitress;
Linda - drums - bus driver;
Lucy - bass guitar - teacher.

No 102

The person from Etheridge is 54 years old (clue 1) and Archie is either 57 or 58. The person from Mannstown (clue 2) is either 57 or 58, and isn't Archie. Thus Maude from Accringtown is 45 (2) and Ethel is 41. Ethel is thus from Blackrock (1), Bill is 58 (3) and Thomas is 54. Archie is 57. Archie isn't from Mannstown (2), so Trowville. Bill is from Mannstown.
Thus:
Archie - Trowville - 57 years old;
Bill - Mannstown - 58 years old;
Ethel - Blackrock - 41 years old;
Maude - Accringtown - 45 years old;
Thomas - Etheridge - 54 years old.

No 103

No entertainment is offered on Wednesday (grid). The entertainment on Tuesday isn't karaoke or the quiz (clue 2), the folk band or the darts match (clue 3), so skittles. The Plough offers the quiz night (1). The Fox hasn't an entertainment night on Tuesday (3). Nor does it offer a folk band or darts match (3), so karaoke. The karaoke night isn't on Sunday (2), so Saturday (3). Sunday's entertainment isn't a folk band or darts match (3), so the quiz night. Thursday's entertainment is the folk band (3) and Friday's is the darts match. The folk band plays at The Ferret (2). The Black Swan's entertainment night is on Tuesday (4) and the King's Head's entertainment night is on Friday.
Thus:
Black Swan - skittles - Tuesday;
King's Head - darts match - Friday;
The Ferret - folk band - Thursday;
The Fox - karaoke - Saturday;
The Plough - quiz night - Sunday.

No 104

The man who finished fourth isn't Eddie (clue 1), Mike (clue 3) or Carl (4), so Tommy. His time was 16m 10s (3). The man whose time was 15m 25s isn't Carl or Mike (4), so Eddie. Mike's time wasn't 16m 05s (2), so 15m 45s. Carl's was 16m 05s, thus he has the ArrowFlite bike (2). Carl finished two places ahead of Eddie (4), so Carl was first and Eddie was third. Mike was second. Tommy owns the JetStream bike (1). Mike's bike isn't the LightningOne (2), so the FlameStreak. Eddie owns the LightningOne bike.
Thus:
Carl - 1st - 16m 05s - ArrowFlite;
Eddie - 3rd - 15m 25s - LightningOne;
Mike - 2nd - 15m 45s - FlameStreak;
Tommy - 4th - 16m 10s - JetStream.

No 105

The 10-year-old (youngest) child isn't Anna (clue 1), David (clue 3) or William (4), so Zoe. Zoe is going to Belgium

(5), so Anna is 14 (1) and the child going to Wales is 11. William is 11 (5). He is setting off on 31st July (1), so the 10-year-old sets off on 13th August (3). David is 13. The trip to France starts on 21st July (2), so the one to Ireland starts on 24th July. David isn't going to France (3), so Ireland. Anna is going to France.

Thus:

Anna - 14 years old - France - 21st July;
David - 13 years old - Ireland - 24th July;
William - 11 years old - Wales - 31st July;
Zoe - 10 years old - Belgium - 13th August.

No 106

Cheryl didn't write 170 lines (clue 2), so her detention wasn't on Wednesday (clue 4), thus Adam's wasn't on Friday (2). The child who received Friday's detention isn't Cheryl (2), Katie or Edward (3), so Gordon. Gordon didn't write 140 lines (1). The child who wrote 170 lines had a detention on Wednesday (4). The child who wrote 140 lines wasn't detained on Monday or Tuesday (3), so Thursday. Katie's detention was thus on Wednesday (3). Cheryl's was on Tuesday and Adam's was on Thursday (2), so Edward's was on Monday. Adam thus wrote 140 lines (above), so Gordon wrote 80 lines (1). Cheryl wrote 110 lines (2), so Edward wrote 50 lines.

Thus:

Adam - Thursday - 140 lines;
Cheryl - Tuesday - 110 lines;
Edward - Monday - 50 lines;
Gordon - Friday - 80 lines;
Katie - Wednesday - 170 lines.

No 107

The mountain in Peru isn't Fallov Peak (clue 2), so Neverest is in Peru (clue 4) and Skaler plans to climb Fallov Peak. Skaler isn't going to Russia (5), so Chile (2), and Bergmann is going to Russia. He and Klamberer are climbing either Pico Rodriguez or Kermet (5),

so Montagnier is climbing Widow's Peak (3) and Klamberer is going to Argentina. The mountain he will climb isn't Kermet (1), so Pico Rodriguez. Bergmann will climb Kermet. Widow's Peak is in Nepal. Tumbla plans to climb Neverest.

Thus:

Bergmann - Kermet - Russia;
Klamberer - Pico Rodriguez - Argentina;
Montagnier - Widow's Peak - Nepal;
Skaler - Fallov Peak - Chile;
Tumbla - Neverest - Peru.

No 108

Nerys wrote *Whirl's End* (clue 4) and Andrew wrote the science fiction story (clue 5). *Zenith Down* is a romance and wasn't written by Bryn (2), so Miranda. Bryn sent his work to Boddis & Ripp (2), thus it isn't the comedy (1), so adventure story. Nerys wrote the comedy and (1) sent it to Booke & Clubb. Bryn didn't write *Window Five* (3), so *Arches*. Andrew wrote *Window Five*. He didn't send it to Paige & Turner (5), so to ParraGraff. Miranda sent her book to Paige & Turner.

Thus:

Andrew - *Window Five* - sci-fi - ParraGraff;
Bryn - *Arches* - adventure - Boddis & Ripp;
Miranda - *Zenith Down* - romance - Paige & Turner;
Nerys - *Whirl's End* - comedy - Booke & Clubb.

No 109

The child surnamed Aster is painting a tree (clue 1). The one surnamed Mitchell isn't painting a car or ducks (clue 2), so his/her mother. He/she is at an easel numbered one higher than Ricky's (3) and one lower than that of the child surnamed Walters. Thus the child surnamed Walters is painting ducks (2). The one surnamed Goring is painting a car. The child at easel No 1 isn't painting a tree (1), ducks (2) or his/her mother (3), so a car. The one at easel No 2 isn't painting a tree (1) or ducks (2), so his/her mother. Ricky is at easel No 1 (3) and the Walters child is at easel No 3. He/she isn't Sara (3) or Holly (1), so Colin. The child surnamed Aster is at No 4 (1) and Holly is at No 2. Thus Sara is at No 4 and Holly's surname is Mitchell. Sara is painting a tree.

Thus:

Colin - Walters - ducks - 3;
Holly - Mitchell - mother - 2;
Ricky - Goring - car - 1;
Sara - Aster - tree - 4.

No 110

The person who saw 52 daffodils isn't Ms Willis or Mr Havelock (clue 2), Mr Mason (clue 3) or Mrs Carter (4), so Miss Stoker, who didn't see 45 crocuses (3). The person who saw 45 crocuses isn't Mr Mason or Ms Willis (1) or Mr Havelock (4), so Mrs Carter. She didn't see 44 daffodils (3) or 46 daffodils (4), so 40 (3) and Mr Mason saw 44 daffodils (3). Ms Willis thus saw 46 (2) and Mr Havelock saw 50 daffodils (4). Mr Havelock saw 40 crocuses (4). Thus Mr Mason saw 43 (1), Miss Stoker saw 44, and Ms Willis saw 39 crocuses.

Thus (crocuses - daffodils):

Mrs Carter - 45 - 40;
Mr Mason - 43 - 44;
Mr Havelock - 40 - 50;
Miss Stoker - 44 - 52;
Ms Willis - 39 - 46.

No 111

PC Chase dealt with the bike theft (clue 3) and PC Peel dealt with the car theft (clue 4). PC Dixon didn't deal with the burglary or mugging (2), so the bar fight. The burglary wasn't dealt with by PC McNab (1), so PC Cooper. PC McNab

was called to the scene of the mugging. His call-out was at 10.55pm (1), thus the man who received the 11.50pm call-out wasn't PC Dixon or PC Cooper (2) or PC Chase (3), so PC Peel. PC Chase's call-out wasn't at 10.10pm (3), so PC Cooper's was at 10.10pm (2) and PC Dixon's was at 9.05pm. PC Chase's call out was at 8.25pm.

Thus:

Chase - bike theft - 8.25pm;
Cooper - burglary - 10.10pm;
Dixon - bar fight - 9.05pm;
McNab - mugging - 10.55pm;
Peel - car theft - 11.50pm.

No 112

Annie read *Hooray!* (clue 1) and the child who did the vacuuming read *Zippo* (clue 3). David who was asked to feed the pets and was given peanuts (2) didn't read *Dash*, so *Whee!*. Annie didn't fold clothes (1), so she did the washing up. Vicky was given chocolate (4). Annie wasn't given potato chips (1), so a lollipop. Peter had potato chips. He didn't read *Dash* (1), so *Zippo*. Vicky read *Dash* and was asked to fold clothes.

Thus:

Annie - washing up - lollipop - *Hooray!*;
David - feed pets - peanuts - *Whee!*;
Peter - vacuuming - potato chips - *Zippo*;
Vicky - fold clothes - chocolate bar - *Dash*.

No 113

Fred works in Vale on Friday (clue 3), so he works in Fieldham on Thursday (clue 1) and does fencing work on Monday. He does gardening in Hilldown (2), so he goes to Hilldown on Tuesday. Monday's work is in Woodley. On Monday he gets $47 (2), so he gets $35 on Thursday (1). Friday's job isn't cutting grass (3), so helping the vet. Thursday's job is cutting grass. The pay for helping the vet is $40 (3), so Tuesday's pay is $52.

Solutions

Thus:
Monday - Woodley - fencing - $47;
Tuesday - Hilldown - gardening - $52;
Thursday - Fieldham - cutting grass -
   $35;
Friday - Vale - helping vet - $40.

No 114

The 4-day job isn't digging ditches
(clue 1), erecting a barn (clue 2),
building walls (3) or digging a pond
(4), so felling trees. Fred will erect the
barn in June (2), taking either 9 or 12
days to do so. Digging ditches will also
take 9 or 12 days (1). The 7-day job is
to dig a pond (4), so the 10-day job will
be to build walls. The ditches will take
two days longer than April's job (1) and
the barn will take two days longer than
the job planned for the month after
the ditching work (2), so April isn't the
month after the ditches are to be dug;
in other words, the ditches won't be
dug in March. Thus (grid) the ditches
will be dug in September. October's job
will take either 7 or 10 days (2), as will
April's (1). By elimination, the 4-day
job (felling trees, above) is scheduled
for March. The walls won't be built in
October (3), so April. October's task is
to dig the pond. Fred will take 12 days to
dig ditches (1), so 9 days to erect a barn.
Thus:
Build walls - April - 10 days;
Dig ditches - September - 12 days;
Dig pond - October - 7 days;
Erect barn - June - 9 days;
Fell trees - March - 4 days.

No 115

Poppy is either 25 or 26 years old
(clue 1), as is Lily (clue 3). So Rosie is
20 (2) and Richard's fiancée is 19. Tansy
is thus 19 (3) and Lily is 25. Poppy is
26. Daisy is 22. Lily is marrying David
(1). Rosie isn't marrying Gerald (2)
or Kenneth (4), so John. Kenneth's

intended bride isn't Poppy (4), so Daisy.
Poppy will be married to Gerald.
Thus:
Daisy - 22 years old - Kenneth;
Lily - 25 years old - David;
Poppy - 26 years old - Gerald;
Rosie - 20 years old - John;
Tansy - 19 years old - Richard.

No 116

Remember throughout that each 'new'
picture is made of pieces of four 'old'
ones. Mr Holt's legs are in the same
picture as the head of a woman (clue 1),
so Mr Lane's head isn't with Mr Holt's
legs. Mr Lane's head is in the same
picture as the feet of a woman (clue 2),
so Mr Lane's head isn't with Mr Holt's
feet. Thus (by elimination) Mr Lane's
head is with Mr Holt's body. They're
not with Mrs Lane's feet (3), so they're
with Mrs Holt's feet and Mrs Lane's legs.
Mrs Holt's head is with Mr Lane's legs
(2), so they're with Mrs Lane's body and
Mr Holt's feet. Thus Mr Holt's head is
with Mrs Holt's legs, Mr Lane's body and
Mrs Lane's feet. Thus Mrs Lane's head is
with Mrs Holt's body, Mr Holt's legs and
Mr Lane's feet.
Thus (head - body - legs - feet):
Mr Holt - Mr Lane - Mrs Holt - Mrs Lane;
Mrs Holt - Mrs Lane - Mr Lane - Mr Holt;
Mr Lane - Mr Holt - Mrs Lane - Mrs Holt;
Mrs Lane - Mrs Holt - Mr Holt - Mr Lane.

No 117

The woman with the 9 of diamonds has
neither the jack nor queen of hearts
(clue 2), so the woman with the jack of
hearts has the 8 of diamonds (clue 1)
and Geri has the 7 of diamonds. Frances
and/or Dawn have the 8 and/or 9 of
diamonds (4), so Ellen has the king of
diamonds. The woman with the ace of
spades isn't Geri (3), so Ellen has the 6
of hearts, and the woman with the ace of
spades has the 8 of diamonds (and the
jack of hearts, above). Dawn's diamond

SOLUTIONS

isn't the 9 (2), so Dawn has the 8 of diamonds (4) and Frances has the 9 of diamonds. Frances has the 5 of hearts (2), so Geri has the queen of hearts. Frances hasn't the 5 of spades (2), so she has the 7 (5) and Geri has the 9 of spades. Ellen has the 5 of spades.

Thus (heart - diamond - spade):
Dawn - jack - 8 - ace;
Ellen - 6 - king - 5;
Frances - 5 - 9 - 7;
Geri - queen - 7 - 9.

No 118

Anthony is from Canada (clue 4). Simon the bricklayer isn't from Mexico or Venezuela (clue 1) or Jamaica (3), so Nicaragua. Joseph is from Mexico (2). The plumber from Jamaica isn't Michael (3), so Samuel. Michael is from Venezuela. He isn't an electrician (3), so Anthony is the electrician (4). The carpenter isn't Joseph (2), so Michael. Joseph is a glazier.

Thus:
Anthony - electrician - Canada;
Joseph - glazier - Mexico;
Michael - carpenter - Venezuela;
Samuel - plumber - Jamaica;
Simon - bricklayer - Nicaragua.

No 119

The parent affected by Mort's spell was either Merfyn or Wanda (3), so Mort changed one of them into a teapot (1) and Plutonia was transformed by Adolph. The other of Mervyn or Wanda was turned into a griffin (3). Uriah changed someone into either a bat or a duck (2), thus his spell affected neither Merfyn nor Wanda. Uriah's didn't affect Algol (2), so Uranius. Plutonia didn't become a bat or duck (2) or griffin (3), so a fairy. Thus Wanda was affected by Herman's spell (4) and (3) became a griffin. Mort's spell affected Merfyn (3). Manfred's affected Algol. He became a bat (2) and Uranius became a duck.

Thus:
Adolph - Plutonia - fairy;
Herman - Wanda - griffin;
Manfred - Algol - bat;
Mort - Merfyn - teapot;
Uriah - Uranius - duck.

No 120

Montjoy is a character in Henry V (clue 1) and Osric is a character in Hamlet (clue 2). Lew Smith is playing Edgar, but not in Macbeth (3), so in King Lear. The character in Macbeth is thus Seyton. He isn't in Westington (4). The production in Westington isn't Henry V (1) or King Lear (3), so Hamlet. The man in Hamlet isn't Ian Burton (1) or Jack Lawes (2), so Derek Fox. Ian Burton isn't in Henry V (1), so Macbeth. Jack Lawes is in Henry V. Macbeth isn't being staged in Eastbank (4) or Bromford (5), so Crawwood. Jack Lawes isn't in Bromford (2), so Eastbank. Lew Smith is in Bromford.

Thus:
Derek Fox - Hamlet - Osric - Westington;
Ian Burton - Macbeth - Seyton - Crawwood;
Jack Lawes - Henry V - Montjoy - Eastbank;
Lew Smith - King Lear - Edgar - Bromford.

No 121

Jeff and Mary found their car in the red area (clue 3). John and Mia found theirs in space No 38 (clue 4). The car in space No 16 in the blue area (1) doesn't belong to Jack and Jo (2), so Jim and Tina. The Hondera in the green area doesn't belong to Jack and Jo (2), so John and Mia. The car in the yellow area thus belongs to Jack and Jo. It was found in space No 82 (2), so the car in space No 25 belonged to Jeff and Mary. Jack and Jo don't own the Royola or Nickan (5), so the Fordson. Jeff and Mary don't

234

Solutions

own the Royola (3), so the Nickan. The Royola belongs to Jim and Tina.

Thus:

Jack and Jo - Fordson - yellow - 82;
Jeff and Mary - Nickan - red - 25;
Jim and Tina - Royola - blue - 16;
John and Mia - Hondera - green - 38.

No 122

Tim got a roast beef sandwich (clue 3). The person who wanted tuna got salad (clue 1) and the one who wanted salmon got chicken. Thus Suzi who wanted pastrami but didn't get egg and cress (2) got ham. The salami sandwich wasn't ordered by Tim (4), so Tim ordered bacon. The person who ordered salami got egg and cress. He/she isn't Philip (4) or Angela (5), so Gary. Angela didn't get the salad sandwich (5), so chicken. Philip got the salad sandwich.

Thus:

Angela - salmon - chicken;
Gary - salami - egg/cress;
Philip - tuna - salad;
Suzi - pastrami - ham;
Tim - bacon - roast beef.

No 123

George likes Schoenberg (clue 1). The Shostakovich fan isn't Barney (clue 1), Rodney or Leila (clue 2), so Penny. The person who went alone on 9th August isn't George (1), Rodney or Leila (2) or Penny (3), so Barney. The one who went on 4th August isn't George (1), Rodney or Leila (2), so Penny. Barney is a fan of Elgar (3). George went alone on 25th July (1), so Rodney went on 30th July (2) and Leila on 20th July. The Wagner fan isn't Rodney (3), so Leila. Rodney likes Stravinsky.

Thus:

Barney - Elgar - 9th August;
George - Schoenberg - 25th July;
Leila - Wagner - 20th July;
Penny - Shostakovich - 4th August;
Rodney - Stravinsky - 30th July.

No 124

Pincher who will be met at Manchester airport isn't accused of kidnapping (clue 4), bank robbery (clue 2) or jewellery theft (3), so drug running. He isn't returning from Spain (1), Italy (5) or France (6), so Greece. Blaggs is being extradited from France (6). The man being flown from Italy to Gatwick isn't Nicks (5), so Scamma. Nicks is being extradited from Spain. Blaggs isn't accused of kidnapping (2) or jewellery theft (6), so bank robbery. The man accused of jewellery theft is returning to Glasgow (3), so (by elimination) he's Nicks. Scamma is accused of kidnapping. Blaggs will be met at Heathrow airport.

Thus:

Blaggs - bank robbery - France - Heathrow;
Nicks - jewellery theft - Spain - Glasgow;
Pincher - drug running - Greece - Manchester;
Scamma - kidnapping - Italy - Gatwick.

No 125

Zemism is the religion led by Cevin who worships Bom (clue 2). It isn't the religion of Buvairya (clue 2), Ducota (3) or Yawkshya (4), so Nawmundi. Zimism is the religion of Kyli whose god isn't Bam or Bem (5), so Bim. Thus Zimism is the religion of Yawkshya (4). The god revered in Ducota isn't Bam (1), so Bem. Bam is worshipped in Buvairya. Zomism isn't the religion of Ducota (3), so Buvairya. The religion of Ducota is Zamism. Its leader isn't Sharen (1), so Daren. Sharen leads the religion in Buvairya.

Thus:

Buvairya - Zomism - Sharen - Bam;
Ducota - Zamism - Daren - Bem;
Nawmundi - Zemism - Cevin - Bom;
Yawkshya - Zimism - Kyli - Bim.

Solutions

No 126

The $290 car wasn't manufactured in 1963 (clue 3), so 1962 (clue 2), thus it's the Zephyr (3). The car priced at $180 was manufactured in 1968 (2). It isn't the Herald (1), so the Herald was manufactured in 1965. The $180/1968 car isn't the Minx (1) or Rapier (4), so the Hunter. The Rapier wasn't manufactured in 1969 (4), so 1963. The Minx was manufactured in 1969. It isn't $200 (5), so the Rapier is for sale at $275 (4) and the Minx at $250. Rusty is asking $200 for the Herald.

Thus:

Herald - 1965 - $200;
Hunter - 1968 - $180;
Minx - 1969 - $250;
Rapier - 1963 - $275;
Zephyr - 1962 - $290.

No 127

Fred didn't drink lager (clue 2), so in clue 3 he's the person who scored 1066. The person who drank lager isn't Derek (2), Jimmy or Wendy (3), so Suzanne. The person who scored 989 isn't Jimmy or Suzanne (1), or Wendy (3), so Derek. He didn't drink bitter beer or gin and tonic (1) or cognac (2), so Scotch whisky. Jimmy didn't drink bitter beer or gin and tonic (1), so cognac. Neither Jimmy nor Suzanne (who drank lager, above) scored 1113 (2), so Wendy scored 1113. Jimmy scored 1091 (2), so Suzanne scored 1005. Wendy drank gin and tonic (1), so Fred chose bitter beer.

Thus:

Derek - 989 - Scotch whisky;
Fred - 1066 - bitter beer;
Jimmy - 1091 - cognac;
Suzanne - 1005 - lager;
Wendy - 1113 - gin and tonic.

No 128

Remember throughout that each family has members whose names begin with different letters (intro). Josephine's son isn't Ian (clue 2), so either Felix or Gordon; thus she isn't married to Frankie (clue 1). Ivana's son isn't Jimmy (3), so either Felix or Gordon; thus she isn't married to Frankie (1). Thus Frankie's wife is Geraldine. Their daughter isn't Jessica (1), so Iona; thus their son is Jimmy. By elimination, Ian's mother is Freda. Ivana's husband isn't Graham (3), so Jude. Thus Ian's father (and Freda's husband) is Graham, whose daughter is thus Jessica. Ivor's wife is Josephine. Their daughter isn't Fenella (2), so Gracie; thus their son is Felix. Jude's son is Gordon and his daughter is Fenella.

Thus (husband - wife - son - daughter):

Frankie - Geraldine - Jimmy - Iona;
Graham - Freda - Ian - Jessica;
Ivor - Josephine - Felix - Gracie;
Jude - Ivana - Gordon - Fenella.

No 129

Remember throughout that each man was born, married and died on three different days (intro). The man who was born on a Friday and died on a Thursday (clue 3) isn't Alex (clue 1), Bob (2) or Max (4), so Sean. Bob died on a Friday (2). Sean married on a Tuesday (4) and Max was born on a Monday and died on a Wednesday. Alex died on a Tuesday. Alex married on a Thursday (1) and was born on a Wednesday. Bob was born on a Tuesday. By elimination, Bob married on a Monday and Max married on a Friday.

Thus (born - married - died):

Alex - Wednesday - Thursday - Tuesday;
Bob - Tuesday - Monday - Friday;
Max - Monday - Friday - Wednesday;
Sean - Friday - Tuesday - Thursday.

SOLUTIONS

No 130

Norman lives at either No 2 or No 5 (clue 2), so Gordon and Harry (clue 4) live at No 4 and No 1 respectively. Thus Norman has lived in his house for one year longer than either Gordon or Harry (2). Jane hasn't lived in her house for 5 or 6 years (3) or 2 years (4), so either 3 or 4 years. If Norman has lived in his house for 4 years, then (2) either Gordon or Harry has lived in his house for 3 years, leaving no time for Jane (above). So Norman hasn't been there for 4 years. The person who has been there for 4 years isn't Gordon (1), Harry (3) or Rosie (5), so Jane. Harry has lived in his house for 6 years (3), so Norman lives at No 5 (2). Norman has lived in his house for 3 years (2) and Gordon has been there for 2 years, so Rosie has lived in her house for 5 years. Jane lives at No 2 (5) and Rosie lives at No 3.

Thus:

No 1 - Harry - 6 years;
No 2 - Jane - 4 years;
No 3 - Rosie - 5 years;
No 4 - Gordon - 2 years;
No 5 - Norman - 3 years.

No 131

Arthur didn't pick 15 pears or 45 apples (clue 3), so he picked 40 apples plus 20 pears, and Wesley picked 45 apples plus either 15 or 18 pears. The man who picked 30 apples also picked 23 pears (5). The man who picked 25 pears didn't pick 25 apples (1), so 35 apples. Thus he's the ONE man who picked ten more apples than pears (1), so the man who picked 25 apples didn't pick 15 pears. By elimination, the man who picked 25 apples picked 18 pears. So Wesley picked 15 pears. The man with 35 apples (and 25 pears, above) isn't Brian (2) or John (4), so Harry. John didn't pick 18 pears (4), so 23. Brian picked 18 pears.

Thus:

Arthur - 40 apples - 20 pears;
Brian - 25 apples - 18 pears;
Harry - 35 apples - 25 pears;
John - 30 apples - 23 pears;
Wesley - 45 apples - 15 pears.

No 132

The mission with 5% accuracy wasn't overseen by Brusilov (clue 1), Nevsky (clue 2) or Simonov (3), so Lazarev. Mission Onega to Mercury wasn't overseen by Brusilov (1) or (since Mercury has seven letters) Simonov (3). Mission Onega's accuracy wasn't 1% or 3% (1), so it wasn't overseen by Nevsky (2). Thus Lazarev was in charge of Onega. Brusilov's mission achieved 4% accuracy (1), thus it wasn't Ladoga (2). Ladoga wasn't overseen by Nevsky (2), so Simonov. Its accuracy was 3% (2) and Nevsky's was 1%. Ladoga didn't go to Mars (2) or (seven letters) Jupiter (3), so Venus. Nevsky wasn't in charge of Baikal (2), so Orel. Orel went to Jupiter (3). Brusilov was in charge of Baikal, which went to Mars.

Thus:

Brusilov - Baikal - Mars - 4%;
Lazarev - Onega - Mercury - 5%;
Nevsky - Orel - Jupiter - 1%;
Simonov - Ladoga - Venus - 3%.

No 133

The person surnamed Wyatt didn't get a letter (clue 1), postcard or catalogue (clue 4), so a birthday card. The person at No 7 didn't get a letter (1), birthday card or postcard (4), so a catalogue. The person who got a letter lives at either No 1 or No 3 (1), as does the person who got a postcard (4), so the person surnamed Wyatt lives at No 5. The one surnamed Moore thus lives at No 1 (3) and Melissa lives at either No 3 or No 7. Nigel thus lives at No 5 (1) and the person surnamed Bourne lives at No 7, so the letter was delivered to

SOLUTIONS

No 3. The person at No 1 got a postcard. The person at No 3 is surnamed Finch. Larry's surname isn't Finch (2), so he lives at No 1 and Karen lives at No 3. Melissa lives at No 7.

Thus:
No 1 - Larry - Moore - postcard;
No 3 - Karen - Finch - letter;
No 5 - Nigel - Wyatt - birthday card;
No 7 - Melissa - Bourne - catalogue.

No 134

Rex's owner isn't Joan (clue 1), so Bill (clue 2). Fido's owner bought Diggo (4), so (by elimination) Quentin owns Fido (3), Sally-Anne's dog is either Mitzi or Rover, and Rex's owner (Bill, above) bought Walkis. Joan didn't buy Rollova (1) or Barko (2), so Waggo. Sally-Anne didn't buy Barko (2), so Rollova. Roberta bought Barko. Joan owns Archie (1). Roberta's dog isn't Rover (2), so Mitzi. Sally-Anne's dog is Rover.

Thus:
Bill - Rex - Walkis;
Joan - Archie - Waggo;
Quentin - Fido - Diggo;
Roberta - Mitzi - Barko;
Sally-Anne - Rover - Rollova.

No 135

The delegate scheduled to speak at 1145 hours isn't Helmut or Anna (clue 1), Sofie (clue 2) or Bernhard (3), so Josef. The 1100 hours presentation won't be given by Anna (1), Sofie (2) or Bernard (3), so Helmut. The person surnamed Krenz will speak at 0930 hours (1). He/she isn't Anna (1) or Sofie (2), so Bernhard. Anna's presentation isn't at 0800 hours (1), so her surname is Strauss (2), Sofie's presentation is at 0800 hours, and Anna's is at 0700 hours. Sofie's surname isn't Schindler (2) or Weber (3), so Popper. Josef's isn't Schindler (3), so Weber. Helmut's surname is Schindler.

Thus:
Anna - Strauss - 0700 hours;
Bernhard - Krenz - 0930 hours;
Helmut - Schindler - 1100 hours;
Josef - Weber - 1145 hours;
Sofie - Popper - 0800 hours.

No 136

Captain Stern's ship isn't the *Walrus* (clue 2), so the gems are aboard the *Siren* (clue 3). Thus Captain Crowe's ship has rum (1) and the *Siren* is going to Trinidad. The rum is on the *Swordfish* (3) and Captain Stern's ship has gold. By elimination, Captain Stern's ship is the *Golden Fox*, and the *Walrus* is carrying silver. The *Walrus* is going to Barbados (2). Captain Dedman's ship isn't the *Walrus* (2), so the *Siren*. Captain Planck's is the *Walrus*. Captain Stern isn't going to Cuba (1), so Antigua. Captain Crowe is thus going to Cuba.

Thus:
Captain Crowe - *Swordfish* - rum - Cuba;
Captain Dedman - *Siren* - gems - Trinidad;
Captain Planck - *Walrus* - silver - Barbados;
Captain Stern - *Golden Fox* - gold - Antigua.

No 137

The girl aged 10 isn't Tracey (clue 1), Heather (clue 4) or Chris (5), so Kathy is 10 and (4) Heather is 12. The boy aged 16 isn't Richard (1) or Dave (6), so Jake is 16 (3) and Micky is 14. Micky's sister is thus Heather (3). Chris's brother isn't Jake (5) or Dave (6), so Richard. Thus Dave is 12 (6) and Richard is 13. Tracey is 15 (1), so Chris is 14. Dave's sister isn't Tracey (6), so Kathy. Jake's sister is Tracey.

Thus (his age - her age):
Dave - Kathy - 12 - 10;
Jake - Tracey - 16 - 15;
Micky - Heather - 14 - 12;
Richard - Chris - 13 - 14.

SOLUTIONS

No 138

The item collected on Friday wasn't the necklace or radio (clue 1), clock (clue 2) or book (3), so the television was collected on Friday and (4) Betty collected her prize on Thursday. Monday's collector wasn't Charles (1), Steve (2) or Miranda (3), so Frederick. Tuesday's collector wasn't Charles (1) or Steve (2), so Miranda. Thus Frederick won the book (3). The radio wasn't collected on Tuesday (1), so Charles didn't collect his prize on Wednesday. Thus the radio was collected on Thursday (by Betty, above) and Charles collected his prize on Friday (1). Steve collected his prize on Wednesday. Steve didn't win the clock (2), so the necklace. Miranda won the clock.

Thus:

Betty - radio - Thursday;
Charles - television - Friday;
Frederick - book - Monday;
Miranda - clock - Tuesday;
Steve - necklace - Wednesday.

No 139

The 4-year-old isn't Bella (clue 1), Lucy or Clarissa (clue 2) or Miranda (3), so Susan. Bella lost a slipper (1) and Lucy lost a wing (2). The girl who lost her magic wand isn't Miranda or Susan (3), so Clarissa. The girl who lost a tiara isn't Susan (3), so Miranda. Susan lost a silver wig. Bella is 5 (1). The 8-year-old isn't Lucy or Miranda (2), so Clarissa. Lucy is 7 (2) and Miranda is 6 years old.

Thus:

Bella - 5 years old - slipper;
Clarissa - 8 years old - magic wand;
Lucy - 7 years old - wing;
Miranda - 6 years old - tiara;
Susan - 4 years old - silver wig.

No 140

The man who went to Dedropp cave descended either 380 or 450 feet (clue 2), as did the man in Buryam cave (clue 3). The man who went to 500 feet didn't do so in the Darkole cave (4), so he was in Forling cave. The man in the Darkole cave went to 600 feet. He suffered from exhaustion (4). The man in Forling cave didn't experience a bat attack (1) or flooding (2), so a rockfall. Karl who experienced flooding wasn't in the Dedropp cave (2), so Buryam. The bat attack was in the Dedropp cave. Rod wasn't in the Darkole or Forling cave (1), so Dedropp. He and Karl descended to either 380 or 450 feet (above), so Alfred went to 500 feet (3). Mitch thus went to 600 feet. Karl didn't descend to 450 feet (2), so 380 feet. Rod descended to 450 feet.

Thus:

Alfred - Forling - 500 feet - rockfall;
Karl - Buryam - 380 feet - flooding;
Mitch - Darkole - 600 feet - exhaustion;
Rod - Dedropp - 450 feet - bat attack.

No 141

Friday's class wasn't taken by Mr Cotter (clue 1), Mr Player (clue 2) or Miss Jones (4), so by Mrs Samson. No class took place on Tuesday (grid). Mr Player's class was on either Monday or Wednesday (2), so not the day after any other. Thus Mr Player didn't give the woodwork lesson (1). Miss Jones gave the basket-making lesson (3). The woodwork lesson wasn't given by Mr Cotter (1), so by Mrs Samson. Mr Cotter took a class on Thursday (1). Mr Player didn't teach spinning (2), so pottery. Mr Cotter taught spinning. Mrs Samson's class gathered leaves and roots (5). Miss Jones's class didn't collect fungi (3) or berries (4), so nuts. Thus her class was on Wednesday (2) and Mr Player's was on Monday. Mr Cotter's class picked berries (4), so Mr Player's gathered fungi.

SOLUTIONS

Thus:

Mr Cotter - Thursday - spinning - berries;

Miss Jones - Wednesday - basket-making - nuts;

Mr Player - Monday - pottery - fungi;

Mrs Samson - Friday - woodwork - leaves and roots.

No 142

Caitlin's gift cost either £110 or £120 (clue 1), as did Barney's. So Caroline's gift cost £125 (clue 3) and the scooter was £120. The games console thus cost £110 and the hi-fi was bought for a boy (nephew, 2) and cost £150, so it was bought for Toby. The iPod cost £160 (1), so it was bought for Sally. Caroline's gift was the watch. Caitlin's gift (1) cost £120 (scooter, above), so Barney's gift was the games console.

Thus:

Barney - games console - £110;

Caitlin - scooter - £120;

Caroline - watch - £125;

Sally - iPod - £160;

Toby - hi-fi - £150.

No 143

The Jones family has bought either apartment 7 or apartment 10 (clue 2), as has the Williams family (clue 3), thus the hold-up caused by the gas supplier is at either apartment 3 or apartment 6 (1). Apartment 3 hasn't been bought by the Evans (1) or Roberts families (4), so by the Hughes. The Jones family is having a problem with the internet subcontractor (2). The Williams' move isn't affected by a problem with the television (2) or phone (3), so with the electricity service. Apartment 9 isn't affected by the television subcontractor (2), so by the phone company. The Williams family has bought apartment 10 (3), so the Joneses have bought apartment 7 and (2) the problem with the television

subcontractor is at apartment 3. The gas supplier is thus causing problems at apartment 6. The Evans family has bought apartment 9 (1), so the Roberts family has bought apartment 6.

Thus:

Apartment 3 - Hughes - television;

Apartment 6 - Roberts - gas;

Apartment 7 - Jones - internet;

Apartment 9 - Evans - phone;

Apartment 10 - Williams - electricity.

No 144

Remember throughout that each 'new' picture is made of pieces of four 'old' ones. Joan's brother's legs and father's feet are in the same picture (clue 2), so not with the head of her brother or her father. Her father's head isn't with her brother's body (3), so (by elimination) her father's head is with either Joan's mother's body or her sister's body; and her father's head is also with either her mother's legs or her sister's legs. Thus her father's head isn't with her mother's feet or her sister's feet. So her father's head is with her brother's feet. Joan's father's feet (and brother's legs, 2) are with either her mother's body or her sister's body, as are her brother's feet and (above) father's head. Her father's body isn't with her sister's legs (1), so her father's body is with her mother's legs; and (by elimination) they're also with her sister's feet. Her mother's feet are thus with her brother's body, so they're also with her sister's head and her father's legs. Her brother's legs are thus with her mother's head and her sister's body. Her brother's head is with her father's body. Her father's head is with her mother's body and sister's legs.

Thus (head - body - legs - feet):

Brother - father - mother - sister;

Father - mother - sister - brother;

Mother - sister - brother - father;

Sister - brother - father - mother.

240

SOLUTIONS

No 145

Jeanne has the 4 of clubs (clue 5), Frank has the 6 of clubs and Martin has the ace of hearts. Frank has the 8 of diamonds and Martin has the 8 of clubs (clue 2), so Louisa has the queen of clubs. Frank has the jack of hearts (4). Louisa has the 3 of diamonds (3) and Martin has the 6 of diamonds. Jeanne has the jack of diamonds. Louisa hasn't the king of hearts (1), so she has the 9 and Jeanne has the king of hearts.
Thus (heart - club - diamond):
Frank - jack - 6 - 8;
Jeanne - king - 4 - jack;
Louisa - 9 - queen - 3;
Martin - ace - 8 - 6.

No 146

Mr Katz doesn't own a kitten or a puppy (clue 2), a rabbit (owned by a woman, clue 4) or a cat (6), so a dog. Mrs Bird doesn't own a kitten or a puppy (2) or a cat (6), so a rabbit. Daisy doesn't belong to Mr Parott, Miss Bull, Mr Katz or Mrs Bird (3), so Mrs Clore owns Daisy. The puppy's owner isn't Mr Parott or Miss Bull (6), so Mrs Clore. The kitten isn't called Lucky (1), Rosie (2) or Fluff (5), so Sam. It doesn't belong to Mr Parott (5), so Miss Bull. Mr Parott has a cat. It isn't called Lucky (1) or Fluff (5), so Rosie. Mrs Bird's rabbit isn't called Lucky (4), so Fluff. Mr Katz's dog is Lucky.
Thus:
Mrs Bird - Fluff - rabbit;
Miss Bull - Sam - kitten;
Mrs Clore - Daisy - puppy;
Mr Katz - Lucky - dog;
Mr Parott - Rosie - cat.

No 147

Remember throughout that each boy traded one country's stamp for that from another country (intro) both of which start with letters that are different to the initial letter of his name (clue 1). The boy who gave a stamp from Denmark got one from Greece (clue 3). Frankie gave a stamp from Estonia but didn't get one from Denmark (2), so from Chile. The boy who gave a stamp from Finland didn't get one from Denmark (5), so from Estonia. Gordon didn't give a stamp from Finland or get one from Denmark (6), so he gave a stamp from Chile and got one from Finland. Thus the boy who gave a stamp from Greece got one from Denmark. He isn't Eddie (4), so Chris. Dave thus gave a stamp from Finland and Eddie gave one from Denmark.
Thus (gave - got):
Chris - Greece - Denmark;
Dave - Finland - Estonia;
Eddie - Denmark - Greece;
Frankie - Estonia - Chile;
Gordon - Chile - Finland.

No 148

The 11.45pm act isn't that of the comedian (clue 1), singer or juggler (clue 2), so the psychic. The 9.00pm act isn't that of the singer or juggler (2), so the comedian. Mr Wundaful will appear at 9.30pm (1). He will be paid either $150 or $170 (1), as will Max Power (2). Thus Max Power will appear at 11.45pm (1). So he will get $150 (3) and Rokki Shaw will get $140. Mr Wundaful will thus get $170, and Sherri Glass will get $125. Mr Wundaful isn't the singer (2), so the juggler. Sherri Glass isn't the singer (2), so the comedian. Rokki Shaw is the singer and will appear at 10.30pm.
Thus:
Max Power - psychic - 11.45pm - $150;
Mr Wundaful - juggler - 9.30pm - $170;
Rokki Shaw - singer - 10.30pm - $140;
Sherri Glass - comedian - 9.00pm - $125.

SOLUTIONS

No 149

The man who went to Bryncir on the 15th didn't take 20 animals (clue 2), so the man who took 20 went on the 22nd (clue 1), the bullocks were taken on the 15th and Eric went on the 8th. The man who took 5 animals went on the 1st (4) and the man who took 15 went on the 15th. So the man who took 10 went on the 8th (Eric, above). Pigs were taken on the 1st (3). Eric didn't take heifers (1), so sheep. Heifers were thus taken on the 22nd. Michael took 20 animals (2). Alan didn't take 5 (4), so 15. Edgar took 5 animals.

Thus:

Alan - bullocks - 15 - 15th;
Edgar - pigs - 5 - 1st;
Eric - sheep - 10 - 8th;
Michael - heifers - 20 - 22nd.

No 150

The girl who came first isn't Esther (clue 1), Harriet (clue 2), Andrea (3) or Jill (4), so Caroline. Her costume isn't pink (3), so Andrea was third, and the girl who wore pink was second. Caroline's costume isn't blue (2), so the girl in blue was third, and Harriet was fifth. Harriet's costume is black (3). The girl in yellow wasn't fourth (1), so first (Caroline, above). Thus the girl in mauve was fourth. She isn't Jill (4), so Esther. Jill was second.

Thus:

Andrea - third - blue;
Caroline - first - yellow;
Esther - fourth - mauve;
Harriet - fifth - black;
Jill - second - pink.

No 151

Lauren's bikini is blue (clue 2). The gold bikini with brown stripes isn't Myra's (clue 4), Jessica's (1) or Noelle's (2), so Kathy's. Noelle's bikini has green stripes (2). The stripes on Jessica's bikini aren't red (1). Jessica's bikini isn't turquoise (1), so it's either pink or white. Thus Jessica's bikini hasn't black stripes (5), so yellow. Jessica's bikini isn't pink (3), so white. Noelle's isn't pink (2), so turquoise. Lauren's bikini thus has black stripes (5). Myra's bikini is pink with red stripes.

Thus (bikini - stripes):

Jessica - white - yellow;
Kathy - gold - brown;
Lauren - blue - black;
Myra - pink - red;
Noelle - turquoise - green.

No 152

The child who brought in 4 nuts isn't Ronald (clue 1), Colin (clue 2) or Tina (4), so Alison. The one who brought the slug had 5 nuts (3), so Colin had 6 nuts (2). Alison brought the toadstool (3), so the child who brought the spider had 6 nuts (1) and Ronald had 7. Tina brought in 5 nuts. Ronald brought the frog. Colin didn't have 10 or 11 leaves (2), so 9 (1) and Ronald had 8 leaves. Tina had 11 leaves (2), so Alison brought in 10 leaves.

Thus:

Alison - 4 nuts - 10 leaves - toadstool;
Colin - 6 nuts - 9 leaves - spider;
Ronald - 7 nuts - 8 leaves - frog;
Tina - 5 nuts - 11 leaves - slug.

No 153

The woman who made 7 calls drank ginger (clue 3), so Lola made 5 calls (clue 4), the woman who drank lemon made 6 calls, and the woman who received 6 calls made 4 calls. The woman who drank honey made one fewer call than the woman who received 8 calls (2), so the woman who received 8 didn't drink ginger. Nor did she drink peppermint (1), so the woman who received 8 calls drank lemon. The woman who made 5 (Lola, above) drank

242

Solutions

honey (2), so the one who made 4 calls drank peppermint. Judy received 8 calls (1). Miriam didn't drink peppermint (1), so ginger. Karen drank peppermint. Miriam didn't receive 5 calls (3), so 7. Lola received 5 calls.

Thus (made - received):
Judy - 6 - 8 - lemon;
Karen - 4 - 6 - peppermint;
Lola - 5 - 5 - honey;
Miriam - 7 - 7 - ginger.

No 154

No-one wants to go in July (grid). The woman who suggested a date in September doesn't want to go to Mexico (clue 1), London (clue 2), California (3) or New England (4), so Rome. Amanda doesn't want to go to Rome (3). Thus either Amanda wants to go in May and the person who suggested California wants to go in April (3), or Amanda wants to go in June and the person who suggested California wants to go in May. Helen suggested New England (4), thus she doesn't want to go in May (above). If Helen wants to go in April (3), then Catherine wants to go in May (4) to California (above), and Amanda wants to go in June. But then there's no possible month for Nia's suggested destination (1). So Helen wants to go in August (4) and Catherine in September. Nia thus hasn't suggested June (1), so April. Yolanda hasn't suggested June (1), so May. Amanda has suggested June and (1) wants to go to Mexico. Yolanda wants to go to California (3), so Nia wants to go to London.

Thus:
Amanda - Mexico - June;
Catherine - Rome - September;
Helen - New England - August;
Nia - London - April;
Yolanda - California - May.

No 155

The boy who said he'd seen 6 sharks isn't Carl (clue 1), Phil (clue 2), Joe or Martin (3), so Hal. No boy said he'd seen 3 whales (grid), so Hal didn't say he'd seen 2 whales (1). The boy who said he'd seen 2 whales isn't Carl (1) or Joe (3), so Martin said he'd seen 2 whales (2) and Phil said he'd seen 5 whales. Thus Carl said he'd seen 7 whales (1) and Hal said he'd seen 6 whales. Joe said he'd seen 4 whales. Carl said he'd seen 4 sharks (1). Phil said he'd seen fewer sharks than Martin (2) and Joe said he'd seen more sharks than Martin (3), so Phil said he'd seen 2 sharks, Martin said he'd seen 3 sharks, and Joe said he'd seen 5 sharks.

Thus (sharks - whales):
Carl - 4 - 7;
Hal - 6 - 6;
Joe - 5 - 4;
Martin - 3 - 2;
Phil - 2 - 5.

No 156

Bertram encountered ice (clue 2). Graham's problem wasn't rain or gales (clue 1), so sleet. The man who took 6 hours 45 minutes wasn't hampered by sleet or gales (1) or ice (2), so rain. The one who took 7 hours 40 minutes wasn't affected by sleet or gales (1), so ice. Thus the man who walked on Saturday took 7 hours 30 minutes (2). Sunday's walk wasn't taken by Malcolm or Bertram (3), so Sunday's walker wasn't affected by ice (above). Nor was rain the problem on Sunday (1). So Sunday's walker took 7 hours 10 minutes. Donald didn't walk on Sunday (4). Thus Graham walked on Sunday. Saturday's walker was affected by gales (1) and Wednesday's walker by rain. So Bertram walked on Tuesday. Wednesday's walk took 6 hours 45 minutes. If Donald walked on Saturday, then Malcolm walked on Wednesday, which (4) isn't possible. So Donald walked on Wednesday and Malcolm walked on Saturday.

Thus:

Bertram - Tuesday - ice -
7 hours 40 minutes;

Donald - Wednesday - rain -
6 hours 45 minutes;

Graham - Sunday - sleet -
7 hours 10 minutes;

Malcolm - Saturday - gales -
7 hours 30 minutes.

No 157

The person who brought wine also brought 7 extra guests (clue 3). Bob didn't bring 5 extra guests (clue 2), so the person who brought sandwiches didn't bring 4 extra guests (1). The person who brought cakes didn't arrive at 7.00pm (2). So the person who arrived at 7.00pm with 4 extra guests (4) brought beer. The person who brought cakes didn't bring 5 extra guests (2), so 6. The one who brought sandwiches brought 5 extra guests. Bob brought 6 extra guests (1). Andy didn't bring 5 (2) or 4 (5), so 7. Michelle didn't bring 4 (5), so 5. Lynne brought 4 extra guests. Bob (6 guests/cakes, above) arrived at 7.30pm (2), Michelle arrived at 7.45pm, and Andy arrived at 7.15pm.

Thus:

Andy - 7.15pm - 7 guests - wine;

Bob - 7.30pm - 6 guests - cakes;

Lynne - 7.00pm - 4 guests - beer;

Michelle - 7.45pm - 5 guests - sandwiches.

No 158

Either Mrs White or Ms North is selling the Foat (clue 2), so since Mr Butcher isn't selling the Foat, Mr Worth is buying a car from Miss French (clue 4) and Mrs Croft is buying the Foat. Mr Worth is buying the Ardi (1) and Mr Smith is selling the Vauxer. It isn't being bought

by Mr Barnes (1) or Mrs Dean (who is buying either a Mavda or a Hondo, 2), so by Mr Young. Mrs Dean is buying a car from Mr Butcher (3) and Mr Barnes is buying the Mavda. Mrs Dean is thus buying the Hondo. Ms North is selling the Foat (2), so Mrs White is selling the Mavda.

Thus (buyer - seller):

Ardi - Mr Worth - Miss French;

Foat - Mrs Croft - Ms North;

Hondo - Mrs Dean - Mr Butcher;

Mavda - Mr Barnes - Mrs White;

Vauxer - Mr Young - Mr Smith.

No 159

The Ed Hobart consignment is leaving from either Plymouth or Dover (clue 4), so the Weelz consignment is leaving from Portsmouth (clue 1) and the truck going to Le Havre is owned by Parsel (3). The Weelz consignment isn't going to Calais (2), so the QuikSend consignment is going to Calais (1). It isn't leaving from Plymouth (2), so Ramsgate (4). Thus the Weelz consignment is going to Ostend (2). The Ed Hobart consignment isn't going to Zeebrugge (5), so Dunkirk. The Van Truk consignment is going to Zeebrugge. It isn't leaving from Newhaven or Plymouth (5), so Dover. The Ed Hobart consignment is leaving from Plymouth (4), so the Parsel consignment is leaving from Newhaven.

Thus:

Ed Hobart - Plymouth - Dunkirk;

Parsel - Newhaven - Le Havre;

QuikSend - Ramsgate - Calais;

Van Truk - Dover - Zeebrugge;

Weelz - Portsmouth - Ostend.

No 160

Cheryl has either 6 or 7 dogs and has more dogs than cats (clue 2), so her brother isn't Brian (clue 1), Gary (3) or Patrick (5), thus he's Desmond. Lavinia has two more dogs than Melanie (4) and

SOLUTIONS

Sharon has two more dogs than Patrick (5), so Melanie's brother isn't Patrick. Patrick's sister isn't Sharon (5), so Lavinia. Thus Sharon has two more dogs than Lavinia (5), who has two more dogs than Melanie (4), so Sharon has 6, Lavinia has 4 and Melanie has 2 dogs. Cheryl has 7 dogs. Brian has 6 dogs and 6 cats (1), so Melanie's brother is Gary. Desmond (Cheryl's brother, above) hasn't 8 cats (2), so 5 (6) and Gary has 4 cats. Patrick has 8 cats.

Thus:

Brian - Sharon - 6 cats - 6 dogs;
Desmond - Cheryl - 5 cats - 7 dogs;
Gary - Melanie - 4 cats - 2 dogs;
Patrick - Lavinia - 8 cats - 4 dogs.

No 161

Raoul's carrots won first prize (clue 2) and Eric's other entry was fruit (clue 3). The man who entered eggs and got first prize for peas isn't Sam (4), so Arthur. Sam didn't get a first prize for his potatoes (4), so Sam's first prize was for onions and Eric's first was for potatoes. Eric's second prize wasn't for potatoes (two different vegetables, intro), peas (1) or carrots (3), so onions. Arthur's second prize wasn't for peas (intro) or potatoes (4), so carrots. Sam's second prize wasn't for potatoes (4), so peas; thus he also entered the cheese (1). Raoul won a second prize for potatoes and also entered flowers.

Thus (first - second):

Arthur - peas - carrots - eggs;
Eric - potatoes - onions - fruit;
Raoul - carrots - potatoes - flowers;
Sam - onions - peas - cheese.

No 162

The 35-mile trip wasn't to Bearwood or West Point (clue 1), Elm Hill (clue 2) or Sandy Bay (3), so Mountford. The trip to West Point was on either Tuesday or Wednesday (2) and the one to Mountford was on either Monday or Tuesday. Bearwood was visited the day after Mountford (1), so the trip to Bearwood was on either Tuesday or Wednesday (as was the trip to West Point, above). So Monday's trip was to Mountford, Tuesday's was to Bearwood and Wednesday's was to West Point. The trip to Elm Hill was on Friday (2), so that to Sandy Bay was on Thursday. The 30-mile trip wasn't on Wednesday (1), Thursday or Friday (3), so Tuesday. Thus Wednesday's journey was 15 miles (1). Thursday's was 10 miles (3) and Friday's was 20 miles.

Thus:

Monday - 35 miles - Mountford;
Tuesday - 30 miles - Bearwood;
Wednesday - 15 miles - West Point;
Thursday - 10 miles - Sandy Bay;
Friday - 20 miles - Elm Hill.

No 163

Remember throughout that each woman's name, hat colour and scarf colour begin with three different letters (intro). The woman with a black hat has an orange scarf (clue 4). The woman with a pink scarf hasn't a red hat (clue 2). The woman with a red hat hasn't a green scarf (3). So the woman with a red hat has a black scarf. Brenda's hat is green (3). By elimination, Pam's hat and Rhoda's scarf (1) are orange. Since the woman with a pink scarf hasn't a pink hat, Pam's scarf isn't red (2). So Pam's scarf is green. The woman with a pink scarf thus has a green hat (Brenda, above). Greta's scarf is red (2), so her hat is pink. Olga's hat is red.

Thus (hat - scarf):

Brenda - green - pink;
Greta - pink - red;
Olga - red - black;
Pam - orange - green;
Rhoda - black - orange.

Solutions

No 164

Mr Morrison had an operation on his duodenum (clue 3). Mr Payne carried out the lung operation (clue 5), but not on Mrs Ferguson (2) or Mrs Johnson (4), so Mr Anderson. Mr Delver left an iPod in his patient (1), who wasn't Mrs Ferguson (2) or Mrs Johnson (4), so Mr Morrison. Mr Sewham operated on Mrs Johnson (4), so Mrs Ferguson was operated on by Mr Cutham who (2) accidentally left the car keys inside her. He didn't perform the liver operation (2), so the appendix operation. Mrs Johnson had the liver operation. Mr Payne didn't leave a wristwatch inside his patient (5), so he left the wallet. The wristwatch was inside Mrs Johnson.

Thus:

Mr Anderson - lung - Mr Payne - wallet;

Mrs Ferguson - appendix - Mr Cutham - car keys;

Mrs Johnson - liver - Mr Sewham - wristwatch;

Mr Morrison - duodenum - Mr Delver - iPod.

No 165

The child who picked up a 5 isn't Nathan (clue 1), Rowena or Laura (clue 3), so Paul. Thus in clue 3, Nathan is the child who picked up a pair of clubs. Paul didn't pick up a pair of hearts (1) or diamonds (2), so spades. He didn't pick up a 7 (1), 8 or 9 (4), so a 6. Rowena didn't pick up an 8 or 9 (4), so a 7; thus she didn't pick up hearts (1), so diamonds. Laura picked up a pair of hearts. Nathan didn't pick up a 9 (3), so an 8. Laura picked up a 9. Rowena didn't pick up a 2 or 4 (2), so a 3. Laura didn't pick up a 2 (1), so a 4. Nathan picked up a 2.

Thus (lowest - highest):

Laura - hearts - 4 - 9;

Nathan - clubs - 2 - 8;

Paul - spades - 5 - 6;

Rowena - diamonds - 3 - 7.

No 166

Peter and Paul didn't work on Wednesday (grid), so didn't work for 8 hours on Monday (clue 2). The 12 feet long section wasn't built on Monday (clue 2), so Monday's section was 15 feet in length (3) and took either 5 or 7 hours to build; and the 18 feet long section took either 3 or 5 hours to build. The length of wall which took 8 hours to build wasn't 20 feet or 12 feet (1), so 16 feet. It was built on either Tuesday or Thursday (2) and the section 12 feet long was built on either Thursday or Saturday. If the 16 feet section was built on Tuesday, then the 12 feet section was built on Thursday (2), leaving no day for the 18 feet section (4). So the 16 feet section was built on Thursday, the 12 feet section was built on Saturday (2) and the 18 feet section was built on Tuesday (4). The 20 feet section was built on Friday. The day on which Peter and Paul worked for three hours wasn't Tuesday (5), so they worked for 5 hours on Tuesday (3) and 7 hours on Monday. They worked for 3 hours on Saturday (5), so 6 hours on Friday.

Thus:

Monday - 7 hours - 15 feet;

Tuesday - 5 hours - 18 feet;

Thursday - 8 hours - 16 feet;

Friday - 6 hours - 20 feet;

Saturday - 3 hours - 12 feet.

No 167

Lenny went to Westlake on either Thursday or Friday (clue 2), so Carl went to Westlake on either Tuesday or Wednesday (clue 1). The person who went to Westlake on Monday also went to Eastlake on Thursday (3), thus he/

she isn't Betsy (1) or Andrew (4), so Michelle. Andrew went to Westlake on Friday (4), so Lenny went there on Thursday (1) and Carl went there on Tuesday. Betsy went to Westlake on Wednesday. Lenny went to Eastlake on Monday (2). Betsy went to Eastlake on Wednesday (1) and Carl went there on Friday. Andrew went to Eastlake on Tuesday.

Thus (Eastlake - Westlake):
Andrew - Tuesday - Friday;
Betsy - Wednesday - Wednesday;
Carl - Friday - Tuesday;
Lenny - Monday - Thursday;
Michelle - Thursday - Monday.

No 168

The child with 5 orange sweets hasn't 5 red sweets (clue 1), so he/she has 8 red (clue 5) and Jenny has 7 red. Thus the child with 4 red has 6 orange (2) and Josie has 7 orange. By elimination, Josie has 5 red and Jenny has 3 orange. Jude has 6 orange (3) and Jim has 5 orange. Jenny has 7 red and Josie has 7 orange (above), so neither has 7 green (1). Thus Josie has 9 green (4) and Jenny has 8 green. Jude (6 orange, above) hasn't 6 green (1), so 7. Jim has 6 green sweets.

Thus (red - orange - green):
Jenny - 7 - 3 - 8;
Jim - 8 - 5 - 6;
Josie - 5 - 7 - 9;
Jude - 4 - 6 - 7.

No 169

The 66 feet tall tree wasn't the beech (clue 1), yew (clue 2) or willow (4), so the ash. The tree which took 2 hours 15 minutes to fell was 61 feet tall (3). The yew didn't take 2 hours 15 minutes to fell (2), so it was 57 feet tall and Mr Hughes felled the 61 feet tall tree. The willow was 64 feet (4) and the beech was 61 feet tall. Thus Mr Barker felled a tree in 2 hours 30 minutes (1). Neither Mr Wood (3) nor Mr Barker

(5) felled the ash, so the ash was felled by Mr Sawyer. Mr Barker felled the 64 feet tall tree (1), so Mr Wood felled the yew. Mr Sawyer didn't take 2 hours 20 minutes (5), so 2 hours 45 minutes. Mr Wood took 2 hours 20 minutes.

Thus:
Mr Barker - willow - 64 feet -
    2 hours 30 minutes;
Mr Hughes - beech - 61 feet -
    2 hours 15 minutes;
Mr Sawyer - ash - 66 feet -
    2 hours 45 minutes;
Mr Wood - yew - 57 feet -
    2 hours 20 minutes.

No 170

Book A isn't on the subject of music (clue 1) or art (clue 3). The gardening book is between books of different sizes (2), so it's either C or D, thus the one on cooking isn't book A. So book A is on mountains. Book D has 176 pages (4). If the music book is D, then the one with 144 pages would be C (1), which (same height) isn't possible. So the music book is either B or C (1) and the one with 144 pages is either A or B. The book on gardening C or D (above) thus hasn't 144 pages. It has 16 fewer pages than the music book (1), so the gardening book has 176 pages and the music book has 192 pages. Book C is on music (2) and E is on cooking. B is on art and (1) has 144 pages. Book A has 128 pages (3), so E has 160 pages.

Thus:
Book A - mountains - 128 pages;
Book B - art - 144 pages;
Book C - music - 192 pages;
Book D - gardening - 176 pages;
Book E - cooking - 160 pages.

No 171

Remember throughout that each bride and groom have names starting with two different letters (intro). Matthew's wife isn't Fiona (clue 3) or Veronica (clue 4), so either Dawn or Simone. Vernon's wife isn't Myra (1) or Fiona (3), so she's also either Dawn or Simone. Freddy's wife isn't Veronica (4), so (by elimination) she's Myra. Fiona's husband isn't Shane (5), so Dean. Veronica married Shane. Dean didn't marry on Monday or Tuesday (2) and Fiona didn't marry on Thursday or Friday (5), so Dean and Fiona married on Wednesday. Dawn was married on Thursday (5) and Shane on Friday. Simone didn't marry on Monday (2), so Tuesday. Myra married on Monday. Matthew didn't marry on Tuesday (1), so Thursday. Vernon was married on Tuesday.

Thus:

Monday - Myra - Freddy;
Tuesday - Simone - Vernon;
Wednesday - Fiona - Dean;
Thursday - Dawn - Matthew;
Friday - Veronica - Shane.

No 172

Remember throughout that each family has members whose names begin with different letters (intro). Rachel's daughter isn't Dawn (clue 1), so either Hannah or Willow. If she's Hannah, then Rachel's husband isn't William (clue 2) and if she's Willow, then Rachel's husband isn't William. Rachel's son isn't Wesley (1), so in Rachel's family, the person whose name begins with 'W' is her daughter, thus Willow. William's wife isn't Diane (3), so Hilary. By elimination, Wesley's mother is Diane. Roy's sister isn't Willow (whose mother is Rachel, above) or Hannah (4), so Dawn. Diane's husband/Wesley's father isn't Des; and Roy's and Dawn's father isn't Des. So Des's son is Harry. By elimination, Hannah's father is Richard. Wendy's son isn't David (5), so either Harry or Roy; thus either way, she isn't married to Richard. So Richard's wife is Diane; thus their daughter is

Hannah, since her brother is Wesley (above). Wendy's husband isn't Horace (6), so Des; thus their daughter is Rosie. Horace's wife is Rachel; thus their son is David. William's son is Roy and his daughter is Dawn.

Thus (husband - wife - son - daughter):

Des - Wendy - Harry - Rosie;
Horace - Rachel - David - Willow;
Richard - Diane - Wesley - Hannah;
William - Hilary - Roy - Dawn.

No 173

The man who retired in 2008 wasn't in a documentary (clue 1), soap opera (clue 2) or sports programme (3), so a quiz programme. Fred Fisher didn't retire in 2008 and wasn't in a documentary or soap opera (1), so he was the sports presenter who (3) now works as a plumber. Fred Fisher didn't retire in 2009 (1), so either he retired in 2009 (3), or he retired in 2011 and Keith King in 2010. In other words, the man who retired in 2010 is either Fred Fisher or Keith King. The teacher retired two years before Fred Fisher (1), so Keith King isn't a teacher. Bob Barnet is now a clerk (2), so Keith King is a journalist. Mike Mole is the teacher. The man who retired in 2011 isn't Mike Mole (1) or Bob Barnet (2), so Fred Fisher. Thus Keith King retired in 2010 (3) and Mike Mole in 2009 (1). Bob Barnet retired in 2008. Keith King was in the documentary (1), so Mike Mole was in the soap opera.

Thus:

Bob Barnet - quiz - 2008 - clerk;
Fred Fisher - sport - 2011 - plumber;
Keith King - documentary - 2010 - journalist;
Mike Mole - soap opera - 2009 - teacher.

No 174

The girl who left the car first wasn't taken to a friend's house or the swimming pool (clue 1), the library

SOLUTIONS

(clue 2) or the cinema (3), so to the shops. The girl who left the car fifth wasn't Juliette (1), Madge (2), Katy or Imelda (3), so Leonie. Juliette wasn't first to leave (1), so she didn't go to the shops (above). Nor did she go to a friend's house or the swimming pool (1) or the library (2), so Juliette went to the cinema. Leonie (fifth, above) didn't visit a friend (4), so Juliette wasn't fourth to leave the car (1). Thus she was third (3), Katy was second and Imelda was first. Madge was fourth. Madge saw her friend (1) and Katy was taken to the swimming pool. Leonie went to the library.

Thus:

Imelda - shops - first;
Juliette - cinema - third;
Katy - swimming pool - second;
Leonie - library - fifth;
Madge - friend - fourth.

No 175

Remember throughout that each door was repainted a different colour (intro). The door that was blue isn't now red (clue 1), green (clue 2) or white (4), so black. The door that was white isn't now green or blue (4), so red. The door that was green isn't now white (4), so blue. The door that was blue and is now black (above) isn't at No 8 or No 9 (1), No 5 or No 6 (3), so No 7. The house where the door was black is No 8 (1) and that where the door is now red is No 9. The house where the door was red isn't No 5 (3), so No 6. Thus (by elimination) the door at No 5 was once green. The door at No 6 isn't now green (4), so white. The door at No 8 is now green.

Thus (was - is now):

No 5 - green - blue;
No 6 - red - white;
No 7 - blue - black;
No 8 - black - green;
No 9 - white - red.

No 176

Remember throughout that each 'new' picture is made of pieces of four 'old' ones. Peter's uncle's head is with his sister's body (clue 2). His grandma's head isn't with his father's body (clue 1), so it's with his uncle's body. Thus his father's head is with his grandma's body, and his sister's head is with his father's body. His uncle's feet aren't with his father's body (1), so (by elimination) his uncle's feet are with his grandma's body (plus father's head, above) and sister's legs. By elimination, his uncle's body is with his father's legs and sister's feet; his sister's head is with his uncle's legs and grandma's feet; and his uncle's head is with his grandma's legs and father's feet.

Thus (head - body - legs - feet):

Father - grandma - sister - uncle;
Grandma - uncle - father - sister;
Sister - father - uncle - grandma;
Uncle - sister - grandma - father.

No 177

Keith has either the 6 or 8 of diamonds (clue 1), as has George (clue 4). The man with the ace of diamonds isn't Dave (1), so Henry. Dave has the queen of diamonds. Dave hasn't the king of spades (2) or the 2 of spades (5), so Dave has either the 5 or 8 of spades. Keith also has either the 5 or 8 of spades (1). Thus Henry (ace of diamonds, above) has the 2 of spades (1) and Keith has the 5 of spades. Dave has the 8 of spades. George has the king of spades, thus he has either the 2 or 4 of clubs (2) and Dave has either the 4 or 6 of clubs. Dave has the queen of diamonds and the 8 of spades (above), thus the man with the jack of clubs isn't Henry (5). So Keith has the jack of clubs. The man with the 2 of clubs isn't Henry (3), so George. Dave has the 4 of clubs (2), so Henry has the 6 of clubs. George has the

SOLUTIONS

8 of diamonds (4), so Keith has the 6 of diamonds.

Thus (club - diamond - spade):
Dave - 4 - queen - 8;
George - 2 - 8 - king;
Henry - 6 - ace - 2;
Keith - jack - 6 - 5.

No 178

Bill visited at either 3.00pm or 3.30pm on Saturday (clue 3). Thursday's and Friday's visitors came at either 3.00pm, 3.15pm or 3.30pm (clue 5). Tuesday's visitor didn't call at 4.00pm (4), so at 2.30pm. Wednesday's caller came at 4.00pm. Tim visited at 3.30pm (2), so Bill visited at 3.00pm (3). The person who visited on Tuesday isn't Harry (1) or George (4), so Brenda. Harry didn't call at 3.15pm (1), so 4.00pm. Thus George called at 3.15pm. Thursday's caller was George (1), so Tim visited on Friday.

Thus:
Bill - 3.00pm - Saturday;
Brenda - 2.30pm - Tuesday;
George - 3.15pm - Thursday;
Harry - 4.00pm - Wednesday;
Tim - 3.30pm - Friday.

No 179

No-one lives directly east or west of No 4 (map). The person at No 1 and the person who lives east of the person who uses electricity are two different people (clue 1), so electricity is used at No 3. The person who uses coal thus lives at No 1 (2). Alan doesn't use coal (2), so he lives at No 5. Thus (since no-one lives north of him) Alan doesn't use wood (1) or gas (3), so oil. By elimination, in clue 1, the person who lives directly north of the neighbour who uses wood lives at No 4; and Greg is the person who lives at No 4. Gas is used at No 2. Deborah doesn't live at No 2 or No 3 (3), so No 1. Claire doesn't live at No 3 (1), so No 2. Edgar lives at No 3.

Thus:
Alan - No 5 - oil;
Claire - No 2 - gas;
Deborah - No 1 - coal;
Edgar - No 3 - electricity;
Greg - No 4 - wood.

No 180

Remember throughout that each woman has had three different surnames (clue 1). Sheila's birth surname was Smith (clue 3). Gloria's current surname is White (clue 4). The woman surnamed Jones at birth isn't currently surnamed Jones, so Gloria's birth surname was Baker (4) and the woman whose current surname is Baker was given the surname Jones at birth. By elimination, Sheila's current surname is Jones. The name given to June at birth and to Gloria when she married her first husband (1) is Jones. Alice's birth surname was thus White. Since June (Jones at birth) is currently surnamed Baker (above), the woman currently surnamed Smith is Alice. Thus the woman whose first husband was surnamed Smith is June. Alice (White at birth, above) wasn't first married to a man surnamed White, so Alice's first husband's surname was Baker. Sheila's first husband's surname was White.

Thus (born - first - current):
Alice - White - Baker - Smith;
Gloria - Baker - Jones - White;
June - Jones - Smith - Baker;
Sheila - Smith - White - Jones.

No 181

The man born on 14th April isn't Theo (clue 3) or Charles (clue 4). Thus Charles was born in February (4), the youngest man (born in 1984) was born in January, and one man's birthday is 10th March. Theo wasn't born in January (1), so March. Ronald is two years younger than Charles (1), who wasn't born in 1982 (2), so Ronald was

SOLUTIONS

born in 1983 and Charles in 1981. By elimination, Theo was born in 1982 and Harry in 1984, so Ronald's birthday is in April. Harry's birthday is on the 16th (2), so Charles's birthday is on the 12th.
Thus:
Charles - 12th - February - 1981;
Harry - 16th - January - 1984;
Ronald - 14th - April - 1983;
Theo - 10th - March - 1982.

No 182

Claire collected either 8 or 9 slugs and either 7 or 8 snails (clue 5). The person who collected 5 snails isn't Antony (clue 1), Felicity (2) or Michael (3), so Pete. The one who collected 4 snails isn't Antony (1) or Michael (3), so Felicity. The one who collected 6 snails isn't Michael (3), so Antony. Felicity collected 8 slugs (1), so Claire collected 9 slugs (above). Pete collected 6 slugs (2). Michael collected 8 snails (3), so Claire collected 7 snails. The person who collected 7 slugs isn't Antony (4), so Michael. Antony collected 5 slugs.
Thus (slugs - snails):
Antony - 5 - 6;
Claire - 9 - 7;
Felicity - 8 - 4;
Michael - 7 - 8;
Pete - 6 - 5.

No 183

No girl is 9 years old (grid). The 7-year-old isn't Sally (clue 1), Lynne (clue 3) Pamela or Cindy (4), so Rose. The girl who owns Sooty is 10 years old (2), so Lynne isn't 11 (3). The 11-year-old isn't Pamela or Cindy (4), so Sally. Katie's owner is 12 years old (1). Neither Sally nor Rose owns Sammy (1), so their kittens are either Lucky or Moppet. Pamela isn't 12 years old and her kitten isn't called Sammy (4), so Pamela's kitten is called Sooty and (above) Pamela is 10 years old. Cindy is 12 years old (4), so Lynne is 8. By elimination,

Lynne's kitten is Sammy. Rose's is Lucky (3), so Sally's is Moppet.
Thus:
Cindy - 12 years old - Katie;
Lynne - 8 years old - Sammy;
Pamela - 10 years old - Sooty;
Rose - 7 years old - Lucky;
Sally - 11 years old - Moppet.

No 184

Remember throughout that each woman has three different numbers of children, grandchildren and great-grandchildren (intro). Edna has either 3 or 6 great-grandchildren (clue 2). The woman with 3 children hasn't 3 (intro) or 6 great-grandchildren (clue 3), so she isn't Edna. Nor is she Diane (1) or Cynthia (2), so she's Barbara. Barbara hasn't 8 great-grandchildren (1), so she has 5 great-grandchildren and Diane has 6 children. Cynthia has 4 children (2), so Edna has 5 children. Cynthia has 8 great-grandchildren (2) and Edna has 6 great-grandchildren. Thus Diane has 3 great-grandchildren. Barbara has two more grandchildren than Edna (3), and Edna (5 children, above) hasn't 5 grandchildren, so Edna has 4 grandchildren and Barbara has 6 grandchildren. Cynthia has 7 grandchildren (2) and Diane has 5 grandchildren.
Thus (children - grandchildren - great-grandchildren):
Barbara - 3 - 6 - 5;
Cynthia - 4 - 7 - 8;
Diane - 6 - 5 - 3;
Edna - 5 - 4 - 6.

No 185

Remember throughout that items were found on the same day as they were lost (intro). Scott lost his wallet (clue 1). The keys were found by Liz (clue 3), thus not lost by her (intro). The person who lost the keys isn't Jeremy (3), so Doreen. She didn't lose them on Monday (3),

SOLUTIONS

so Doreen's loss was on Wednesday (2), the book was lost on Friday and Doreen found something on Sunday. Jeremy's item was lost on Monday (3), so (by elimination) it was found by Scott. Jeremy found an item on Friday (book, above), so Liz lost the book and Jeremy lost the mobile phone. The wallet was lost on Sunday.

Thus (lost by - found by):
Book - Liz - Jeremy - Friday;
Keys - Jeremy - Liz - Wednesday;
Mobile phone - Jeremy - Scott - Monday;
Wallet - Scott - Doreen - Sunday.

No 186

Denise is marrying in September (clue 2). The woman marrying in May isn't Lara or Penny (clue 1) or Hannah (3) so Mandy, who is marrying Ross (1). Joe's wedding isn't in September (2), so Hannah and Eddie (3) will marry in July, Joe will marry in August, and Kevin will marry in June. Bob's wedding will be in September, so his fiancée is Denise (2). Lara's wedding will be in June (1) and Penny's will be in August.

Thus:
Bob - Denise - September;
Eddie - Hannah - July;
Joe - Penny - August;
Kevin - Lara - June;
Ross - Mandy - May.

No 187

The person surnamed Dawkins isn't 93 years old (clue 5), so Kenneth isn't 93 or 94 (clue 2). Edith isn't 96 (2), but she's older than Kenneth. So Edith is 97. In clue 1, she's one of the two women with an age difference of one year; thus neither Gregory nor Kenneth is 96. Kenneth is thus 95 (2) and another woman is 94 (1), so Gregory is 93. His surname isn't Barton (3), Mallett (4), Dawkins or Price (5), so Ford.

The person surnamed Dawkins isn't Edith or Kenneth (2) or Doris (3), so Margaret. Margaret is 94 (2), so Doris is 96. Kenneth's surname is Mallett (4). Edith's surname is Barton (3), so Doris's surname is Price.

Thus:
Doris - Price - 96 years old;
Edith - Barton - 97 years old;
Gregory - Ford - 93 years old;
Kenneth - Mallett - 95 years old;
Margaret - Dawkins - 94 years old.

No 188

The first try resulted in a cherry in the middle panel (clue 3), thus the cherry in the right panel plus lemon in the left panel showed on a different try (intro). The try which showed a bar in the left and orange in the middle wasn't the fourth (4), so either the second or third. The one which showed a cherry in the right panel and lemon in the left panel wasn't the second try (1) or the fourth (2), so the third. Thus the fourth try showed a lemon in the right panel (2). By elimination, the bar in the left and orange in the middle (4) was on the second try. The first try showed a bar in the right panel (1), so Keith's second try showed a bell in the right panel. The melon was in the middle on the third try (5), so the orange in the left panel appeared on the fourth try. The bell in the left was on the first try. The plum in the middle was on the fourth try.

Thus (left - middle - right):
First - bell - cherry - bar;
Second - bar - orange - bell;
Third - lemon - melon - cherry;
Fourth - orange - plum - lemon.

No 189

The diary kept for 42 days (shortest time) wasn't a gift from Dora's aunt (clue 2), brother or sister (clue 5), so her father. The blue diary was from her aunt (2). The green diary wasn't from

SOLUTIONS

her brother or sister (5), so her father. Thus the black diary given by a man (4) was from her brother, so the red diary was from her sister. The 2002 (oldest) diary wasn't from her aunt (2), sister or father (3), so her brother. Her father's diary wasn't given in 2003 (3) or 2004 (4), so 2005. The diary kept for 63 days (9 weeks, 1) wasn't written in 2002 (2) or 2004 (4), so 2003. If it's red (and from her sister, above), then the one kept for 56 days (8 weeks, 1) is black (3). But the black diary was given by Dora's brother and dates to 2002 (above), so the blue diary from her aunt would also have been kept for 63 days (2). Thus the 2003 diary is blue, the 2002 diary was kept for 56 days (2), and the 2004 diary was kept for 49 days and is red.

Thus:
2002 - black - brother - 56 pages;
2003 - blue - aunt - 63 pages;
2004 - red - sister - 49 pages;
2005 - green - father - 42 pages.

No 190
Postcard A (highest) wasn't placed by Miss Tarrant or Mr Palmer (clue 1), Mr Mitchell (clue 2) or Mr Fox (3), so Mrs Greaves. Postcard E wasn't placed by Miss Tarrant (1), Mr Mitchell (2) or Mr Palmer (3), so Mr Fox. Mr Palmer placed D (3), so Mr Fox isn't selling the lawnmower (2). Nor is Mr Fox selling the clock (1), motorbike (2) or table (3), so the bed. The clock is on either A or B (1), as is the motorbike (2). The lawnmower and table are thus on either C or D. The lawnmower isn't being advertised by Mr Mitchell or Miss Tarrant (2), so Mr Palmer. Thus C is advertising the table. Mr Mitchell placed C (2), so Miss Tarrant placed B. Postcard A is advertising the clock (1), so Miss Tarrant's postcard is advertising the motorbike.

Thus:
Card A - Mrs Greaves - clock;
Card B - Miss Tarrant - motorbike;
Card C - Mr Mitchell - table;
Card D - Mr Palmer - lawnmower;
Card E - Mr Fox - bed.

No 191
The white cushion is either A or B (clue 4), the diamond-patterned cushion is either C or D, and the cushion with circles is either D or E. If the yellow cushion is E, then D is black with squares (clue 3). But D has a pattern of either diamonds or circles (4 and above), so E isn't yellow. Nor is E green or mauve (1). So E is black and has a pattern of squares (3) and D is yellow. By elimination, D has circles, C has diamonds (4) and A is white. Cushion A has a pattern of zigzags (2) and cushion B has stripes. Cushion B is mauve (1) and C is green.

Thus:
Cushion A - white - zigzags;
Cushion B - mauve - stripes;
Cushion C - green - diamonds;
Cushion D - yellow - circles;
Cushion E - black - squares.

No 192
Yacht D doesn't belong to Adam or Thomas (clue 2) or Larry (clue 3), so Ian, who (1) is either 6 or 9 years old. Thus Ian isn't two years younger than any other boy, so Thomas's yacht is further left than that of a boy who isn't Ian (2). Yacht C therefore isn't Thomas's. So B belongs to Thomas (2) and Adam's yacht is A. Yacht C belongs to Larry and (3) is white. Larry is two years younger than Adam (2). Ian is one year older than the owner of the green yacht (3), so Ian is 6 and the owner of the green yacht is 5. By elimination, Thomas is 5, so Larry is 7 (2) and Adam is 9. Yacht A is blue (1), so yacht D is red.

Solutions

Thus:

Yacht A - Adam - blue - 9 years old;
Yacht B - Thomas - green - 5 years old;
Yacht C - Larry - white - 7 years old;
Yacht D - Ian - red - 6 years old.

No 193

Of the two men who threw something east (clue 3), neither lives at No 7 (map), so Mrs Hale doesn't live at No 5. Thus she lives at No 3 (clue 3) and Mrs Lang lives at No 7. Mr Penny threw something on Friday (4), so Mrs Hale threw something on Wednesday (1) and something was thrown into the garden of No 3 on Monday. Mrs Lang thus threw something on Tuesday (2) and Mr James threw something on Monday. Whatever he threw landed at No 3 (1), so Mrs Lang is the woman (4) into whose garden (No 7, above) Mr Penny threw something. Mrs Hale didn't throw anything into the garden of No 1 (1), so No 5. Mrs Lang threw something into the garden of No 1. Since Mr James threw something into the garden of No 3, he lives west of Mrs Hale (3), so at No 1. Mr Penny lives at No 5.

Thus (lives at - landed at):

Mrs Hale - No 3 - Wednesday - No 5;
Mr James - No 1 - Monday - No 3;
Mrs Lang - No 7 - Tuesday - No 1;
Mr Penny - No 5 - Friday - No 7.

No 194

Remember throughout that each plane was diverted to an airport different to its destination airport (intro). Flight No 509 was diverted to Morneton (clue 3) and flight No 255 was diverted to Rayford (clue 4). Flight No 276's destination was Newfort (2), so it wasn't diverted to Newfort. The plane diverted to Newfort wasn't flight No 799 (3), so flight No 147. The flights diverted to Berryham and Westwick were thus either flight No 276 or flight No 799. So Berryham and Westwick were the destination airports of either flight No 147 (1) or flight No 509 (3). By elimination, flight No 255's destination was Morneton, and flight No 799's destination was Rayford. The flight bound for Berryham was diverted to either Morneton or Newfort, thus (5) the flight bound for Newfort was diverted to Berryham and the one bound for Berryham was diverted to Newfort. Flight No 799 was diverted to Westwick. Flight No 509's original destination was Westwick.

Thus (destination - diverted to):

Flight No 147 - Berryham - Newfort;
Flight No 255 - Morneton - Rayford;
Flight No 276 - Newfort - Berryham;
Flight No 509 - Westwick - Morneton;
Flight No 799 - Rayford - Westwick.

No 195

The person who paid $200 isn't Mr Hughes (clue 1), Mrs Roberts (clue 2), Mr Williams or Mr Thomas (4), so Mrs Parry. The person who paid $100 isn't Mr Thomas (1), Mrs Roberts (3) or Mr Williams (4), so Mr Hughes. Mr Thomas paid $125 (1). The work done for Mr Hughes wasn't shed repairs (1), a new door (2), fencing (3) or concreting (4), so for chimney pots. The new door cost either $175 or $200 (2) as did the concreting (4); so the fencing and shed repairs cost either $125 or $150. The fencing wasn't done for Mrs Roberts or Mr Williams (3), so for Mr Thomas. Mrs Roberts paid $150 (3), so Mr Williams paid $175. The shed repairs cost $150. Mrs Parry's job was concreting (4), so the new door was for Mr Williams.

Thus:

Mr Hughes - chimney pots - $100;
Mrs Parry - concreting - $200;
Mrs Roberts - shed repairs - $150;
Mr Thomas - fencing - $125;
Mr Williams - new door - $175.

SOLUTIONS

No 196

The woman whose birthday was on Tuesday didn't receive a watch (clue 1), necklace (clue 2) or flowers (3), so perfume and (5) Nancy's birthday was on Wednesday. Thus Maxine's was on Tuesday (3) and the woman who received flowers had her birthday on either Wednesday or Thursday. Laura's birthday wasn't on Thursday (4), so Saturday. Olivia's birthday was on Thursday. Her husband isn't Graham (2), nor is Maxine (perfume/birthday on Tuesday, above) married to Graham (5), thus Graham's wife's birthday was on Wednesday (2). He didn't give his wife (Nancy, above) a necklace (2). Nor did Olivia receive a necklace (2), so Laura got the necklace. Her husband isn't Philip (1) or Dave (4), so Martin. Olivia's husband isn't Dave (2), so Philip; thus (1) she received the watch. Maxine's husband is Dave. Nancy received flowers.

Thus:
Laura - Martin - necklace - Saturday;
Maxine - Dave - perfume - Tuesday;
Nancy - Graham - flowers - Wednesday;
Olivia - Philip - watch - Thursday.

No 197

The men due to start at 1.00pm and 2.00pm were either 22 or 30 minutes late (clue 1) and the ones due to start at 8.00am and 9.00am were either 7 or 15 minutes late due to either car or traffic problems: thus the men due to start at 2.00pm and 3.00pm had problems with either a dog or a wife. One man was eight minutes later than Jeff Ball who had a problem with his dog (clue 2), so Jeff Ball was 22 minutes late. The person whose wife was ill was thus 30 minutes late. He's Ted Stump (3) whose shift thus started at 1.00pm; and Jeff Ball's started at 2.00pm. The man

held up by traffic should have started at 8.00am (2), so the one who had a car breakdown should have started at 9.00am. Sam Fielder wasn't 7 minutes late (4), so 15. Fred Bale was 7 minutes late. Sam Fielder's shift didn't start at 8.00am (4), so 9.00am. Fred Bale's shift started at 8.00am.

Thus:
Fred Bale - 8.00am - 7 minutes - traffic;
Jeff Ball - 2.00pm - 22 minutes - dog;
Sam Fielder - 9.00am - 15 minutes - car;
Ted Stump - 1.00pm - 30 minutes - wife.

No 198

Seat C isn't occupied by either Alison (clue 3), the person drinking coffee or the person drinking lemonade. So either the lemonade drinker is in E, Alison is in A and the person with coffee is in B (clue 3), or the lemonade drinker is in D, Alison is in E and the person with coffee is in A. In other words, the person in seat E is either Alison or the lemonade drinker, and the person in A is either Alison or the coffee drinker. Donald has cola (2), so isn't in seats A or E. The person with tea isn't in seat C (2), so Donald isn't in B. So either Donald with cola is in C and the tea drinker is in D (2) or Donald with cola is in D and the tea drinker is in E. In other words, the person in seat D is drinking either cola or tea. Thus the lemonade drinker is in E (above), Alison is in A and the person with coffee is in B. By elimination, Alison is drinking water, Donald is in seat C, and the tea drinker is in D. Sally is in E (1) and Vanessa is in B. Raymond is in seat D.

Thus:
Seat A - Alison - water;
Seat B - Vanessa - coffee;
Seat C - Donald - cola;
Seat D - Raymond - tea;
Seat E - Sally - lemonade.

No 199

The expense for which Mr and Mrs Cannie saved $200 wasn't life insurance 1 or life insurance 2 (clue 1), home or car insurance (clue 2), so the car service. They didn't save $230 towards life insurance 1 or life insurance 2 (1) or car insurance (3), so home insurance. July's saving was for the car service (2). The car insurance money amounted to $400 (3) and the $300 sum was set aside six months after the home insurance (3), so the home insurance money was saved in either February or May. Thus the life insurance monies weren't set aside in February and May (1) respectively. Thus they were saved for in either May and August, or August and November. In other words, August's saving was towards one of the life insurances. The car insurance money wasn't put aside in either February or May (4), so in November. Thus they saved towards life insurance 1 in May (1) and life insurance 2 in August. By elimination, they saved towards home insurance in February. The amount put aside for life insurance 2 was $300 (3), so they put aside $350 in May.

Thus:

February - home insurance - $230;
May - life insurance 1 - $350;
July - car service - $200;
August - life insurance 2 - $300;
November - car insurance - $400.

No 200

Herrero finished one place behind the driver of the Blue Cow (clue 1) and the Laurent finished one place behind the Boyota (clue 2), so Herrero didn't drive the Laurent. Nor did he drive the Boyota (1), so Herrero drove the Motus. The Blue Cow started in either position 2 or 6 (1), as did the Boyota (2), so the Laurent and Motus started in either positions 3 or 7. Schmidt drove the Laurent (1). Smith didn't drive the Boyota (2), so he drove the Blue Cow and Forgeron drove the Boyota. Herrero finished one place behind Smith (1). Schmidt finished one place behind Forgeron (2), who wasn't 3rd (3), so Schmidt wasn't 4th. Thus Herrero was 4th (1) and Smith was 3rd. Forgeron was 1st (2) and Schmidt was 2nd. Smith's starting position wasn't 2 (3), so 6. Forgeron's was 2. Schmidt started in position 7 (1), so Herrero started in position 3.

Thus:

Forgeron - 1st - Boyota - position 2;
Herrero - 4th - Motus - position 3;
Schmidt - 2nd - Laurent - position 7;
Smith - 3rd - Blue Cow - position 6.